A PRIMER OF ADLERIAN PSYCHOLOGY

The Analytic-Behavioral-
Cognitive Psychology
of Alfred Adler

Harold H. Mosak
Michael P. Maniacci

USA	Publishing Office:	BRUNNER/MAZEL *A member of the Taylor & Francis Group* 325 Chestnut Street Philadelphia, PA 19106 Tel: (215) 625–8900 Fax: (215) 625–2940
	Distribution Center:	BRUNNER/MAZEL *A member of the Taylor & Francis Group* 47 Runway Road, Suite G Levittown, PA 19057 Tel: (215) 269–0400 Fax: (215) 269–0363
UK		BRUNNER/MAZEL *A member of the Taylor & Francis Group* 1 Gunpowder Square London EC4A 3DE Tel: +44 171 583 0490 Fax: +44 171 583 0581

A PRIMER OF ADLERIAN PSYCHOLOGY: The Analytic-Behavioral-Cognitive Psychology of Alfred Adler

1   2   3   4   5   6   7   8   9   0

Printed by Braun-Brumfield, Ann Arbor, MI, 1999
Cover design by Marja Walker.
Cover photo courtesy of Sanford J. Greenburger Associates
Edited by Hilary Ward and Mark Eggerts

A CIP catalog record for this book is available from the British Library.
  The paper in this publication meets the requirements of the ANSI Standard Z39.48–1984 (Permanence of Paper).

Library of Congress Cataloging-in-Publication Data
Mosak, Harold H.
      A primer of Adlerian pyschology: the analytic-behavioral-cognitive pyschology of Alfred Adler/Harold H. Mosak, Michael P. Maniacci.
      p. cm.
      Includes bibliographical references and index.
      ISBN 1–58391–003–4 (pbk.: alk. paper)
      1. Adlerian psychology.   2. Adler, Alfred, 1870–1937.
I. Maniacci, Michael.   II. Title.
BF175.5.A33M68   1999
150.19'53--dc21   99-25738
                                                                                                    CIP

ISBN 1-58391-003-4 (paper)

Dedication

Harold H. Mosak: To Ada, a class act . . .
Michael P. Maniacci: To the two women of my life, Laurie and Emily . . .

CONTENTS

PREFACE

All men by nature desire to know.
Aristotle (circa 350 BC)

BELIEVING is what we humans do best.
Michael S. Gazzaniga (1985)

Who am I? Where do I come from? What is all of this about? Questions like these have been on the minds and in the hearts of humanity for what seems to be an eternity. Aristotle (350 BC/1941), in *The Metaphysics*, posed just such questions and attempted to lay the foundation for those answers in philosophy and logic well over 2000 years ago. He was the founder of a school that trained some of the greatest minds of ancient Greece, he himself having graduated from Plato's Academy several years earlier. In *The Metaphysics*, Aristotle attempts to explore how to understand "being," that is, the nature of all that exists. In the very first paragraph of this monumental work, he turns his attention to human beings and their ability to sense and perceive, and how that perception leads them to search for answers to such eternal questions. "All men by nature desire to know" is the first line of the book (p. 689).

Some 2000 years later, a cognitive neuroscientist, Gazzaniga, begins his book, *The Social Brain* (1985), with "BELIEVING is what humans do best" (p. 3). In it, he attempts to understand how the neural networks of the brain have both reflected and created the social networks of our community, culture, and environment. Much like Aristotle before him, Gazzaniga finds himself intertwined with the issue of our senses and human perception.

Human beings, as a species, have been, and continue to be, preoccupied with these issues. Though our answers to these questions have varied across time and culture, with technology allowing us more precision in our responses (but no less rigorous answers than philosophers), the mere fact that we continue to ask these questions may be one of the fundamental distinguishing characteristics of human nature. The nature of what is "known" is difficult, if not impossible, to distinguish from the nature of those who are seeking to know; or, put more simply, what is "seen" is often influenced by who is "looking." This book is written by two psychologists, and our "answers" are couched in the science and philosophy of psychology. Though both of us have been trained in fields of inquiry other than psychology, and other disciplines and theories within psychology, our primary affiliation is with the system of psychology and psychotherapy of the psychiatrist Alfred Adler. It is through this perspective that we practice and teach.

Alfred Adler, and those who have joined him in a similar world view, have built a system of psychology called *Individual Psychology*. It provides not only a strategy of psychotherapy but a philosophical framework with which to interpret and comprehend information relevant to an understanding of human nature. In fact, Adler's most popular book, written in 1927, was entitled *Understanding Human Nature* (1927/1957). Adler's system is a growing, evolving, vibrant system, whose basic tenets have been gradually incorporated into diverse fields, not only within the disciplines of psychology and psychiatry, but in anthropology, sociology, social psychology, and education. His insights have gained widespread acceptance, even though his name has often been forgotten. As Adler himself wrote in a book foreword in 1933,

> Individual Psychology, which is essentially a child of this age, will have a permanent influence on the thought, poetry, and dreams of humanity. It will attract many enlightened disciples, and many more who will hardly know the names of its pioneers. It will be understood by some, but the numbers of those who misunderstand it will be greater. It will have many adherents, and still more enemies. Because of its simplicity many will think it too easy, whereas those who know it will recognize how difficult it is. (Dreikurs, 1933/1950a, p. vii)

Adler's words have been prophetic. Many of the insights he articulated have become "mainstreamed" into contemporary thought, particularly in psychology. As is evident throughout this work, psychoanalysis (particularly self-psychology and object relations theory), cognitive therapy, systems theory and family therapy, existential psychotherapy and philosophy, and social psychology, to mention only a few therapy systems, have incorporated much of what Adler espoused as early as the turn of the century. This book is an attempt to clearly articulate the system Adler began building at that time.

There have been other attempts to systematize Adler's work in the form of introductory textbooks. Dreikurs (1933/1950a), Manaster and Corsini (1982), Wexberg (1929), and Wolfe (1932) have written such texts, but all, except Manaster and Corsini, have (at the time of this writing) gone out of print. Many of Adler's original works are out of print as well, but the work of Ansbacher and Ansbacher has served to collect, edit, and systematize Adler's writings (Adler, 1956, 1964g, 1978). This book is an attempt to provide those in the field of Adlerian psychology with an introductory text and those who are as yet unfamiliar with the work of Adler a single source from which to evaluate his system as it stands today. It is not a book about Adlerian counseling and psychotherapy per se; rather it is a theoretical book that will touch upon counseling and psychotherapy as some of its topics. It is a text about the *theory* of Individual Psychology.

This book is an exploration and elaboration of the theory and system of Individual Psychology. Chapter 1 reviews the historical background of Adlerian psychology.

Chapter 2 begins with an analysis of the basic assumptions and philosophy of Individual Psychology. It is intended to familiarize readers with the underlying assumptions of the system, in much the same way Chapter 1 attempts to acquaint readers with Adler himself.

Chapter 3 examines human personality development as conceptualized by Adlerians. The development of the life style entails taking into account the biological, psychological, and social influences upon personality development in light of the aforementioned assumptions of Adlerian theory.

Chapter 4 provides an overview of the style of life, Adler's phrase for what is now known as personality. What it is and how it is used is detailed.

Chapter 5 is, for all practical purposes, a continuation of Chapter 4 and is called "Typology." Certain life styles have themes, or clusters of issues, that can form recognizable patterns theorists call "types." Adler's original four types, with some current additions, are detailed.

Chapter 6 is titled "Inferiorities, Inferiority Feelings, and Inferiority Complexes." This chapter discusses how individuals respond to challenges posed by life and the social situations they both find themselves in and help to create and maintain. The general challenges people face can be clustered into six key areas, and these are discussed in Chapter 7, "The Tasks of Life."

In "Psychopathology," Chapter 8, various pathological methods of functioning are analyzed. Topics such as diagnosis, symptoms, and psychodynamics are viewed from the interpersonal, goal-oriented perspective of Adlerian psychology. A detailed case history is presented that highlights the topics addressed in the chapter.

Chapter 9 is an overview of what Adlerians assess when they begin understanding a person. How the individual's style of life is assessed, the person's current movement in regards to his or her social field, and the meaning and purpose of behavior are the focus of this section.

Intervention strategies is the topic of Chapter 10. Issues of prevention, parenting, parent and family education, counseling, psychotherapy, and psychoanalysis, including the reconceptualization of Adlerian psychotherapy as an "analytic-behavioral-cognitive" system, are explored.

Finally, in Chapter 11, a critique of Individual Psychology is presented, along with an annotated bibliography of Adlerian works that readers may wish to examine for themselves, and a glossary of key terms. If Adlerian theory is to flourish, its strengths need to be highlighted and its limitations noted and corrected. Although Individual Psychology is a comprehensive, broad-based system, there are many areas future Adlerians must address if the system is to remain viable. Also, we examine Adler's influence as it continues today, particularly as it relates to one of the newest trends in clinical psychology and psychotherapy, cognitive constructionism. The chapter concludes with some comments upon the future of Individual Psychology.

This is intended to be an introductory text; therefore at the end of each chapter, we have some questions that may be useful for instructors and students in classroom settings. In addition, summary points highlighting the key issues of each chapter are found immediately before the review questions.

Because, as we have stated previously, the answers people find are intimately related to the "natures" of those who do the "looking," an appropriate place to begin a textbook of Adlerian psychology is with the individual himself, the man who "did the looking," Alfred Adler.

Harold H. Mosak
Michael P. Maniacci

CHAPTER 1

Alfred Adler and Adlerian Psychology: An Overview

It is one of the peculiar ironies of history that there are no limits to the mis-understanding and distortion of theories. . . .

Erich Fromm (1961)

☐ Alfred Adler: A Biographical Sketch

Adler was the second of six children born to a Jewish family on February 7, 1870. He was a sickly child who had rickets and suffered from spasms of the glottis. At the age of 3 years, his younger brother died in bed next to him (Mosak & Kopp, 1973). A year later, he contracted pneumonia and became seriously ill. Later, as an adult, he remembered the physician saying at that time to his father, "Your boy is lost" (Orgler, 1939/ 1963, p. 16). As if these experiences were not enough to impress him, he was *twice* run over in the streets. Though he reported no memory for how these incidents happened, he did remember recovering consciousness on the family sofa. Adler became very aware of death and vowed to become a physician in order to overcome it (Adler, 1947).

Adler was raised on the outskirts of the intellectual capital of his day, Vienna. The area in which he lived was not predominantly Jewish, and he and his family were minority-group members.

These issues of belonging, inferiority, and weakness had a large influence upon the young Adler. He was a poor student with bad eyesight who was physically clumsy and felt uncoordinated, primarily because of his numerous physical ailments. His mathematics teacher recommended to his father that Adler leave school and apprentice himself as a shoemaker. Adler's father objected, and Adler embarked upon bettering his academic skills. Within a relatively short time, he became the best math student in the class. Adler became embroiled in a conflict with a classmate, and a fight broke out. Adler struck the boy, and hurt him. He vowed not to fight again.

Adler studied medicine at the University of Vienna and in 1895 graduated with his medical degree and a specialization in ophthalmology.[1] He became interested in politics and began attending meetings of the rising socialist movement. Through these meetings, he met Raissa Timofeyewna Epstein, and they were married in 1897. She was a socialist and a feminist (R. Adler, 1899) who continued her active interest in political affairs throughout their marriage (Hoffman, 1994).

He started his private practice. His practice soon switched to internal medicine, and he observed that many of the patients who sought his services suffered from diseases that traced their origin to the social situations in which they lived and worked. As Ansbacher (1992a, b) notes, Adler's practice was located in an area that exposed him to lower socioeconomic classes, and his first publication was on the health of tailors (Adler, 1898). In it, Adler noted how the social conditions in which people worked and lived greatly influenced the diseases and disease processes that affected them. This seems to have been historically the first essay into community outreach (Papanek, 1965a). Along a similar line, Adler often treated the performers from the local circus, what used to be referred to as the "sideshow freaks," and Adler was greatly impressed by how their physical abnormalities influenced their choice of vocation and how their bodies appeared to "compensate" for such abnormalities.

☐ Adler and Freud: Adler as a Psychoanalyst

Freud's life and work has been documented and detailed in numerous biographies, for example by Jones (1953, 1955, 1957) and Stone (1971). It is also referred to by Ellenberger (1970).

Freud was an eldest son of an upperclass Jewish family. He was brilliant, and as Mosak and Kopp (1973) note, provocative in personality. An early recollection of his suggests long self-training in this direction. At age 7 or 8 years, "Freud recalls having urinated [deliberately] in his parents' bedroom and being reprimanded by his father, who said, 'That boy will never amount to anything'" (Jones, 1953, p. 16; Mosak & Kopp, 1973).

He was unafraid of being negatively perceived. Freud wanted to be a scientist, and his intellectual "forefathers" were men who were bound to the scientific tradition.

Freud (1900/1965) published his seminal work, *The Interpretation of Dreams,* in 1899 (though the work carried the year 1900, it was published in the Winter of 1899 but postdated). As the editor of the English translation, Strachey notes in the introduction, it sold poorly (only 351 copies in the first 6 years) and was roundly criticized. Freud fell into a depression shortly after its publication and general rejection. It was into this atmosphere Adler stepped.

Legend has it that amidst all the criticism and negativity surrounding *The Interpretation of Dreams,* Adler published a vigorous defense of it in a local paper; this "paper" has never been found. Freud, reportedly, was grateful to have found someone who was willing to openly defend his position and, in 1902, invited Adler to meet with him on a Wednesday evening, to discuss these and similar issues. The Wednesday Night Meetings, as they became known, led to the development of the Psychoanalytic Society. Adler became its first president, though he was 14 years younger than Freud. Adler (1931/1964b), even years after their split, had this to say about those early "meetings" and Freud's initial attempts to understand human nature:

> Despite the many scientific contrasts between Freud and myself, I have always been willing to recognize that he has clarified much through his endeavors; especially, he has severely shaken the position of positivistically [*materialistisch*] oriented neurology and opened a wide door to psychology as an auxiliary science to medicine. This is his chief merit, next to his detective art of guessing. (pp. 217–218)

In two footnotes to that paper, Adler continues to note that:

> I remember very well when as a young student and medical man I was very worried about and discontented with the state of psychiatry and tried to discover other ways, and found Freud was courageous enough, actually to go another way to explore the importance of psychological reasons for physical disturbances and for neuroses. (p. 218)

and that

> A psychological system has an inseparable connection with the life philosophy of its formulator. As soon as he offers his system to the world, it appeals to individuals, both laymen and scientists, with a similar trend of

mind and provides them with a scientific foundation for an attitude towards life which they had achieved previously. (p. 218)

Adler was not a "disciple" of Freud; he was a collaborator (Ansbacher,
1962; Hoffman, 1994; Maslow, 1962). The comments by Ansbacher and
Ansbacher, found in Adler (1956), clarify this position. Adler had his
own philosophy and was beginning to develop it *before* his association
with Freud. As Adler astutely noted, the clash between him and Freud
had to do with their respective personalities as much as with their respective theories, for their theories were outgrowths of their personalities (Stepansky, 1983). Adler became a "Freudian" and attempted to
continue his train of thought within orthodox Freudian guidelines. He
found, however, that his fundamental assumptions were different than
Freud's, and tensions began to increase between the two men. As Ansbacher and Ansbacher (Adler, 1956, pp. 21–75) detail, even within the
Freudian system, Adler *originated* these concepts within psychoanalysis,
and Freud readily adopted them (sometimes, years after having split
with Adler):

> The confluence of drives (Adler, 1908)
> The transformation of a drive into its opposite (Adler, 1908)
> The direction of a drive to one's own person (Adler, 1908)
> The aggression drive and the relationship of aggression to anxiety
> (Adler, 1908)
> Safeguarding tendencies (defense mechanisms) (Adler, 1912/1983b)
> The concept of the "ego-ideal" (Adler, 1912/1983b)
> The emphasis upon "ego" psychology (Colby, 1951)

Colby (1951) and Furtmüller (1964) discuss the notes of the meetings
of the Vienna Psychoanalytic Society, and the eventual split of the group,
with Adler and nine other members resigning their membership and
Adler resigning not only his presidency but his position as coeditor of the
psychoanalytic journal, in February of 1911.

Adler was a subjectivistic, socially oriented theorist who had a feel
for the "common people" (Ansbacher, 1959b), and he placed a great
deal of emphasis upon philosophy. He cited, as his principle influences,
the works of Kant, Nietzsche, Vaihinger, Goethe, Shakespeare, and
the Bible. His early work was concerned with public health, medical
and psychological prevention, and social welfare (Ansbacher, 1992b).
As he continued his work, he wrote papers on and lectured extensively
about:

> Children at risk, especially delinquency (Adler, 1930/1963, 1930/
> 1983c, 1935)
> Women's rights and the equality of the sexes (Adler, 1978)

Women's rights to abortion (Adler, 1978)
Adult education (Hoffman, 1994)
Teacher training (Adler, 1924a, 1929b)
Community mental health and the establishment of family counseling clinics (Adler, 1929b)
Experimental schools for public students (Birnbaum, 1935; Hoffman, 1994; Spiel, 1956)
Brief psychotherapy ("The Father of Self-Help," 1995; Maniacci, 1996a)
Family counseling and education (Sherman & Dinkmeyer, 1987)

This work stands in sharp contrast to Freud, who maintained a relatively neutral stance towards many of these issues and never openly addressed most of them. Adler's split with Freud was as much about Adler returning to the doctrines that had preoccupied him prior to his association with the psychoanalytic movement as it was about the theoretical and technical issues he and Freud debated.

The final break with Freud centered around two key issues that are touched on only briefly here—the masculine protest (Adler, 1939; Mosak & Schneider, 1977) and the nature and origin of repression (Adler, 1911, 1956). Adler felt that the "driving force" behind "psychic disturbances" was the "masculine protest." The masculine protest was the attempt of some people to deal with society's overvaluation of masculinity. Men who subscribed to this overvaluation wanted to be "like a real man" or, in other words, powerful. If they failed to meet this standard, they became discouraged, became resigned, "withdrew," or overcompensated. Women who similarly overvalued masculinity competed with men, identified with men, overcompensated, became resigned, or "withdrew." Adler felt that the striving of the disturbed individual was of a socially useless nature, and that this striving "to be above others" had its roots in the prevailing social orientation of the day; that is, masculinity was viewed as dominant, and those who felt "weak, or inferior" viewed themselves as "feminine."[2] Adler felt that this was a result of both psychological dynamics taking place within the individuals and the social values of the day. Freud wholeheartedly disagreed and responded that the masculine protest was, in reality, nothing other than "penis envy" or "the fear of castration." For Freud, social influences played little, if any, role in the etiology of psychic disturbances.

Adler felt that "repression," or the ability to not deal with certain issues or actually "remove them from consciousness" was not the *result* of culture, but actually a sign of poor *adjustment to* society. Freud felt that repression resulted from individuals having to adapt to culture and hence "repress" their instinctual life. Freud felt that neurosis was the price we pay for civilization. Adler felt it was the price we pay for our lack of civilization. Adler felt that healthy adaptation came *because of* an adjustment to society, and repression was therefore a sign of poor adjustment. Individuals who were "well adjusted" learned to adapt their "drives" to society, in constructive, prosocial ways and had no need to repress them. Hence, for Adler, repression was but one of many "safeguarding mechanisms" (Adler, 1911; Credner, 1936) individuals employed if "neurotic." For Freud, at the time of the break, repression was *the* cause of neurotic disturbance, and not simply one particular defense mechanism (fascinatingly enough, many years later, he reversed his position and adopted Adler's).

For the first time in the history of science, these two contrasting positions (Freud's and Adler's) were put to a vote by members of the society, and "scientific facts" were decided by majority vote (Colby, 1951, 1956; Furtmüller, 1964; Nunberg & Federn, 1962). Adler "lost" the vote and left the society.

Adler was an important coworker, whom Freud considered to be a "serious opponent" to psychoanalysis. He may have been Freud's personal physician, and Freud himself turned over many of his patients to Adler prior to Adler's resignation. Thus, Freud lost the first of his "disciples," although Adler did not regard himself as one.

Adler originally entitled his new group The Society for Free Psychoanalytic Research.[3] Later, the name was changed to *Individual Psychology*, with "individual" meaning "indivisible," that is, holistic (derived from the Latin *individuum*). Adler and coworkers founded their own journal, started their own Adlerian organization, and began accepting members.

Early in its inception, its primary focus was upon psychoanalysis. Adler himself maintained his private practice as a psychiatrist, but after World War I (during which time Adler served as a military physician) Adler turned much more social in his orientation and began working full force for many of the social issues listed previously. Hence, his work falls approximately into two periods: Prior to the First World War, Adler was a psychoanalyst, and that can be seen in his two most important, early works—*The Neurotic Constitution* (1912/1983b), and *The Practice and Theory of Individual Psychology* (1920/1983d).

These are the only two works Adler himself wrote on his own, with the latter being a collection of his papers that he assembled. After World War I, Adler wrote increasingly as a philosopher, social psychologist, and educator, with works such as *Understanding Human Nature* (1927/1957), *The Science of Living* (1929c), *The Education of Children* (1930/1970), *What Life Should Mean to You* (1931/1958), and *Social Interest: A Challenge to Mankind*

(1933/1964f) being directed to the lay public. These works are primarily based upon lectures and notebooks of Adler and were assembled by members of his group, with his approval.

☐ Adler and America: The Early American Movement

In 1926 Adler made his first trip to the United States. Though he was 56 years old, he began to learn English, and soon he was not only proficient but fluent. He lectured, did public demonstrations, and began to write and publish in English. As the Fascists came to power in Austria (Hoffman, 1994), he and his wife and family moved to America, at first part-time as he continued to lecture worldwide in 1932; then by 1935, he settled in New York City and accepted the first chair of medical psychology at Long Island Medical College. He also served as visiting professor at Columbia University. Adler wrote, maintained his practice, lectured on an international circuit, and did numerous demonstrations and public education seminars. He died of heart failure while on a lecture tour in Aberdeen, Scotland, on May 28, 1937, while he was on a walk (Feldmann, 1972). His work was carried on in this country by his followers, most notably Rudolf Dreikurs, a psychiatrist who originally studied with Adler in Vienna and later relocated to Chicago; Dreikurs' colleagues, Bernard Shulman and Harold Mosak; Adler's children, Alexandra and Kurt; and Lydia Sicher.

Adler was very popular with American audiences. His work was well received. His pragmatic, socially oriented system seemed easy to grasp and nicely fit the prevailing *Zeitgeist*. After Adler's death, the movement, particularly in America, lost its momentum. The behaviorists had a stronghold in the universities and psychology departments; the psychoanalysts held virtually a monopoly in the psychiatric training centers and hospitals. Adlerians were without a place to train and educate new members, and by and large they either "died off" or practiced in silence, so as not to draw the wrath of the prevailing psychoanalysts who were still opposed to Adler's system.

Dreikurs fought hard to change this situation (Terner & Pew, 1978). He was a psychiatrist with a forceful personality and a strong, determined sense of rightness. Dreikurs lectured, did public demonstrations, and openly challenged not only the psychiatric community but psychologists and educators as well. Through his writings, his beginning of a new American journal, and his teaching, Dreikurs began to revive the Adlerian movement in this country.

☐ Individual Psychology: Its Current Status

Adlerian psychology is alive and well as we enter the turn of the century. In America, its principal organization is the North American Society of Adlerian Psychology (NASAP), with its conferences, workshops, newsletters, and journal, the *Journal of Individual Psychology*, published quarterly by the University of Texas Press. There is an international journal; international organizations such as the International Association of Individual Psychology (IAIP) and the International Congress of Adlerian Summer Schools and Institutes (ICASSI), which offers yearly conferences throughout the world; and numerous member organizations throughout the world.

Training in Adlerian psychology can be found at many universities and colleges in the United States and abroad as well as at numerous free-standing, postgraduate training institutes throughout the United States and Canada. In addition, the Adler School of Professional Psychology in Chicago is one of the oldest Adlerian training sites in the United States. Originally founded by Dreikurs, Shulman, and Mosak in 1952 as the Alfred Adler Institute of Chicago, it was, in its early years, a postgraduate training center. In 1972, it began offering a Master of Arts degree in counseling psychology, and in 1987 an accredited Doctor of Psychology (Psy.D.) degree in clinical psychology. Through these and other training sites and institutions, Adlerians are growing in numbers and becoming increasingly integrated into mainstream practice.

☐ The "Friends of Adler" Phenomenon

O'Connell (1976) coined the phrase, "friends of Adler phenomenon." By this he meant many theorists have borrowed extensively from Adler without giving him due credit. Indeed, as Ellenberger (1970) has stated, "It would not be easy to find another author from which so much has been borrowed from all sides without acknowledgment than Adler" (p. 645). Similarly, Wilder (Adler & Deutsch, 1959, p. xv) has observed, "Most observations and ideas of Alfred Adler have subtly and quietly permeated modern psychological thinking to such a degree that the proper question is not whether one is an Adlerian but how much of an Adlerian one is." With the increasing trend to psychotherapy integration (cf. Norcross & Goldfried, 1992, for example), Adler's system is gaining even greater recognition. As is evident throughout the remainder of this text, Adlerian psychology provides a basis for integrating many diverse systems and strategies of psychotherapy and counseling. A recent study by Sherman and Dinkmeyer (1987) found that

> Adlerian theory in particular overlaps to a high degree with most other theories . . . [a fact that] is well borne out by the fact that on over 92% of the items, the Adlerians were in agreement with the majority of the other theorists on the degree to which these items were accepted or rejected. (p. 105)

The family therapy work of Minuchin (1974) and Haley (1976); the existential work of Frankl (1983), May (1983), Yalom (1980), and Sartre (1943/1956) (Frankl and May studied with Adler [Ansbacher, 1959a]); the self-psychology of Kohut (1971, 1977) and Basch (1988); the cognitive therapy of Ellis (1973) and Beck (1976); Kernberg's (1975) object relations theory; the "cultural schools" of Fromm (1941), Horney (1945, 1950) and Sullivan (1953, 1964); and the integrationist/constructionist viewpoints of Guidano and Liotti (1983), Mahoney (1991), Safran and Segal (1990), and Wachtel (1977) all share striking similarities to Adler's work. The commentaries by Ansbacher and Ansbacher (Adler, 1956, 1964g, 1978), Ellenberger (1970), and Ford and Urban (1963) offer possible explanations for such oversight of Adler's name while "borrowing" heavily from his theory. Our point in mentioning such trends is to make readers aware that Adler's theory and system has more to offer students and practitioners than historical significance. By learning the principles and applications of Adlerian psychology, it is *easier* to make the transition to contemporary clinical practice within other systems of thought.

☐ Summary

This chapter commences by stating that all people desire to know, and that believing is what we humans do best. Our quest for understanding ourselves, our world, and our future may be the single most distinguishing feature of human nature. This book attempts to provide answers to some of these timeless questions, but from a perspective, for no one can see without seeing from somewhere. Adler (1937/1964b), in the last year of his life, wrote that

> Everyone subordinates all experiences and problems to his own conception. This conception is usually a tacit assumption and as such unknown to the person. Yet he lives and dies for the inferences he draws from such a conception. It is amusing, and sad at the same time, to see how even scientists—especially philosophers, sociologists, and psychologists—are caught in this net. In that it also has its assumptions, its conception of life, its style

of life, Individual Psychology is no exception. But it differs in that it is well aware of this fact. (p. 24)

It is against this "awareness," this background of a man who was small, poor sighted, physically ill and near death on several occasions, and considered poor in school, that we present this text. Adler overcame his fear of death by becoming a physician; he studied hard to overcome his academic troubles; he became interested in social causes and the influence the environment had upon those less fortunate or privileged; and he was attracted to and married a strong, politically active woman. He stressed social and sexual equality, finding a place in life in useful, prosocial ways and coming to grips with the challenges life presents us in cooperative, egalitarian ways. That was the background of Alfred Adler, the man. What follows is the philosophy and system of psychology of Adler the theorist, philosopher, social scientist, educator and psychiatrist.

☐ Points to Consider

It is difficult to separate a theory from the person creating the theory. The personality of the theorist often "spills into" his or her theory.

Adler was not a disciple of Freud, but rather an important coworker. He had his own theory about human nature before he began working with Freud.

Many of Adler's key concepts and insights have been absorbed into other systems, often without credit to their originator. With this realization, theoretical integration of diverse systems can be facilitated by learning the principles of Adlerian psychology.

☐ Questions

1. What was Adler's original choice of a medical specialty? How might this have influenced his theory?
2. What were some of the contributions Adler made to psychoanalysis which were later adopted by Freud?
3. What were the two issues Adler and Freud debated during their break-up?
4. Adler's theorizing can be divided into two periods. What are those two periods?
5. What were some of the social issues Adler addressed and incorporated into his system?

☐ Notes

[1]This is consonant with Adler's early theory expressed in *Study of Organ Inferiority and Its Psychical Compensation* (1907/1917). His specialization in ophthalmology, according to this theory, could have been a compensation for his poor eyesight.

[2]Although Adler described the premises underlying the masculine protest, he totally disagreed with them and endorsed the notion of sexual equality (Mosak & Schneider, 1977).

[3]This was essentially a Freudian society that was "free" of Freud.

Basic Assumptions and Philosophy of Individual Psychology

We have absolutely no experience of a cause; psychologically considered, we derive the entire concept from the subjective conviction that we are causes, namely, that the arm moves—but that is an error. We separate ourselves, the doers, from the deed, and we make use of this pattern everywhere— . . . . There is no such thing as a "cause". . . .

Friedrich Nietzsche (1888/1967)

. . . a mind not to be chang'd by Place or Time. The mind is its own place, and in itself Can make a Heav'n of Hell, and Hell of Heav'n. What matter where, if I be still the same. . . .

John Milton (1674/1957)

Theory, be it psychological, theological, or historical, is constructed by individuals. As Mahoney has chronicled in his massive work, *Human Change Processes* (1991), humans are not only passive recipients of sensory data from the environment; they are active agents in *constructing* the data perceived. This shift, called *constructionism*, is evident not only in psychology, but in numerous other disciplines and, as Mahoney documents, has been in circulation, in some form or another, since antiquity. Only recently has it gained popularity and more general acceptance from the "mainstream" scientific community.

As Shulman (1985) and Forgus and Shulman (1979) have detailed, Adler was a constructionist. He believed that people actively interpreted data according to biases that resided within the "cognitive map" of the individuals themselves (Mosak, 1995a). Hence, as documented in Chapter 1, Adler felt that theory was as much an outgrowth of the person's style of life as it was a statement of "truth."

What is the role of psychological theory? An analogy might clarify the issue. Theory is analogous to a pair of glasses (Adler, 1924b; Beecher & Beecher, 1951; Dreikurs, 1960), to the lenses we use to clarify our vision of life. With lenses we can better see. Some people need lenses that fit *them* and no one else. Others have lenses that can readily fit several others. The lenses that fit me may not fit you—because I can see better with them, it is not a given that you will see "equally" as well with my lenses. My "eyes" suit me to different lenses than yours. The key becomes to find lenses that fit one's "biases." If they fit you, wonderful. If not, it is wise to keep looking for another pair of lenses.

What follows are the basic assumptions of Individual Psychology. They are not "truth," but rather the lenses Adlerians use to construe life. Assumptions are not the "ends"; they are the *means* to an *end.* They are assumptions because if we "assume" these, they help us to proceeed further. If we assume that $2 + 2 = 4$ in a base-10 system, then we can proceed to $2 + 2 + 1 = 5$. However, this is only true if we assume a decimal system; it is not true in Boolian algebra, which uses other assumptions.

Try watching a ballgame without knowing the rules (i.e., the underlying assumptions). It is difficult, to say the least. Knowing the rules "up front" makes watching the game more enjoyable, primarily because it is more understandable. One does not have to scramble around, attempt to infer what is going on, and therefore miss much of the action. One can "sit back" and concentrate on the game itself.

Knowing the assumptions of a theory also allows another process to take place, that is, critical evaluation. In our culture (particularly among students), criticism commonly precedes scholarliness; in other words, we are all too ready to criticize without a thorough understanding. By understanding the assumptions *first,* and not simply the postulates, one can adopt a scholarly stance and then be in a better position to evaluate and, finally, criticize, a theory. For instance, a more fruitful approach to evaluating baseball is to know the game and its rules: Should there be a designated hitter or not? Have relief pitchers radically changed the nature of batting averages? A far less useful approach to evaluating baseball might be to criticize it for not having enough touchdowns. A system should be evaluated—and hence criticized—based upon the integrity of its system and assumptions, not upon another set of assumptions. "Drives," a basic assumption of classical psychoanalysis, are *not* part of the assumptions of Individual Psychology. Similarly, striving for superiority is a key assumption of Adler's theory but has little direct relevance to Freud's system. "Don't," the old saying states, "confuse apples with oranges."

☐ The Basic Assumptions of Individual Psychology

In Chapter 1, we explored the "style of life" of Adler and how his background influenced the development of the person (Mosak & Kopp, 1973). Adler astutely noted that a system, or theory, frequently has a life style of its own (Adler, 1931/1964b). That style reflects the personality of its originator and those who are attracted to it. What is about to be discussed is the life style of a theory—the underlying "schemas" that organize its structure.

Holism

Adlerians postulate that the person is an indivisible unit, that the person needs to be understood in his or her totality. From this vantage point, dividing the person into id, ego, and superego, or parent, child, and adult states, is not beneficial. As Adler (1956) stated:

> Very early in my work, I found man to be a [self-consistent] unity. The foremost task of Individual Psychology is to prove this unity in each individual—in his thinking, feeling, acting, in his so-called conscious and unconscious, in every expression of his personality. (p. 175)

What exactly is holism? In more concrete terms, holism can be conceptualized in the following ways.

The whole is *different* than the sum of its parts (Smuts, 1926/1961). For instance, imagine three parallel lines of equal length. In their present configuration, one "sees" one pattern; these same three lines can be reconfigured to form an equilateral triangle or the letter N or the letter Z and other configurations. One must know the *Gestalt* in order to understand the particular item, for in each case, we have three lines of equal length. If we focus too exclusively upon the parts, we lose the

Gestalt and, hence, we may "miss the boat." We do not see the forest for the trees.

Similarly, to allude to the opening quote of this chapter from Nietzsche, to say "the arm moves" is to assign to "it" (i.e., the arm) a "mind" and "will" of its own. "I raised my arm" is a very different statement philosophically than "my arm rose." The first statement awards responsibility to the person; the latter gives responsibility to the arm. Hence, Freud's emphasis upon drives and instincts originating from the id raised all sorts of "sticky" issues with regard to personal responsibility. Who, if anybody, was responsible for directing the instincts? If they "directed themselves," as Freud typically implied, that meant they had to have some sort of "ego-functions," a point Adler (1956) duly noted and called into question during his early days as a psychoanalyst.

Finally, as we demonstrate in our teaching, imagine this: For a moment, hold your hands out in front of your chest, with elbows bent, hands close to your body, and hold your hands. Now, pull. Notice something? Your hands, to paraphrase Nietzsche, stay dead center. No matter how hard you pull, with your left hand pulling left, right hand pulling right, they stay center. Why? Because you *choose* to keep them there. As long as we conceptualize the "hands"—that is, the parts—as being the focus of our attention, we formulate the idea of internal conflict or intrapsychic conflict with the person expressing him- or herself as a victim of the conflict (Mosak & LeFevre, 1976). Actually, we have *decided* to keep our hands "in conflict." Rather than victims of conflict, we are creators of conflict. The conflict is only apparent from an atomistic, reductionistic perspective (a different set of assumptions). From a holistic perspective, the hands are not in conflict with each other because "they" are exhibiting equal force in opposing directions; the hands stay dead center because we have decided to keep them there by exerting equal force. Conflict is a decision not to make a decision, to stay "dead center." The "pain" we feel is the price we pay for not making the decision (and perhaps "look good" to ourselves and others). If you "allow" one hand to pull harder (i.e., if you make a decision), notice how easily they move.

Teleology

Given this emphasis upon holism, and the fact the "intrapsychic conflict," or conflict that is related to a reductionistic perspective, is a function of choice, why would one choose to remain "in conflict?" It serves a purpose. In Aristotle's work, *The Metaphysics* (350 BC/1941), this is referred to as the final cause. Aristotle delineated four causes and believed that in order to understand the nature of something (i.e., anything), we must know the:

Material cause—what it is made of
Efficient cause—how it came to be
Formal cause—what shape or essence it is
Final cause—for what sake, or purpose, it is

A clinical example clarifies. A woman is depressed:

Material cause: A sad presentation, with lethargy, diurnal variation, psychomotor retardation.

Efficient cause: She may have a biological vulnerability she inherited. She suffered a loss in childhood of a parent. Her husband has just left her.

Formal cause: A mood (affective) disorder. She dislikes it and it causes suffering to herself and those around her. She complains and feels "horrible" and is self-critical.

Final cause: It places others into her service. With it, she can get others to move toward her and allow her to seek revenge upon her husband ("Look how that bastard has ruined my life!").

The various "schools" of psychotherapy have emphasized different causes. The first three causes (the material, efficient, and formal) are well known, at least in applications, to most clinicians. Adler's emphasis was upon the fourth, the final, cause. To emphasize any one to the exclusion of the others would be reductionistic, and Adlerian psychology is holistic; we stress all four causes, particularly the final cause (Ansbacher, 1951).

As Adler (1927/1957) wrote, the "first thing we discover in the psychic trends is that the movements are directed toward a goal . . . .This teleology, this striving for a goal, is innate in the concept of adaptation" (p. 28). In order to understand a person's goal, we need to understand his or her line of movement. People move towards goals in various ways; the most common goal is to belong. The importance of belonging is stressed by Horney (1950) in one of her central concepts, that of "basic anxiety," which she defines as "the feeling of being isolated and helpless in a potentially hostile world" (p. 18). All of us want to belong, and we establish a final, fictional goal that directs us as to what we should be or accomplish in order to belong (Adler, 1956). Goals are generally differentiated along two dimensions: concrete versus fictional, and long-range versus short-range. Fictional goals are subjective and state what must be achieved—fame, power, perfection, money, sexual attractiveness, performance, conquest, or so forth—in order to have a place in life. Because one can achieve significance in other ways, these goals are fictional.

An example clarifies the matter. Carl establishes early during his development (see Chapter 3) that the way for him to "fit in," to bond with his family, is to be "the best." This is unarticulated—it is learned preverbally (Rogers, 1951). To be the best is a "fictional goal." It becomes concretized in many diverse ways, such as to be the smartest student, the swiftest runner, the most popular classmate, and so forth. Even the concrete, "tangible" manifestations can be further broken down. If his long-term goal is to be the number-one student, many short-term goals can be envisioned: to study hard, to be "teacher's pet," or to have no one answer more questions than he does when in class. The final, fictional goal, therefore, can have many permutations and components. Also, there can be more than one final fictional goal (Mosak, 1979). Carl may want to be the best *and* he may crave excitement as well. The competition to be number one is certainly important, but the feelings of excitement and the thrill of competing may be "addictive" for him as well. This second final, fictional goal can have the same kind of permutations and variations mentioned about being the best.

To return to the issue from the beginning of this section, why would someone choose to be "in conflict?" What purpose could that serve? A more complete discussion is presented in the chapters on inferiority complexes and psychopathology, but for present purposes, a brief rationale can be offered. Sometimes, it seems beneficial "not to move," to "stay put" (Mosak & LeFevre, 1976). A man who cannot decide between his wife and his mistress can be conceptualized as in conflict. The purpose: As long as he "cannot" choose, he keeps both. If he "suffers" enough, they feel sorry for him and continue to wait for his decision. It is apparent that not to decide is to make a choice.

The Creative Self

Adlerians view people as actors, not merely reactors. We are more than the product of heredity and environment, more than simply reactive organisms; as Mahoney (1991) has stated, the prevailing trend in the social sciences is to see individuals as actively constructing their experiences, not simply passively responding to what is presented.

Adlerian psychology has been erroneously characterized as one that advocates merely reactive adjustment to society. Adler (1933/1964f), to the contrary, indicated that if we do not live in a suitable societal situation, we have the obligation to change it.

Adler (1929b, p. 34) noted that the child "strives to develop, and it [the child] strives to develop along a line of direction fixed by the goal which it chooses for itself." Although heredity and environment do provide parameters (see subsequent discussion of "soft determinism"), they do not take into account how the person will perceive his or her heredity or background.

Two processes are worth noting: feedback and feedforward mechanisms. Feedback mechanisms are (generally) homeostatic in function; they interpret data and determine what adjustments need to be made in order to maintain the status quo or adjust accordingly. Feedforward mechanisms are proactive; they anticipate and modify the situation in order to produce feedback that is already in line with the organism's requirements. The creativity we speak of is related to feedforward mechanisms. Children, for example, not only passively receive input from their caregivers, but actively elicit responses from those same individuals (Mosak, 1980). Similarly, anyone can be victimized; life can, and does, "kick us in the teeth" on occasion. Whether or not one chooses to become a victim, however, is not so automatic. As Frankl (1983) has discussed, life challenges us, but the *meaning* we derive from life is up to us. Life deals the cards; we only get a chance to play the hand.

Soft Determinism

This assumption becomes evident at this point. The classic philosophical debate has been between determinism and nondeterminism. The former assumes that causality (in the sense Nietzsche referred to at the opening of this chapter) is a fact, and that A implies (leads to) B. Nondeterminism assumes no causal connections whatsoever. Soft determinism is the middle ground. It stresses influences, not causes, and speaks of probabilities and possibilities, not givens. According to Adler (1933/1964f), the givens of a person's life situation and biologic constitution "are events of statistical probability. The evidence of their existence should never be allowed to degenerate into the setting up of a fixed rule" (p. 27). As Adler (1936) was fond of pointing out, "Everything can also be different" (p. 14).

Several clarifications need to be made, for the subtle distinctions of this issue have fostered considerable misunderstandings, even among Adlerians. First, choosing does *not* always mean wanting. I may choose a broken leg, even though I do not want it, if it means jumping from this burning building in order to save my life. Similarly, one may choose to go to graduate school to get one's doctorate, but one may not want to have to do all the work and read all the texts.

Second, freedom to choose *is not the same* as freedom of choice. Life does impose certain limits, and within those limits I am free to choose. Freedom of choice typically implies unlimited choice. That rarely exists. Nonetheless, we are always free to choose, at least how we feel about what is presented, in other words, our attitude (see Frankl, 1983, for a cogent discussion of this topic).

Third, the dynamics of responsibility, choice, and blame need to be explored. Although Adlerians hold them responsible for their actions (Maniacci, 1991; Mosak, 1987a), they do not blame people. Given the assumptions of holism, creativity, teleology, and soft determinism, people choose; they, and they alone, are responsible for their choices. They may not be aware of making the choices or of the consequences of their choices and many of the implications that those choices entail, particularly the social implications, but they are responsible for them. Adlerians do not believe that "the Devil made me do it." People are not to be blamed but to be educated, and Adler (1956) considered his therapy to be strongly reeducative (see the discussion of this issue by Ford & Urban, 1963; and Mosak, 1995a).

Phenomenology

"I am convinced," Adler (1933/1964f, p. 19) stated unequivocally, "that a person's behavior springs from his idea . . . because our senses do not receive actual facts, but merely a subjective image of them." Technically speaking, we do not see the world, we apprehend it. Adler (1956, p. 182) spoke of a "schema of apperception [*Apperzeptionsschema*]." An apperception is a perception with meaning, a conclusion, attached to it. Whereas Freud operated from the premise (vantage point) of an objective psychologist, Adler was a subjective psychologist (Ford & Urban, 1963). Adler was not interested in facts per se, but the individual's perceptions of the facts.

The cognitive map we form to guide us through life, to direct our line of movement toward our final, fictional goal, is based upon our phenomenological interpretation of experience (Mosak, 1995a). A story clarifies:

> A child turns to his father and asks, "Which is closer, the moon or China?" His father, being a man who values logic, replies, "China." The child forcefully disagrees. Upon questioning, the child explains that the moon must be closer, because he can see the moon, and he's never seen China.

An interesting historical note is in order. It is generally considered that the founder of the "school" of phenomenology was the mathematician/philosopher Edmund Husserl, who first detailed his system in his book, *Ideas: General Introduction to Pure Phenomenology* (1913/1962). Adler was writing at the same time and had published his book *The Neurotic Constitution* a year earlier (1912/1983b). Though it is not commonly known, Husserl was a classmate of Freud; the only nonmedical course Freud took at the University of Vienna was from Franz Brentano, Husserl's mentor. Husserl's "star pupil" was a young theology student who switched to philosophy, Martin Heidegger, the founder of the school of existentialism. The phenomenological method is the cornerstone of existential psychology (Yalom, 1980), and one of the key assumptions of Individual Psychology (Allers, 1961; van Dusen, 1959). The interrelatedness of the two schools has been well documented (Ansbacher, 1959a; Birnbaum, 1961; Ellenberger, 1970; Farau, 1964; Holt, 1967; Johnson, 1966; Radl, 1959; Schaffer, 1974, 1976; Stern, 1958; van Dusen, 1959).

If the person is continually acting on, and not simply reacting to, his or her environment, and that person is actively creating his or her own perceptions, goals, and movements through life, then the Adlerian conception sees development as an ongoing process; the person is continually creating (or recreating) him- or herself. He or she is always in the process of becoming (K. Adler, 1963; Allport, 1955). As is evident in Chapter 4, the influences, not causes, from the past may have had phenomenological reality for us, but conditions do change, and we have the capacity to change with them. We may have "had to," from our phenomenological reality, react a certain way "back then," but if the situation has changed, we are responsible if we continue to act as we did in the past. As a patient eloquently put it, "You mean I'm giving conditioned responses to conditions which no longer exist." Time moves on, life changes, but we have a stubborn, tenacious ability to continue to see things "in the future," as "they were." Hence, as May (1983, p. 140) aptly phrased it, "What an individual seeks *to become* determines what he remembers of this *has been*. In this sense the future determines the past."

Social-field Theory

Individuals develop and live in a social context. The idea of a person living outside of a world is incomprehensible. People have challenges; that is part and parcel of being human. Whether or not the challenges become problems is an issue that is contingent upon the individual's phenomenology, goals, and creativity. Not all problems are social problems, for some are genuinely within the province of the individual; but all problems are capable of becoming social problems. For example, if my toe aches, that is a challenge with which I must deal. I may choose to see it as a problem but not bother anybody about it. I can make it a social problem, however, quite easily: I can whine and complain, demand special services, and in general expect an "exemption" from life—and in a social context, that means that if I fail to pull my share of the load, sooner or later, someone will have to pull it for me or it will be left undone.

Adler (1927/1957, p. 34) stated it this way: "In order to know how a man thinks, we have to examine his relationship to his fellow men . . . . We cannot comprehend the psychic activities without at the same time understanding those social relationships" (p. 34). Adler was against classification and labeling. He cautioned that

> the student may very easily fall into the error of imagining that a type is something ordained and independent, and that it has as its basis anything more than a structure that is to a large extent homogeneous. If he stops at this point and believes that when he hears the word "criminal," or "anxiety neurosis," or "schizophrenia," he has gained some understanding of the individual case, he not only deprives himself of the possibility of individual research, but he will never be free from misunderstandings that will arise between him and the person whom he is treating. (Adler, 1933/1964f, p. 127)

Flexibility is one key to adaptation, survival, and, as Gazzaniga (1985) postulates, human evolution. To say someone is phobic does not tell you much. Where is he or she phobic? With whom? For how long? What appears to precipitate it? To stop it? How does he or she feel about being phobic? These types of questions help elucidate the phenomenological field, and therefore provide a better grasp of the person. A characteristic of maladaptive behavior is its inflexibility (Krausz, 1973). To continue with our phobic patient: He or she may have been afraid of a particular dog that provided a rather nasty bite when our patient was quite young. If overgeneralization occurs (Mosak, 1995a), all dogs may be perceived as threatening. If overgeneralization occurs, the phobia may be extended to any fur. The underlying assumption (or schema) may be too rigid. A more extreme example would be the man who feels he has to be "The Boss." At work, this may be fine, but it can cause him some grief at home or with his friends.

A somewhat different, but related, issue revolves around preparation for practice as a psychotherapist. If, given this assumption, one needs to know not only the person but the person's social field, therapists need to be versed in more than psychology. Literature, myths, religion, ethnicity, history, movies, and the like all help to illuminate the person's picture.

Striving for Superiority

Motivation, from some Adlerian perspectives, is conceptualized as moving from a perceived minus situation to a perceived plus situation. As Ansbacher and Ansbacher have documented (Adler, 1956), Adler gave this movement several different names throughout his writings, with the phenomenological "plus" situation being variously described as being:

A real man
A will to power
Self-esteem
Security
Perfection
Completion
Overcoming
Superiority

The first four phrases were characteristic of early Adler, when he wrote primarily as a psychoanalyst, and his concepts were about abnormal individuals. The last group evolved as Adler wrote more and more as a philosopher, educator and social psychologist. During this period, he was more interested in describing normal development. A useful distinction is made by Lazarsfeld (1927/1991). She differentiates the normal individual who strives for perfection from the maladaptive person who tries to be perfect. In the first case, one realizes it is a goal that can never be totally achieved; but in the latter, one actually attempts to become perfect. Adler (1933/1964f) states it this way: "The material of life has been constantly bent on reaching a plus from a minus situation" (p. 97).

In practice, it can be difficult to see how some people are moving towards a plus situation, or towards what Adler (1937/1964e), in one of his last papers, finally referred to as superiority. Some elaboration clarifies.

Adler (1937/1964e) felt that everyone strives for superiority. That is the single, motivating force for all living organisms. The final, fictional goal is a goal that the person perceives as bringing him or her that superiority. The degree of social interest that the person displays (see Chapter 7) sets the direction to the striving. If he or she is very interested in the welfare of others, then the striving is on the socially useful side of life, as manifested in caring, compassion, social cooperation, and contribution to the common welfare (Mosak, 1991). If there is a low degree of social interest, then the striving is not prosocial, but rather antisocial (in the broad sense of the term). Those individuals attempt to gain their superiority at the expense of those around them, rather than for the betterment of all involved.

Sometimes, the price one pays to get to the perceived plus (i.e., superiority), may be a "real" (i.e., concrete) minus. First, a relatively common example. In order to have a clean house, I may have to work very hard and sacrifice some of my free time. Similarly, in order to earn a degree, I may have to spend a lot of money and time and put myself through considerable anxiety and discomfort. In the short term, I experience a "minus," but the "plus" will come. A more clinical example: How can self-mutilation move someone toward a plus situation? Once again, that may be a "real" minus, especially in the short-term situation. Long-term, however, that person may receive attention, others may "walk on eggshells" when near that person (so as to not "upset" him or her), and he or she may gain some sense of subjective relief from the act, including a sense of being able to tolerate pain. The self-mutilator may even develop moral superiority, quoting Jesus (Mark 9:47): "And if your eye causes you to stumble, cast it out; it is better for you to enter the kingdom of God with one eye, than having two eyes, to be cast into hell."

The striving for superiority that takes into account the long-term good, or welfare, of those in life can seldom go wrong. If striving for superiority takes place at the expense of others, or on too short a term, others are not very likely to benefit.

Idiographic Orientation

Adlerians tend to emphasize the idiographic nature of individuals, that is, the particulars of the specific person. This is relatively evident, given the assumptions of phenomenology, teleology, soft determinism, holism, and creativity. "Certainly we cannot altogether avoid using it (the general law), for it enables us to generalize . . . but it can give us very little idea of any particular case or its treatment" (Adler, 1933/1964f, p. 127). The general, or nomothetic, laws place us "in the ballpark," but only by knowing the particular person in his or her phenomenological idiosyncrasies can we know a person. This applies to all people, normal or abnormal.

Research, for instance, has validated Adler's (1956) assumption that agoraphobic persons tend to value control (see Guidano & Liotti, 1983). That is the nomothetic principle. That does not tell us much about the particular person sitting across from us, in our office, seeking our help because the agoraphobia is becoming unbearable. All of us feel inferior at one time or another; that makes us human (Wolfe, 1932). How we feel inferior, what we define as inferior (e.g., being short, fat, dumb, ugly, too tall, too smart), when, and under what circumstances, all of this fleshes out the idiographic dynamics. Remediation in general, and psychotherapy in particular, is greatly enhanced by knowing the person as a person, not as a cluster of signs, symptoms, and syndromes. The various diagnostic labels place us in the ballpark but do not describe the individual patient. Given the phenomenolgical and idiographic assumptions, it follows that one cannot completely interpret a dream unless one knows the dreamer.

Psychology of Use

Adler (1929c) stressed that "it is not what one has inherited that is important, but what one does with his inheritance" (p. 37). Mosak (1995a) has noted that life does, to some extent, provide limits to what one can do, but within those limits, the opinion one has of one's situation, and, hence, the use one makes of it, can be rather startling. A person born without legs will probably never be a high jumper in the Olympics; but Bo Jackson, with his artificial hip, can play for a pennant-contending major league baseball team. As Maniacci (1993, 1996b) points out, a distinction between impairment and disability can prove useful. Two individuals with the same impairment may not be equally disabled. The stances they take toward their situation can be crucial determinants.

Adler's early work led him to study the biological substrates of organic compensation. Published in 1907, *Study of Organ Inferiority and its Psychical Compensation* was given considerable praise by Freud as having contributed greatly to understanding the biological origins of neurotic dynamics. In it, Adler discussed how certain organs or organ systems tended to compensate for deficiencies. One kidney is removed, and the other enlarges and assumes the missing kidney's function. As Adler progressed in this thinking, this original biological, mechanistic view became replaced with a more psychological, holistic one. Although organ inferiority still retained its biological definition (an inherited deficiency or weakness of the body or organ or organ system), the compensations became more psychodynamic. Dreikurs (1948b) has elaborated upon this issue at length, and interested readers are referred to that work for a more complete discussion. But for present purposes, those Adlerians who are medically trained (or sensitive) can often quite accurately find biological correlates to many psychological conditions, such as an organ inferiority of the gastrointestinal system leading to personality traits of a getter (Adler, 1956).

Three areas of special interest with reference to the assumption of psychology of use are memory, emotions, and cognitive processes. We examine each in turn.

Adler (1927/1957) noted that what we remember is greatly influenced by where we are going (hence May's comment noted previously about our future determining our past). As Adler stated, "We remember those events whose recollection is important for a specific psychic tendency" (p. 49). If I want to move toward someone, I will remember nice, pleasant things about that person; but as soon as I want to move away from or against that person (Horney, 1945), I will remember negative, unpleasant things. These serve to justify my movement to my goal. Not only will I remember what suits my purpose, but I will forget what does not suit it as well. The role of memory, and early recollections specifically, is discussed in greater detail in Chapter 9, in which the process of assessment is detailed. For the present discussion, suffice to say that memory, like many other tendencies, is greatly influenced and used according to the goal we set for ourselves.

Emotions are much the same. Adler (1927/1957, 1956) spoke of disjunctive and conjunctive emotions. Like other psychological processes, emotions are used according to the goals people establish (Beecher & Beecher, 1971/1987; Dreikurs, 1951). Some emotions move us towards others; others move us away. Adlerians tend to view emotions as motivators for behavior; to use a metaphor, they are the gasoline we use to power us to our goals. Interestingly enough, contemporary psychoanalysts such as Basch (1988, p. 68) state that "the affect attached to a particular perceptual goal moves a person to engage in behavior that will fulfill or reach it." This is strikingly similar to Adler's formulation. Once again, the idiographic component of Individual Psychology is important, for to know what purpose a particular emotion serves one needs to know the person. Some general guidelines about two particular emotions can offer some clarity: anger and hurt.

If one is angry, it generally serves the purpose of motivating one to change something. It is as if one is saying, "There is something about it or me that needs changing." However, for various reasons the person may fear or be unwilling to attempt that change. By being hurt the person avoids changing *it* then because she or he first has to get over the hurt. The person shifts her or his focus from changing *it* to changing her or his feelings. More clinical examples, such as anxiety, fear, depression, and aggression are discussed in Chapter 8.

Finally, Adler (1956) made a distinction between common sense and private sense (private intelligence) or what has more recently been referred to as private logic. Ansbacher (1965) and Dreikurs (1973) have provided detailed analyses.

Common sense is that which is shared with others, the ability to speak a common language and share perceptions with others. One ingredient of common sense is consensuality; we all agree upon it. A second is that what we all agree upon may be a fiction (Vaihinger, 1911/1965). In reality, a paper dollar is only a piece of paper. We can tear it, burn it, write on it, and the like. But our society has created the fiction that it has worth, and as long as we observe that fiction and behave *as if* it has worth, it makes commerce easier. Private logic has three components: immediate goals, hidden reasons, and life style goals.

Life style goals or long-term, personality goals, are the final, fictional goals. As mentioned previously, those are generally nonconscious, nonverbal, and not clearly understood by individuals. Immediate goals are those short-term goals that are more readily attainable. These too are often not clearly understood and were discussed previously. The hidden reason is the explanation we give ourselves for what we are doing. Maniacci (1993) has provided a clinical example of how all three operate in a case formulation, and a brief example is provided to illustrate:

> Life style goal
>> To be perfect
> Frequent Immediate Goals
>> To look good
>> To be without error
>> To never be corrected
> Frequent hidden reasons
>> "I'm always right."
>> "Who are you to judge me?"
>> "I can't let anybody see me as weak."

Imagine a client with this private logic. In his striving to be perfect, he does not allow anyone to contradict him; he is difficult and moody if "crossed" (and remember, given his phenomenology, he may perceive "crossed" quite differently than others). His hidden reasons (what many cognitive therapists term "self-statements" or "automatic thoughts") reflect this bias. A more detailed analysis of private logic is presented in the chapters on development, life style, and psychopathology.

Finally, cognitive processes such as intelligence are greatly influenced by the person's private logic. For instance, if it does not suit a person's goal to use his or her intelligence, than that person may choose to fail in school if it furthers him or her along towards his or her goal. As one student gleefully announced after flunking out of medical school, "That's the first decision I ever made without my parents in all my life."

Acting "As If"

Adler (1956) was greatly influenced by the work of the philosopher, Hans Vaihinger (1911/1965). According to Vaihinger, people construct "fictions" that help move them through life. These fictions are like lines drawn on a map. They do not exist in reality, but they provide useful guidelines for navigating. Adler applied this philosophical insight to his clinical work. It soon became a cornerstone of his theory.

Given the aforementioned assumptions, people select goals, perceive according to those goals, and move throughout life as if all of this were "true." From a phenomenological standpoint, for the particular person, all of it *is* true. But as Adler (1912/1983b) stated on the first page of his first psychological book, "Everything is a matter of opinion." People act according to their fictions, their beliefs, and even set out to have life (and other people) conform to their expectations or construct life in terms of their expectations. Hence, someone who feels inferior tends to act that way, or to compensate so as to appear superior.

Self-fulfilling Prophecy

This is a natural outgrowth of the tendency to act "as if." As Festinger (1957) attempted to establish, if given a discrepancy between what we believe and what "is," cognitive dissonance occurs. We tend to stick to our beliefs. Adler (1933/1964f, pp. 19–20) provides an example:

> In a word, I am convinced that a person's behaviour springs from his idea . . . . As a matter of fact, it has the same effect on one whether a poisonous snake is actually approaching my foot or whether I merely believe it is a poisonous snake.

If I believe "it's a dog-eat-dog world out there," I act as if it is, construe events to support my belief, and probably provoke others to take a cold, if not hostile, stance toward me. I then feel justified in declaring, "See! I was right!" As Milton stated over 300 years ago, the mind can make a heaven of hell, or a hell of heaven.

Optimism

The last assumption of Individual Psychology is that of optimism. Freud's system is basically pessimistic; it postulates a different set of assumptions about human nature, assumptions that view individuals as in conflict, not only within themselves but with each other. Adler's system is much more optimistic. People can, and do, change. They can, and do, take responsibility for themselves and are quite capable of working cooperatively for the greater good. Adler (1978) was rather clear about one point, however, that is frequently overlooked. People are neither good nor bad; *human nature is neutral.* This view was enunciated by the 12th-century physician and philosopher Maimonides (1180/1944), who wrote,

> Pay no attention to the view . . . that at man's birth God decrees whether he shall be righteous or wicked. That is not so! Every person has the power of becoming as righteous as Moses or wicked as Jeroboam—wise or stupid, tender or cruel, miserly or generous. (5:1–2)

Heredity, environment, and the choice of the creative self all interact to help the person produce the final, fictional goal, which can be socially useful or useless, or neutral itself, with the nature of the movement towards that goal being "good" or "bad." Adler was not naive. He lived through a world war, worked with criminals, psychotics, and the underprivileged. He knew the extremes of human nature as well as did Freud. Freud came out of World War I and postulated the death instinct. He felt that the ultimate aim of human life was to return to an inorganic state. Adler came out of the same war, a war in which he served as a physician, and postulated the concept of social interest, more recently called community feeling (Ansbacher, 1992a). We, as a species, have the potential for good. Whether or not we actualize it is up to us. We are responsible for our fate—the best of it, or the worst of it.

☐ Summary

The assumptions of Individual Psychology are not very complex. Adler (1956) disliked technical jargon, and he was determined to avoid making his system too complicated. To paraphrase him, on the surface it appears simple, but to those who know the system, it is comprehensive, broad in scope, and sophisticated in breadth.

Having established the foundation, let us now turn our attention to how individuals develop. The development of the life style is examined in the next chapter, and with that, the assumptions that have been presented in static form can be seen in action, as they apply to the understanding of personality.

☐ Points to Consider

By knowing the assumptions of a system, one is in a better position to evaluate that system. Systems should be evaluated based upon their adherence to their assumptions, not from the basis of another set of assumptions.

Adlerians emphasize the final cause of people's behavior. Although they consider all four causes (as detailed by Aristotle), they believe the final cause is crucial.

Adler was neutral with regard to human nature. He felt that people could be either good or bad.

Adlerians tend to speak of probable outcomes of certain backgrounds. This is known as soft determinism.

Although it is important to understand what a person has, it is more important to understand the use she or he makes of her or his qualities.

☐ Questions

1. What is phenomenology? How is it incorporated into Adlerian psychology?
2. What did Adler mean by "fictions?"
3. What are some of the various terms Adler used to describe the "plus" position people strive for?
4. What is the difference between freedom to choose and freedom of choice?
5. How do Adlerians introduce teleology into their system?
6. How do Adlerians tend to view "intrapsychic conflict?"

3

The Development of the Life Style

Blest the infant Babe
(For with my best conjectures I would trace
Our Being's earthly progress), blest the Babe,
Nursed in his Mother's arms, who sinks to sleep
Rocked on his Mother's breast; who with his soul
Drinks in the feelings of his Mother's eye! . . .
Emphatically such a Being lives . . .
For feeling has to him imparted power
That through the growing faculties of sense
Doth like an agent of the one great Mind
Create, creator and received both,
Working but in alliance with the works
Which it beholds. . . .

William Wordsworth (1850/1979)

Just as all psychologies have theories of human nature and how to comprehend them, people have their theories, their lenses, for understanding life, people, and themselves. In this chapter, we examine how Adlerians view human personality development. The "facts" of personality development are not the question; people are born, grow, achieve maturity, suffer losses, succeed and fail, and eventually die. It is the way Adlerians perceive these facts to which we now turn.

☐ An Overview of the Concept of Life Style

The life style is the individual's characteristic way of thinking, seeing, and feeling towards life and is synonymous with what other theorists call "personality." Adler (1956, pp. 187–188) wrote that

> [The child's] opinion of life, which is at the bottom of his attitude to life and is neither shaped into words nor expressed in thought, is his own masterpiece. Thus, the child arrives at his law of movement which aids him after a certain amount of training to obtain a style of life, in accordance with which we see the individual thinking, feeling, and acting throughout his whole life.

From this passage and throughout Adler's writings, it becomes evident that Adler conceived of the child as both the receiver *and* the creator of his or her own world. As Wordsworth alluded to in the opening quote for this chapter, the child is "creator and receiver both,/Working . . . in alliance with [that]/Which it beholds." The child is exposed to "a certain amount of training," but that same child is active in his or her creation of the meaning of that training. A story might clarify the issue:

> Two brothers, a 6-year-old and a 5-year-old, decide that today is the day they will learn how to swear. The 6-year-old says, "I'm gonna say the word 'damn,' " and the 5-year-old replies with glee, "I'll say the word 'ass,' " and they giggle and wait for their opportunity. Mother calls for them to come down for breakfast. They run downstairs, into the kitchen, and jump on the stools. "What would you like for breakfast?" Mother asks the oldest. "Give me some cereal, damn it!" the 6-year-old replies, and without skipping a beat, Mother slaps him with the back of her hand across his face. He runs crying and embarrassed to his room. She turns to the 5-year-old and with a stern grimace says, "And what would you like?" to which he replies with a tremor in his voice, "I don't know, but you can bet your ass it won't be cereal."

The message Mother was intending to send was "clear," to her: Don't swear! The message the 5-year-old heard was just as clear: Don't order cereal! As we explore here, development is an interactive process between people, not just from parents *to* children (Mosak, 1980). Parents may do everything "right," but that does not mean that that is how the children perceive it. Many times we have heard clients turn to spouses during marital sessions and utter something akin to, "But that's not how I meant it. I was trying to protect you," to which the other typically replies, "I didn't know that. I thought you were telling me I was stupid." It is not an instance of parent to child, but the principle still applies. People are affected by their perceptions of the facts, not the facts themselves.

In his introduction to Adler's (1929/1964d) *Problems of Neurosis,* Ansbacher (1964) articulates a crucial distinction Adler made to his theory of human development. In Adler's early writings, he was still formulating his theory of development from a drive-reduction perspective. Initially, Adler believed and wrote that children feel inferior, attempt to compensate, and then strive for superiority in any of its manifold forms. Thus, schematically presented, the general developmental picture is this:

> *Feelings of inferiority* are noticed, leading to
>   *Compensatory mechanisms,* which lead to
>   *Striving for superiority*

Later Adler changed this sequence (cf. Adler, 1937/1964e). The emphasis upon drive reduction was replaced with a growth motivation that states that children strive for superiority. When Adler speaks of superiority, he does not literally mean superiority but a more advantageous position. Although many people do strive for actual superiority, Adler was really referring to the striving for competence, significance, and community feeling. Ansbacher (Dubelle, 1997) explains:

> The basic striving, according to Adler, is the striving for *Vollkommenheit.* The translation of *Vollkommenheit* is completeness, but it can also be translated as excellence. In English, only the second translation was considered; it was only the striving for excellence. The delimitation of the striving for excellence is the striving for superiority.
>
> Basically, it all comes from the striving for completeness, and there he said that it is all a part of life in general, and that is very true. Even a flower or anything that grows, any form of life, strives to reach its completeness. And perfection is not right, because the being does not strive—one cannot say to be perfect—what is a perfect being? It is striving for completeness, and that is very basic and very true (p. 6).

Children become frustrated, feel inferior, and then compensate with additional striving. Schematically presented, it looks like this:

> *Striving* leads to
>   *Inferiority feelings,* which lead to
>   *Compensation* and further *striving*

The change is crucial, and not simply cosmetic. The initial formulation implied that a tension was produced that the children "had to" reduce. This is similar to Freud's system, only "feelings of inferiority" are used instead of sexual energy (i.e., libido). Adler's second formulation emphasizes growth processes (cf. Rogers, 1951), and research has tended to support the view of the infant as a growth-motivated, competence-seeking organism (Basch, 1988; Stern, 1985).

As Dreikurs and Soltz (1964) have discussed, children are excellent observers, but horrible interpreters. As we have attempted to point out, this comment applies not only to children, but to adults as well. We, like children, "see" a lot of what goes on around us, but the meaning we attach to it can vary tremendously. The life style is the set of rules, the cognitive map (Mosak, 1995a), that guides us through life. It is the "rule of rules" (Shulman, 1973a, b) in that it directs us not only with reference to the feedback we receive, but the feedforward mechanisms we send out. Its development by children is an attempt to make sense out of and control the data from the environment and their own bodies; they receive information, both internally and externally, that needs to be processed, and the life style is the key to how those data are used.

Forgus and Shulman (1979) have discussed, at length, how the perceptual program of the infant modifies needs and turns them into motives. Innate programs for interacting with the environment are slowly replaced by rules that the infant puts in place in order to achieve goals that the infant forms. Thus, according to Forgus and Shulman, an innate need for nourishment and contact is modified, through interaction with the environment and significant others, into a motive for attachment (Bowlby, 1983). How the infant decides to attach him- or herself becomes a matter of choice, training, biological equipment, and the like. The life style would be the general pattern, or theme, to which the infant coordinates his or her striving for significance.

☐ Factors Influencing Development of the Life Style

The human infant is a complex, highly sophisticated organism, yet it is one of the most dependent, slowly developing infants in the animal world. As we alluded to previously, holism is a key concept in Adlerian psychology, and Adlerians approach development from a similar stance. For ease of presentation, however, a distinction is made between biological factors and psychosocial factors that affect development. In reality, both are intimately connected with one another. This connection itself is not necessarily holistic; it could be, and often is, dualistic in other psychological systems. One factor, however, transcends both biological and psychosocial factors, and it is to it that we turn first.

Degree of Activity

The degree of activity is the amount of energy an individual uses in meeting the challenges of life. According to Adler (1956, p. 164), "The individual degree of activity is created somewhat arbitrarily by the personality during earliest childhood." Some people display a high degree of it, and others a low degree, with numerous shades of difference in between. Generally speaking, the more active the individual was in meeting the tasks and challenges of life, the healthier Adler believed the individual to be.

Biological Factors

Adler (1956) considered there to be three overburdening situations that could elicit behavior and psychopathology in individuals: being born with inferior organs (i.e., organ inferiority), pampering, and neglect.[1] Adler (1907/1917) defined an organ inferiority as an inherited[2] weakness of an organ or organ system. What an individual is born with does play some part in development, and his or her biological equipment is affected by not only inherited (i.e., genetic) factors, but by prenatal factors as well. Dreikurs (1948b) pointed out that Adler's final formulation of organ inferiority had three components. If presented with an inferior organ, the individual could compensate along any of three dimensions: a somatic level, a sympathetic level, and a psychic level. An example of each clarifies. John, born with a dysfunctional limb, may compensate somatically by consciously or unconsciously developing the unaffected limb to an even greater degree than normal. If his left leg is deformed, his right may become very strong. A sympathetic level of compensation might be how he carries himself; he may walk and move in such a way that others hardly notice his impairment. On the psychic level, he may form a goal of being supercompetent in sports, activities, and "masculine" activities. John is not so unusual. This is the actual case of the British romantic poet George Gordon, otherwise known as Lord Byron. He had a deformed foot from birth but carried himself in such a way that others hardly ever noticed, and he became internationally known for his love of swimming, horseback riding, and military adventures, as well as his poetry. Although Adler in his theoretical writings emphasized the compensatory aspects almost to the exclusion of other responses, in his discussion of cases he also alludes to the possibility of retreat and withdrawal. Children may "declare bankruptcy," quit striving, feel sorry for themselves, and gain attention, sympathy, and service from others.

Not only is the organ itself to be considered, but the person's perception of the organ inferiority as well. John may not consider his leg a handicap even if others may consider it an "overburdening situation." One person may consider being tall a plus; another may consider the same height a minus. This affects the developing life style as much as the organic component itself.

Another biological factor, in addition to organ inferiority, relates to brain and central nervous system development. Adler (1956, p. 188) alluded to it in a quote cited earlier: The life style is "neither shaped into words nor expressed in thought." As Gazzaniga (1985) and Miller (1990) have written, the brain is modular in function. The left hemisphere is primarily interpretive; the right is mostly emotive and interactive. Gazzaniga writes,

> The dominant left hemisphere is committed to the task of interpreting our overt behaviors as well as the more covert emotional responses produced by these separate mental modules of our brain. It constructs theories as to why these behaviors occurred and does so because of that brain system's need to maintain a sense of consistency for all of our behaviors. It is a uniquely human endeavor, and upon it rests not only the mechanism that generates our sense of subjective reality but also a mental capacity to free us from the binding controls of external contingencies. (p. 80)

In a similar vein, Miller (1990) describes the function of the frontal lobes. He states that the frontal lobes allow individuals to judge and regulate ongoing external perceptions and to "calculate appropriate responses" to those perceptions (p. 57). He extends his view by remarking that

> The frontal lobe system is certainly important in social behavior . . . . Sociability is the form of *adaptive* behavior most appropriate to the *human* environment, and this, its situational adaptiveness, is what I think accounts for its dependence on frontal lobe functioning. (p. 59)

and that

> [the frontal lobes] synthesize information received about the outside world (appointment dates, plane and train schedules) and information about internal states of the mind and body (financial goals, personal values). This provides the means by which . . . behavior is regulated according to the effects produced by . . . actions. (p. 57)

From a neurodevelopmental perspective, what does all this mean? Children are receiving input from the world at least from birth (Skolnick, 1986), typically via the visual, auditory, tactile (Harlow, 1958), and sensorimotor systems, which are mostly innate, "hard wired" programs.

Their ability to linguistically sort, retrieve, and analyze that data (left-hemisphere functions) and plan, regulate, and execute behavior that moves them towards goals in socially appropriate ways (frontal-lobe functions) are not better developed until a much later time, typically around the age of 5 to 7 years (Skolnick, 1986). Learning, especially learning that occurs between the ages of 8 and 24 months, is of a trial-and-error type, spatial, and imagistic (Skolnick, 1986). As Miller (1990) elaborates, the "unconscious"[3] may be the early learning that took place preverbally, through trial and error, in spatial, imagistic, right-hemisphere processing. It is not particularly accessible to verbal, interpretive, typically left-hemisphere processing. Lessons learned prior to frontal-lobe, left-hemisphere maturation may not be "pulled back" via verbal means—in other words, we know much more than we seem to understand (Adler, 1956). This neurodevelopmental perspective sheds interesting light upon a technique Adler (1956) pioneered for assessing individuals—the use of early recollections in order to determine the life style of the individual. Early recollections are those memories of incidents that can be visualized as having occurred prior to the age of 8 or 9 years (Mosak, 1958). This is explored in much greater detail in Chapter 9, but for present purposes, suffice it to say that Adlerians have long considered these as being indicative of the core issues of the person's style.

Children develop and learn rules about how to move towards goals, but they learn them in nonverbal, sensorimotor, action-oriented ways. Private logic (Adler, 1956; Ansbacher, 1965; Dreikurs, 1973), reconceptualized from a neurodevelopmental perspective, may be just that: early learning prior to frontal-lobe, left-hemisphere processing. As Skolnick (1986) cites, research has verified a point that Adler, Freud, and Piaget noted through their observational, case-study methodology, that the personalities of children appear to be "fixed" around the age of 5 to 7 years. That is approximately when children begin to behave "as if" their early learning were "true" and set in stone ("concrete operations"). They set out to confirm their expectations and apply them in ever increasingly wider social fields. Although these are seemingly "set in stone," slight modifications continue to occur throughout the life span; however, the core convictions remain constant unless the person has a therapeutic experience. A therapeutic experience is not necessarily limited to formal psychotherapy. Life itself may be therapeutic. A prototypic example is the transformation of Saul of Tarsus to St. Paul on the road to Damascus.

The last biological factor we consider, albeit briefly, is the role of "needs" or "drives." In their extensive literature review, Forgus and Shulman (1979) have postulated that there are four primary needs that appear to be "hard wired" into infants at birth, and these are nourishment and contact, protection and safety, mastery, and sensory variation (cf. Maslow's [1970]"hierarchy of needs"). These four needs are biological. Without sufficient attention given to them, infants either perish or fail to thrive. Through the socialization process these four needs become goals that become hierarchically arranged into the following four motives: attachment, security, competence, and cognition. Throughout development, these goals become more and more articulated; for instance, the attachment motive can become a goal to have unfailing love from those around, or the competence motive can become articulated to be the best at whatever is attempted (cf. Rogers, 1951). The particular arrangement of the motives (or goals) varies from person to person; some have attachment and security first; others may have cognition and competence as primary. How each becomes particularly differentiated is a matter of particular (i.e., idiographic) development. Two factors that may influence whether or not a motive is given an overt preference are the overindulgence of a particular need or the neglect of it (e.g., too much or too little contact leading to an overemphasis upon the attachment motive and some of its specific variations).

Psychosocial Factors

As Sherman and Dinkmeyer (1987) aptly detail, Adler can be considered one of the first family therapists and systems theorists. Unlike Freud, he worked directly with children and families and wrote extensively about it (Mosak & Maniacci, 1993). A useful distinction can be made. Adler interpreted personality from an individual-system perspective, rather than a group-system perspective. In the latter view, individuals are secondary to the system to which they belong; the parts cannot be understood without the whole, or, by and large, the system determines the dynamics of the individual. In the former view, the individual is both a reactor to and a creator of the system, and they mutually influence each other; the person is not merely a reactor to the system but "helped create" the dysfunctional system, for example, in which he or she is currently "suffering."

There are numerous psychosocial factors that influence the life style, and Adler (1956) was particularly interested in not only how parents affected children but how children affected parents, children affected each other, and the educational system reinforced or altered all of this. A thorough, in-depth discussion is beyond the scope of this chapter, but some general dynamics can be overviewed.

The family atmosphere is one factor (Dewey, 1971). The emotional "tone" of the home, the family climate (Dewey, 1971; Shulman & Mosak, 1988), can have a very large effect upon the developing mood of individuals. In stormy, conflictual atmospheres, children may develop anxious, guarded styles. Perhaps nowhere is the idiographic, phenomenological perspective of Individual Psychology more evident than in situations such as this, for as soon as we write this, it becomes clear that *just the opposite* may happen. In that same atmosphere, children may develop a hostile, aggressive posture and style. We, as practicing psychotherapists, never cease to be amazed by our observations of families. *In the same family,* one child perceives the atmosphere as tense and emotionally abusive, but another perceives the "same" atmosphere as "typical" or "the way Italians are" or "no big deal," and just "the way things are" and he or she does not seem to be "stressed out" at all. As noted in the story of the two brothers learning to swear, what message is sent may be very different than the message that is perceived. The family atmosphere can be set by any member of the family and can change. Siblings, aunts, uncles, grandparents, and the like can all influence the prevailing tone of the family. Even a teacher can affect the tone, for example by sending home notes. The parental relationship, in particular, can have a profound effect. How the parents get along with each other can have powerful influence upon the mood of the household and provide a model for man-woman relations. For example, if they are perceived as loving and supportive of each other, a calm atmosphere may prevail, and the children's mood may be calmer and more secure. As mentioned previously, Adlerian psychology advocates a soft determinism; one can only speak of probabilities, not certainties. If it is a male-dominated atmosphere, the children may develop what Adler (1956) referred to as masculine protests, in which they overvalue masculinity and their ability to "live up to" the masculine standard (and this would apply to both the male and female children) (Adler, 1978; Bieliauskas, 1974; Mosak & Schneider, 1977). If it is a female-dominated atmosphere, children of either gender may develop feminine protests in which they overvalue femininity (Ronge, 1956).

How values are acquired and "passed on" (Scheibe, 1970), therefore, becomes yet another psychosocial factor we note. Generally speaking, there are four types of values children are exposed to: family, paternal, maternal, and societal. Although once again aunts, uncles, and grandparents, peers, and so forth can (and frequently do) have roles in imparting values to children (not to mention music and television, which are touched upon subsequently), in order to keep this chapter manageable, only these four are touched upon presently. Something that is perceived as an issue to the father typically becomes a paternal value; similarly, if it is perceived as important to the mother, it becomes a maternal value. If it is an issue for *both* parents, either positively or negatively (i.e., by its presence *or* overly strong denial), it becomes a family value. An example clarifies.

Father loves to drink. He feels that children should be inculcated to the world of alcohol early. Thus far, it is a *paternal* value. Mother strongly opposes it, a *maternal* value, so much so that she frequently argues with Father about it. Drinking, therefore, for this family, may be perceived as a *family* value. If Mother were truly indifferent to it, it would remain a paternal value only. Although values that are held by one of the parents are important, they typically do not have the same impact upon children that family values do. With family values, the children are typically "forced" into taking a stand, one way or the other. In this case, to be for drinking implies an alliance with Father; to be indifferent, or neutral, may be seen as siding with either parent or neither; to be against it implies siding with Mother. Family values typically entail taking some sort of stance, and it is difficult to do otherwise.

Such dynamics of value acquisition can lead to individuals who incorporate some issues "whole" and others, even in the same family, who confuse being opposite with being different; hence, they assume that by being opposed to the family values, they are being their "own people." They may, in fact, simply be oppositional. We refer to these as "reverse puppets"; that is, when the right string is pulled, the left arm goes up.

Another psychosocial factor that is relevant in development relates to parenting styles. Adler (1956, 1964g) delineated two that are particularly troublesome, pampering and neglect. He felt that doing too much for children, or not enough, can lead to detrimental effects. However, as has been mentioned repeatedly, children are not passive recipients of data, and Adler noted that pampering may be seen objectively as characteristic of the parents and subjectively as the attitude of children. Adler noted that, in general, pampering was "worse" than neglect. How so? Not all neglected children feel neglected. They may, like so many children from the Depression era, not notice they are lacking (even affection). Pampered children, that is, children who have things done for them that they can do for themselves, can, and often do, feel neglected. They are accustomed to getting, and as soon as they are denied, they feel (i.e., perceive themselves as) neglected.

There are many more parenting styles than Adler noted, such as overprotection, overindulgence, overdomination, inconsistency in one parent, inconsistencies between the parents, overambition, excessive standards of morality, denigration, and punishment. Again, the perception of the parental style by the child is more crucial than the objective style. Dreikurs (1958), Dreikurs & Soltz (1964), and many other Adlerians (Corsini & Painter, 1975; Dinkmeyer & McKay, 1982; Grunwald &

McAbee, 1985) have written extensively on parent education and provided manuals for working with parents to alter their styles in order to influence children. This topic is presented in greater detail in Chapter 10. In general, parenting styles that are *perceived* as overcontrolling might produce children who are either very conforming or rebellious. Parenting styles that are *interpreted* as permissive could produce children who are irresponsible and do not learn from consequences. Once again, the particulars of the situation and the total picture needs to be taken into account before such generalizations can be taken too literally.

The sibling constellation is yet another factor in development. Adler (1920/1983d) was one of the first to note how children affect children. He emphasized that how siblings relate to each other frequently influenced their development. For example, an only girl growing up with several brothers (Mandell, 1942) might develop quite differently than one girl among other girls. An older sibling who is particularly dominant and aggressive will probably have a profound effect upon his or her siblings. Mosak (1972) and Shulman and Mosak (1988) discuss the "teeter-totter" effect. Where one sibling succeeds, his or her nearest competitor fails or gets out of the race. In the family constellation, children frequently map out territories to call their own. They develop characteristic ways of behaving that, subsequently in development, can become typical of how they manifest their social roles. For example, if Mary is particularly smart and uses it (i.e., she decides to find her place in life through her intelligence), her nearest sibling, Sharon, has an interesting choice ahead of her: Should she attempt to be "as smart" as Mary? Because they probably have similar biological equipment, that may be possible. Or should she try and be smarter? After all, if she is "just" as smart as her big sister, she may not feel as noticed. To be smarter is more difficult, however, especially because Mary had a "head start" by being older. Sharon may decide to "be dumber" in order to "be smarter"; in other words, if she acts "as if" she were not as smart, she may get more attention. The teeter-totter effect occurs if siblings appear to act opposite each other on particular traits: Where one goes "up," the other goes "down." In this case, Sharon may avoid anything that smacks of being "intellectual," or she may become intellectual in an area other than Mary's in order to stake out her claim as being different than Mary. She will also "watch" for where Mary fails, or does not try, and she may become a master in that area, such as sports. Similarly, Mary will "watch" Sharon, and she will (probably) adjust her behavior accordingly, constantly reminding her "little sister" how much smarter she (Mary) is. Many other variations are common (Hapworth, Hapworth, & Heilman, 1993; Shulman & Mosak, 1988).

Finally, the last psychosocial factor we examine is the effect of the culture, neighborhood, and school upon development. There are many ethnic issues that have lasting effects upon personality formation (Arciniega & Newlon, 1983; Manaster, 1973). For example, the family atmospheres, parenting styles, and values of traditional Japanese families are different than those of Italian ones. Various religious practices, too, have effects. The household of an Orthodox Jewish family is probably going to be much different from that of an Irish Catholic one. Socioeconomic factors, the type of neighborhood in which children perceive themselves as growing up and the like, effect personality development as well (Davis & Havighurst, 1947). The type of school in general, and teachers in particular, is important, also. Adler (1956) wrote about school reform and Spiel (1956) established an experimental school that was based upon some of the principles that we discuss in Chapter 10. The music and television to which children are exposed can modify values and establish what the peer groups determine to be "required" in order to "fit in." All of these issues play their parts in providing stimuli that children can evaluate and to which they can respond.

The Concept of Life Style Reexamined with Reference to Development

As Wolfe (1932) aptly notes, the human child is perhaps the only infant that experiences his or her own inferiority. The psychomotor skills, Wolfe notes, generally progress differently than conceptual ones, and hence children can be caught in an interesting predicament: *Every human being experiences his incompleteness as a child.*[4] He cannot talk and he cannot walk and he cannot satisfy his hunger, but he can see that his parents and other adults are capable of all these mysterious actions. Thus there arises a sense of incompleteness or inadequacy. The physiological basis of this law is the fact that the human brains and apperceptive powers of children develop out of all proportion to their motor abilities to satisfy their wants. Also, the dependence of the human infant is relatively greater than the dependence of the young of any other species (Wolfe, 1932, p. 29).

A young child attempts to move forward, to do things for him- or herself, and becomes frustrated. Because of physiological and neurodevelopmental factors (including organ inferiorities), certain parenting styles, family atmospheres, his or her place in the family constellation, family values, and cultural, religious, socioeconomic, and early peer-group issues, that child develops specific ways of perceiving and moving through life. A final, fictional goal that organizes behavior is selected *unconsciously,* and skills that reinforce movement toward that goal are emphasized, and those that subjectively appear to be irrelevant are discarded. The child's life style is a mixture of all these factors, *plus* that child's perception of those factors, *and* the choices that the child makes in reference to those factors.

☐ An Example of a Life Style

What follows is a detailed analysis of a case. The names and relevant identifying factors have, of course, been altered to protect the person. We present a case because, though this chapter has had (at least what appears to us as) an abundance of information, we recognize its generalities. That is an issue that Adler often addressed. Individual Psychology places such emphasis upon holism, idiographic dynamics, phenomenology, and the social field that it is difficult to discuss issues such as developmental factors in any great detail without having specific reference points. We examine each of the factors discussed in this chapter in turn.

Liz was born to her parents when they were in their mid-20s. Mother had a normal pregnancy and Liz was born on time and healthy. Her severe migraine headaches were apparently familial because her mother, sisters, aunts, and grandparents had them. If under enough stress, either biologically, such as through sleeping too much or not enough or eating certain foods (e.g., those having tyramine, such as eggplant or Chianti wine), or psychologically, such as if she pushed herself too hard in school, she would experience headaches. She admitted that she could "use" these headaches, or even bring them on, in order to get attention, excuse herself from certain tasks, or seek revenge on her sisters if it suited her (e.g., she would complain they were making too much noise and have them "quieted" down by Mother or Father). This is an example of how one person can set the family atmosphere.

Her perception of her family was that it was "uncomfortable" and, at times, abusive. The children could be beaten quite violently, usually by Mother for having lost a button on their clothes, particularly because Mother sewed most of their clothes for them. Liz recalled, rather vividly, being beaten for having her feet grow too fast and her parents having to spend money on new shoes at a time when money was scarce.

Mother generally was described as given to violent mood swings (she was probably cyclothymic), periods of intense alcohol abuse, and periods of calm, almost loving tenderness. Father was a perfectionist who spent most of his time out of the house, working two jobs. When home, he might be totally disengaged from the family, or he might lord over them and have them pick up lint off the floor with their hands. Mother would observe but not intervene.

Liz, the oldest child, had a sister 2 years younger, a brother 3 years younger, another brother 7 years younger, and a sister 12 years younger. She perceived herself as the oldest of three in what Adlerians call a 3–2 subgrouping (Liz, Shari, and George being in one subgroup, and John and Carol in another). All of the children were described as strong-willed and stubborn, to one extent or another—a family value. Her nearest competitor, Shari, was athletic and into cheerleading. Shari was described as being emotional and more "female-acting." True to teeter-totter form, Liz described herself as tomboyish, stoic, and an exceptional student.

Liz reported that she worked hard to try to fit into the lower class neighborhood of her childhood, but it did not work. She was too oddly dressed, even for her neighborhood, and too "smart." Perhaps because of her feelings of alienation and isolation, she found herself attracted to animals, and because she could not afford pets, she collected whatever she could catch. Frogs, mice, snakes, and the like became her pets, and her friends.

Because of the unpredictability of Mother, the extended family rarely, if ever, came to visit. The parents' social life was virtually nonexistent.

What might Liz, as a child, make of this? How could this background (or more accurately put, this perceived background) influence her cognitive map?

Liz developed a final, fictional goal of staying in control, like Father, and achieving and being as successful as she could be. She believed that to lose control was to appear like Mother. Still, she found it useful to assert herself and to be determined, something she learned from being the oldest of her siblings, but to do so quietly. Imitating Father, she unconsciously decided to become perfectionistic and emotionally detached. She worked hard to be different than Mother, so much so that she began to repudiate what she perceived to be "feminine" traits. With regards to her needs, two became crucial to her: safety and mastery. These eventually led to her striving to become (not as she perceived it) overly controlled (a variation of the competence motive) and overly perfectionistic and guarded (variations of the security and cognitive motives). She learned to find her place in her social field through being smart, controlled, and always on guard.

An early memory she retains taps into many of these themes. She reports this from when she was 3 years old:

> I was wearing a dress Mother had made. I had to go to the bathroom and when I did, I had to pull it down. I lost a button. Mother saw the button was missing and spanked me, really badly. She then realized it would have

fallen off anyway, and she started to cry, becoming very emotional. She realized she had overreacted.

The feeling with the recollection was one of fear and pain initially, and then calmness and soothing. The part that stands out as most vivid for her is her mother crying and apologizing. What lessons could this visual, nonverbal, imagistic learning be teaching to her? Why would she hold onto it into adulthood?

Many of the aforementioned issues are evident. It was important to not lose control. In a metaphorical sense it is important "to have all your buttons." She had to watch what she did and not let little things slip by her unnoticed. Perhaps the only time she can conceive of being cared for is if she is hurting. Women can be hurtful, and at times it might be better to not be one of them, or at least to act like one of them (i.e., from her vantage point, "emotional").

Presently, she was in an unhappy marriage. She, like her mother, had five children and a husband who works too much. She kept the children home with her and provided them with home schooling. After all, too many bad things can happen with the other school children. She suffered numerous psychosomatic complaints, with migraines being the major one, particularly around the time of her period. The issue of hormonal imbalance is a biological trigger; however, her feeling too "feminine" at those times is a psychosocial issue that was difficult for her to handle, possibly making her "incapacity" at those times harder to bear. She still acted on the basis of her childhood script.

☐ Summary

This chapter examines how the life style is developed. The biological and psychosocial factors are touched upon, and a case is presented that articulates many of the factors discussed.

People do not develop in a vacuum. They respond to cues from both their internal and external environments, and they actively set out to influence and arrange life to meet their expectations. They form rules about themselves, other people, and life that they use to guide them through their worlds, but these rules are typically nonverbal and not easily accessible to linguistic processing. They act "as if" these rules were true, and for all practical purposes, for them, they are.

We now examine the nature of those rules, in particular, the "rule of rules" (Shulman, 1973b), the life style. Having detailed how it develops, we can begin to understand what it is in its developed, mature form. It is to that task that we turn next.

☐ **Points to Consider**

Given the assumption of holism, Adlerians emphasize the biological, psychological, and social systems dynamics of personality development. All factors play a part in development.

Though originally stating that inferiority feelings preceded striving, Adler later inverted this position. The move solidified his position as a growth-oriented theorist.

The three key factors Adler noted that were crucial to personality development were organ inferiority, pampering, and neglect. Even these factors, however, were under the influence of the perception of the child and were more than mere "objective facts" the child experienced.

☐ **Questions**

1. How does choice play a part in the "objective facts" of individual development?
2. Early Adlerians such as Wolfe noted that human infants experience their own sense of inferiority. If this is true, how might this influence personality development?
3. What might be the effect of being an only boy growing up amongst sisters? What about being an only girl growing up with brothers?
4. What is meant by the "teeter-totter effect?"
5. Can you think of examples of famous people who overcompensated for their childhood inferiorities?
6. What degree of activity did Adler typically associate with healthy individuals?

☐ **Notes**

[1]As stated, this is a limited view, and although this view has been transmitted from generation to generation, Adler and subsequent Adlerians describe other forms of "overburdening situations" that are described in this chapter.

[2]By this definition, a handicap is not necessarily an organ inferiority, nor does every organ inferiority manifest itself in a handicap.

[3]Adlerians use *unconscious* as an adjective rather than a noun, a reified concept. That is, we speak of unconscious processes, not "the unconscious" as if it were a place.

[4]Janet (1924) speaks of the *sentiment d'incomplétude*, and Zeigarnik (1927), in her seminal study of completed and uncompleted tasks that coined the term "Zeigarnik effect," was also described in Gestalt terms as a striving for closure.

The Style of Life

This . . . allows us to understand better what an existential psychoanalysis must be if it is entitled to exist. It is a method destined to bring to light . . . the subjective choice by which each living person makes himself a person. . . . The behavior studied by this psychoanalysis will include not only dreams, failures, obsessions, and neuroses, but also and especially the thoughts of waking life, successfully adjusted acts, style, etc. This psychoanalysis has not yet found its Freud. . . . But it matters little to us whether it now exists; the important thing is that it is possible.

Jean-Paul Sartre (1943/1956)

. . . How could Sartre be unaware that this method already existed and had Alfred Adler for its author?

Henri F. Ellenberger (1970)

Perhaps the crowning achievement of Adler's thinking as a clinician was his concept of the style of life. Adler (1956), Ansbacher (1967), Dreikurs (1967), Mosak (1977b), Shulman (1973a, b), Powers and Griffith (1987), and Shulman and Mosak (1988) have written extensively on the topic of life style, and this chapter is an attempt to present an overview of that concept.

Life Style: What Does It Do?

The life style can be conceived of as the "rule of rules" (Shulman, 1973a, b). It is the subjective, unarticulated set of guidelines individuals develop and use to move them through life and toward their goals. It develops, as we examined in Chapter 3, through the interactions children have with their significant others, peers, and social world; through their experience of culture and community; through their biological growth and dysfunction; and, perhaps most significantly, through their perceptions and choices.

It is both conscious and nonconscious, in that it exists on what current theorists call a tacit-implicit level as well as an explicit, verbal level (Guidano & Liotti, 1984; Mahoney, 1991). As Adler (1933/1964f) noted, "Man knows much more than he understands"; by that he meant that people frequently have an awareness of basic processes and issues that is not readily accessible to conscious, consensual thought (Sullivan, 1953). In fact, for the life style to function most effectively, Dreikurs (1933/ 1950a, 1967) believed that nonconsciousness was actually beneficial. This topic requires some greater exploration.

If we were conscious of all of our actions and intentions, we would have a difficult time functioning, not just effectively, but at all. It is analogous to learning to drive a car—during the initial period of learning (skill acquisition), we tend to be all too aware of what we are doing. The overemphasis upon conscious rehearsal and implementation hinders "smooth" performance. As a rule of thumb, we tend to become better at doing what we are doing the *less* we are conscious of it. We have all had the experience of driving for a period of time and suddenly realizing we have not been "conscious" of what we were doing or what we were about to do. The life style operates, in effect, upon the economy principle; it allows us to conserve energy and focus our attention to other, more important matters. Various skills, attitudes, convictions, and the like become "habits" and function almost in a reflex-like manner. We do not need to process every bit of data about driving a car each time we sit behind a wheel and drive home at night. That would constitute a waste of time and energy and would be a major impediment to future learning.

In essence, the life style is the set of convictions, the *attitudinal* set (Mosak, 1954), we create in order to help us find our place in the world. Although these convictions may not be objectively true, "All opinions are correct from the point of view of the observer" (Dreikurs, 1972, p. 41). As we explore in the chapter on development, Adlerians believe children (and people in general) are attempting to find their place. This initial project occurs within the family and early social network. The early social network, in particular the family, helps teach us what life is about, how we should fit in, what we are all about, ideas of masculinity and femininity, and ethics and values. These concepts are transmitted to us, and we perceive them according to our biases (our biased apperceptions) and our particular vantage point. Their adoption or rejection gives us a feeling of place. As we biologically mature and psychosocially expand our learning and experiences, we begin to believe that our conceptions about ourselves, life, and others are not *our* conceptions, but *everyone's* convictions ("Doesn't everyone?"). What we create as truths for ourselves and our early social world we assume are truths for people in general, for our friends, family, and the world at large. We grow up, grow old, and move through life as if we know *the* answers when in reality, psychologically speaking, we know only *our* reality.

If our training (Adler, 1924a; Freund, 1928) and self-training (Seif & Zilahi, 1930) have been broad enough and consensual enough and exposed us to enough, our "reality" closely matches others' reality. The views I hold have some semblance of validity with regards to the views you hold. In Adlerian terms, my private logic[1] has its own rules and assumptions that are mine and mine alone; but overall, I have common sense as well—my thinking blends my perceptions and conceptions into a weave, a tapestry, which has room enough for your conceptions and perceptions. We share some commonalities by virtue of being human, some by virtue of being of the same time, place, and culture, and some by virtue of chance. This forms the basis of our common language, culture, and world view. We are separate yet tied to each other, with our own personal worlds that overlap to create common, shared worlds.

The greater the overlap, the greater the chances of "successful" adaptation. As we chronicle in Chapter 8, Adlerians hold that some maps do not overlap very much with others. The private logic of some people, for example, psychotics and sociopaths, is very private, so private that they have a hard time sharing their reality with us. They cling to their private logic so tightly, so desperately, that they often choose it over reality, and over common sense. We, as fellow humans, know them, for they are not so removed that they are "alien" to us, but they seem to speak different languages at times (Mosak & Maniacci, 1989), and to hold views we find hard to grasp. Sometimes, they believe that to hurt themselves is natural; to believe they are the devil is a matter of fact; to see themselves as horrible, worthless, and totally unlovable is the nature of their reality. To a lesser, removed extent, some people believe that they belong only to the extent that they satisfy others, or that they are praised and admired by others, or that they win unconditional approval or love. For some others, their private logic tells them that to love somebody is to hurt them or to be hurt by the ones you love. As Oscar Wilde (1898/1992) wrote, "Yet each man kills the thing he loves." These and other styles are examined in Chapter 8; these are the styles that sometimes lead people to difficulty.

All of us have private logic that is not shared with others. That is part of the human condition. As Thoreau (1854/1991) observed, "If a man does not keep pace with his companions, perhaps it is because he hears a different drummer." All of us have common sense, the ability to think in common with others and share a consensual view of life and its demands. To understand these maps, these blueprints for existence, we need to explore the details of their instructions. The details of the instructions are called convictions.

☐ Life Style Convictions

The convictions of the life style are similar to what Kelly (1955) referred to as the constructs of the personality. They can be broken down into four basic components: self-concept, self-ideal, *Weltbild* (a German term for "picture of the world"), and ethical convictions. In actuality, they are intimately intertwined with each other and cannot be as cleanly and artificially segmented as theoreticians show them to be. For heuristic and pragmatic purposes, however, such a division clarifies the task before us.

The style of life is composed of these four clusters of beliefs. Each major section has numerous subsections and permutations. In some individuals, one set is emphasized more than others; in others all are equally weighted. In some persons, the degree of congruence between the various convictions is great; in others, the amount of incongruity is huge. As becomes evident here, most are learned roughly at the same time of development, but some can be, and frequently are, learned at different times, thus creating the possibility of incongruity once again. For example, Jack's self-concept may fall short of his self-ideal, what Rogerians called the self/ideal self discrepancy. That is one form of incongruity. He may not be what he feels he should be, or he may feel that he is something he should not be. A frequent, but not often discussed, issue may be that he learned his view of himself (self-concept) at an earlier age than he learned his ideal of himself (self-ideal). For instance, Jack may have been relatively happy with himself (i.e., his self-concept/self-ideal had a high degree of congruence) until kindergarten;

at that time, his self-ideal underwent revision when he "discovered" he could not hit a baseball as well as his peers during playtime at lunch. Similarly, some children learn that they can live up to what life expects of them (for the most part); there is congruence between their self-concepts and *Weltbild* convictions. Then, life "kicks them in the teeth," and their views of the world undergo radical revision, such as if children who are relatively happy and productive experience a traumatic event such as a dethronement by the birth of another child, death, or severe accident. At that time, their *Weltbild* convictions may undergo revisions.

A closer examination of the various components of the convictions provides more detail. Each is examined in turn. With reference to psychopathology, Adler (1956) stated that every neurotic is partly right, and before we examine the implications of the dynamic interplay of convictions, it might be useful to explore the significance of that assertion.

Children, from their subjective perception, have "accurately" constructed what they believe to be necessary to find their places in their families of origin. To one degree or another, individuals' life styles are "adequate" to the task of finding a place within the family, for after all, they did survive. What may have worked for them, in their family, they attempt to recreate in "the world," so to speak, and hence they try to encourage others to react in ways that validate their expectations. Hence, if an adult's goal is to be a caretaker, it is not surprising to find out that, as a child, that same person was a caretaker and, to some extent, was rewarded for it. To put it rather colloquially, if it worked at home, why shouldn't it work everywhere else?

Finally, Adlerian psychology, as is probably becoming increasingly evident throughout this text, is difficult to categorize in any particular theoretical niche. It can be characterized as existential, cognitive, systemic, client-centered, and interpersonal in many of its features and, given its emphasis upon psychogenetic reconstruction and understanding of past influences, as analytic. In comprehending the life style of an individual, Adlerian psychology can be seen in its two central foci: its cognitive and motivational interaction. Adlerian psychology is cognitive in that it clearly focuses upon the cognitive structures that underlie personality; it is psychodynamic in that it stresses not just cognitive bases of personality, but motivational issues. In Adlerian psychology, motivation is not caused by libido, but rather the striving for significance. The goals people select for themselves (not always consciously) and how they move toward those goals add the psychodynamic component to the cognitive perspective. As we are characterizing it, Adlerian psychology is an *analytic-behavioral-cognitive* psychology, as contrasted with a more traditional cognitive-behavioral psychology. Perhaps this curious blend is nowhere more apparent than in how we understand and conceptualize the life style of a person.

☐ Self-concept

The self-concept contains all of the convictions about the "I." It is how a person defines him- or herself. "I am . . ." or "I am not . . . ," or "I do . . ." or "I do not . . ." are the sentence stems that are typically found. Body images, too, are found in this conviction. "I am small" and "I am fat," are some of the self-concepts that people have. Other convictions include self-esteem statements such as "I like myself," "I'm a good person," and "I never feel deserving."

The self-concept is the anchor upon which we make our comparisons, appraisals, and assessments (Rogers, 1951; Snygg & Combs, 1959). Modern psychoanalysts such as Basch (1988) and Stern (1985) have followed the direction (though without apparently acknowledging it) of Adler (1912/1983b), who postulated the basis of personality as being the self. Horney (1945), Sullivan (1953), and Kohut (1971, 1977) also were early pioneers in emphasizing the concept of self as central in personality, and like Adler before them they built their systems upon interpersonal, "cultural" perspectives. Adler (1956) noted that the first task of the mother was to bond with the child; their relationship should be a cooperative one, in which the child fills needs for the mother as well as the mother caring for the child. The next task is for the mother to "spread" this interest to the father, and they, in turn, to the rest of the family and the world. What Basch and Stern refer to as "affective attunement" Adler called empathy. As Shulman (personal communication, April 23, 1993) has aptly pointed out, Adler stressed not only the need for affective attunement (matching and validating the child's emotions), but the need for teaching social responsibility and appropriate limits as well. From the Adlerian viewpoint, empathy encourages the child's self-concept to develop in a healthy,[2] prosocial manner, but the awareness of consequences and responsibility encourages a resilient and cooperative self-concept that takes into account others' needs and perspectives.

The self-concept contains the convictions about the "I." That has been stated and is self-evident; the self, however, is part of a social matrix. As discussed in the basic assumptions, my view of myself is my business, but it can (and frequently does) have larger social implications. "I am lazy" is a static, psychology-of-possession statement. Rephrased into a psychology-of-use perspective, its social dynamics become clearer: "I am good at putting others into my service or getting others to push me, to be involved with me," or "I use laziness in order to find my place in this world." With this clarification, Adlerians' emphasis upon not only empathy but responsibility in child development and rearing becomes understandable. Yes, it is important, perhaps crucial to mirror children's feelings in order to validate their emerging sense of self (Kohut, 1971), but it is just as important to develop an awareness of that sense of self in relation to others and their vantage points.

☐ Self-ideal

Adler (1912/1983b) coined the phrase "self-ideal," but the English translation in his first, crucial Adlerian book is poor (Adler, 1978, pp. 416–417). "Self-ideal" is translated as "ego-ideal," and "character" is translated as "constitution," to name but two instances. Rogers (1951) and his group renamed the "self/ideal" as the "ideal self" and explored this issue, particularly the self/ideal self discrepancy in their research. Both Adler and Rogers were interested in how people viewed themselves, and in particular how they measured up to their own standards.

The sentence stems that characterize the self-ideal typically are as follows: "In order to have a place, I should (or should not) . . ." or "in order to belong/to be significant/ to have people have regard for or take notice of me, I should (or should not) . . ." or "in order for me to have regard for myself, I should (or should not) . . ." The long-range goals of the personality usually reside in the self-ideal. They have an imperative quality to them, and people generally develop a sense of what Ellis (1973) terms "catastrophic expectations" should their time table not be kept to. For example, a 6-year-old girl may develop the self-ideal that she should be a married woman with children. If she is not married by age 9, it is hardly catastrophic; if she feels, perhaps by watching her mother and nonconsciously making note of the age at which Mother married (Powers & Griffith, 1987), that she should be married by age 21, then she may begin to feel pressured or pressure herself by her late teens if she has not yet met "Mr. Right." The pressure may become subjectively catastrophic if she passes that age without being married.

Within the self-ideal reside the issues that are central to adaptation. The hopes, dreams, and creations to which humanity has aspired find their sources in this conviction. Unlike the self-concept, which is squarely rooted in the here and now of experience, along with some key elements of the past (our subjectively remembered past, that is), the self-ideal is teleological in direction. It points to the future and "pulls" us toward what could be, what might be, and, often with discouraging consequences, what *should* be (cf. Horney's [1950] "tyranny of the shoulds"). Humanity's brightest ideas and most painful failures rest upon this concept. Our ability to change what we are, to build better worlds, and to envision grander possibilities finds its source in the self-ideal; by the same token, our ability to make our lives living hells also rests here, for it is through the self-ideal that we can mercilessly discourage and cruelly punish ourselves for not attaining what we dream about. Adler (1956) commented that the greatest tragedy of human nature might be that we make such great decisions about ourselves and our world when we are so small and know so little, but he added that it is just this same predicament that is humanity's greatest strength. The overreaching ideals, the high-flown goals, the unrealistic aspirations are part and parcel of being human, but so is the ability to dream and envision what can be, and hence the possibility to actualize those dreams.[3]

Whereas the self-concept forms out of empathy and responsibility, the self-ideal forms out of a sense of inferiority. We become aware of what we are not, and the object of that "not" becomes what we would ideally desire. That desire fosters the formation of the self-as-it-would-like-to-be, and it is a short step from that position to what-it-should-be. If children are aware of what they cannot be, have, or do, they strive to become, attain, or accomplish. The self-ideal thus emerges.

☐ *Weltbild*

The *Weltbild* contains all the convictions about the "not-self." In terms of sheer number, it is possibly the most complex and detailed cluster of convictions. Once again, whereas the classical psychoanalysts paid no attention to the "ego" and only later evolved an awareness of self or self-objects, Adler considered that individuals also develop opinions about the world, others, and life. This concept has been somewhat touched upon by the object relation theorists (e.g., Kernberg, 1975), but the object to which "object" refers is human. Adlerians consider there to be much more to the personality, or life style, than people's views of themselves and others; they also develop views about life, the world, nature, institutions, and so forth. Some of the sentence stems frequently found in the *Weltbild* include:

> "Life is . . ."
> "The meaning of life is . . ." (including issues of spirituality)
> "People are . . ."
> "Men/women are . . ."
> "Classes/types of people are . . ."
> "The world is . . ." (including ideas of nature, the physical world)
> "School/work/government is . . ." (to name but three)

The *Weltbild* is the background upon which the self-concept becomes illuminated. Just as it is difficult, if not impossible, to conceive of a person without others, in total isolation, it is perhaps even more ludicrous to imagine a self without a world. As the existentialists have discussed, the person is a person within a particular context at a particular time—being is being-in-the-world (Heidegger, 1927/1962). A brief overview of some of the dynamics of each clarifies.

"Life is . . ." typically entails judgments about what life is *as it is* (perceived). "The meaning of life is . . ." entails the evaluations about what life is about. For example, the statement that "life is a bowl of cherries," implies that life is good; its meaning may be, "and it should be eaten as often as possible." For some, life is hard, and they believe it should be. Issues of God, spirituality, religion, and such existential, cosmic concerns add (or detract, in some instances) to life's meaning.

"People are . . ." and "Women/men are . . ." determine how we see others. Our conceptions of masculinity, femininity, social obligations, and the like also reside here. "Real men don't cry" and "ladies must not swear" are examples of some of the issues. Similarly, our ideas about various classes of people, such as "kids should be seen and not heard," "a cop is a crook turned inside out," "blondes have more fun," "Yon Cassius has a lean and hungry look. Such men are dangerous," or assorted judgments about various races, religions, ethnic groups are located in the *Weltbild*.

"A country life is for me," and "city life is the only place to live," are common variations of the convictions about the natural or physical world. Convictions about nature, the environment, and other such topics are part of this conviction. Our beliefs about institutions also are found here, though these tend to develop later in the developmental cycle than most other convictions. Why? Whereas most of us experience ourselves, life, other people, and nature early in development, many of us may not begin to form opinions about institutions such as school, work, church, or government until later, typically around the age of 5 or 6 years. That is when we are usually "launched" into the world of school. With that, our education about how institutions operate, where certain types of people fit in, and what is appealing or not begin to be formed in more concrete, readily apparent terms.

☐ Ethical Convictions

The last set of convictions to which we turn our attention are those that provide direction with regards to what is perceived as right and wrong. Our ethical convictions are learned not only at home, but through school, peer interaction, religion, and the like. These, similar to the convictions held in the self-ideal, typically have an imperative quality to them. They contain "shoulds." "This is right to do . . ." and "you should not do this . . ." are common stems. Also found in this cluster are convictions about the consequences of our behavior, such as "if I do this, I'll get punished," or "if I maintain this, I'll be rewarded," or "if you're a good little boy or girl, Santa will leave something in your stocking." These are personal convictions, but by and large they are shared and do overlap with other people's views, for if they did not, we would have what is clinically referred to as a sociopathic style, or antisocial personality. For these individuals, their ethical convictions do not overlap to any great degree with those of others. This may not hold at a cross-cultural, ethnic, or religious level.

At this point it is worth making a distinction to which we return subsequently and that is that these convictions (ethical ones, in particular) do not necessarily translate into actual behavior. We can know full well the "right" thing to do but not do it. Many people quote Oscar Wilde: "I can resist everything except temptation." Similarly, some people have convictions that are ethical but are not part of the larger (i.e., popular) *Zeitgeist* or society. These people are not sociopathic; they are simply different. For some religions, it is an ethical issue to seek or not seek medical treatment if ill. They are operating upon ethical principles, just not popular ones (or, more precisely phrased, commonly shared ones).

☐ Congruence Reexamined

We can now return to an issue touched upon in the opening of this chapter. How do these convictions interact and form the style of life? How can these four main convictions (self-concept, self-ideal, *Weltbild*, and ethical convictions) account for all of the complexities of personality? What happens if they are not congruent with each other?

These convictions exist in infinite variety and combinations. One does not have to be a statistician to begin to appreciate the complexity of combinations that can be formed. Personality, in all of its splendid diversity, can be readily accounted for via varied combinations of assorted convictions (in Chapter 5, we explore just such an issue).

Adler (1927/1957) frequently stated that no two life styles are identical. Even identical twins reared in the same family have slightly different views of life, each other, and themselves. Hence, he repeatedly emphasized the importance of idiographic dynamics.

Given that no two life styles are the same, certain common patterns between convictions can be explored. First, the concept of inferiority must be more closely presented.

Inferiority

An inferiority is objective. It is based upon an external criterion and therefore is measurable. If the external criterion is height, it is relatively simple to determine that one's height is "superior" or "inferior" to another. More concretely, I am not as good a basketball player as Michael Jordan, and if that is used as a criterion or measure, I am inferior to him. Inferiority is context-dependent and situationally determined. It is not necessarily a value judgment.

Inferiority Feelings

The inferiority feeling is a subjective evaluation; it is not necessarily a feeling in the affective sense. It may or may not have any relevance to reality. I may be shorter than you (an objective inferiority if height is the criterion), but I do not have to feel inferior to you because of it. I may choose to, but I do not have to. If I feel inferior, the world may not be aware of it, for I can compensate, hide the feeling or hide myself (cf. "the impostor phenomenon" [Clance, 1986; Harvey & Katz, 1986]), or otherwise distance myself, retreat, or escape.

Inferiority Complex

An inferiority complex is a behavioral presentation of a subjective feeling of inferiority. I may choose to let the world know that I am inferior, and then I am displaying an inferiority complex. For the most part, the *Diagnostic and Statistical Manual of Mental Disorders* (4th edition; American Psychiatric Association, 1994) is a catalogue of inferiority complexes, that is, behavioral presentations of subjectively perceived inferiorities, that allow one to not function (this issue is addressed in considerable detail in Chapter 8). On a more normal side, there are many inferiority complexes that are not psychopathological. The most common inferiority complex in the United States, we believe, is about mathematics. "I never could do math," people say, and therefore they translate a feeling of inferiority into a reason, a justification, for not doing mathematics (at least without a calculator). This inferiority complex is endemic with psychology students facing a course in statistics. This issue is the focus of greater analysis in Chapter 6, but for present purposes, suffice it to say that:

An inferiority is objective.

An inferiority feeling is a subjective appraisal of inferiority. Inferiority feelings and inferiorities are not necessarily correlated. One may be inferior and not feel inferior. One may also feel inferior although there is no actual inferiority, only a perceived one.

An inferiority complex is a behavioral manifestation of feelings of inferiority.

Why the emphasis upon these issues? Because they yield insight into the dynamics of life style convictions that are incongruent.

If the *self-concept falls short of the self-ideal,* people experience *feelings of inferiority.* If the *self-concept does not measure up to the* Weltbild, people experience *feelings of inadequacy.* Finally, if the *self-concept fails to meet the expectations in the ethical convictions,* people have *feelings of guilt.* Guilt feelings and feelings of inadequacy are no more than variations upon inferiority feelings. Adler (1929/1964c) postulated a unitary theory of psychopathology, and on the surface it appears too simple. How can all problems people experience about themselves be boiled down to feeling inferior? It only appears simple. Once the psychodynamics of the life style are elucidated, the complexities begin to emerge. When Adler stated that all neurotics, psychotics, problem children, and criminals were the result of inferiority feelings, he was speaking in nomothetic, general terms. Once the particular life style is understood, grasped in all its complexity, then how this particular person feels inferior becomes visible. Some feel insecure, some inadequate, some weak, some vulnerable, some guilty. Others feel poor, hated, abused, and picked on; still others feel unmanly ("castrated"), unladylike, or inconsequential. All of these can be conceptualized as variations of inferiority *feelings* that are the result of incongruence between convictions in the style of life.

The life style *does not* define behavior. It acts as a limiter and expander of behavior (Mosak & Shulman, 1967). Given this attitudinal set, these convictions, individuals either develop or restrict their repertoires of behaviors. If I believe "real men don't show emotions," I seek out and develop behaviors that reinforce movement toward that goal. Simultaneously, I avoid or constrict the emotional behavior that runs counter to that conviction. I may become an "emotional illiterate," so to speak.

Similarly, knowing the behavior does not automatically lead to an understanding of the conviction. "Life is dangerous" can cause many, many diverse behaviors. I can hide under my bed or ride motorcycles at 120 miles per hour. I can act as if I am strong, invincible, or timid and in need of support. Once we comprehend the convictions, then the behavior is understandable. To work the other way, that is, from the behavior to the convictions, can only put us in "the ballpark" (see Chapter 8 and Adler's distinction between the general diagnosis and the specific diagnosis, in particular).

Adler (1927/1957) wrote about useful versus useless behavior. By that he meant socially useful (today we refer to it as "prosocial") or socially useless behavior. Behavior that is for the common good, in line with what he labeled "social interest" (see Chapter 7), he considered useful. That which ran counter to social interest he deemed useless. For Adler, there was no "normal" life style. Every life style was adequate, until life presented it with a task for which it was not prepared; it was at those times that its "weak points" emerged. Under stress, any structure's design flaws begin to emerge, and Adler felt that the human personality was no different. We prefer to speak of behavior not in terms of useful or useless, a two-dimensional concept, but rather as constructive, nonconstructive, or destructive.

Behavior that moves people toward their goals in cooperative, socially beneficial ways we call constructive. There are behaviors that move people toward goals in nonconstructive ways, that is, ways that do not directly or necessarily benefit others, but do not harm the person or others either. And there are ways of moving toward goals that are destructive to others. That style of movement is at the expense of others or self.

☐ The Core Functions of the Life Style

Why do we develop a life style? Perhaps we will never know the objective truth, but three guesses can be formulated.

1. The life style helps us to understand life. We are thinking creatures. We communicate and explore and hypothesize. The life style allows us to make sense not only of what we are but of what life and other people are all about.
2. It gives us a chance to predict life. Without a life style, we would have to learn, and relearn, each time. Life would become a neverending recursive loop; we would be forced to reexperience the same mistakes and failures over and over again. By having a map, a plan, we can anticipate, plan for the future, and adjust, that is, decide accordingly.
3. It provides us with the opportunity to control life. Although, in an existential sense, no one can control life, on a pragmatic level we can control it to some degree. I can get to what I want. I can prevent certain things from happening to me. We can order situations to get our way.

☐ The Concept of Equipotentiality of Growth

Adlerian psychology is optimistic. As we discussed in the chapter on the basic assumptions, Adler (1937/1964e) felt that human nature was neutral, that it had the potential for "good or bad," and that made redemption, salvation, happiness, or whatever one chooses to call it possible. *Equipotentiality* (Bertallanfy, 1968) is the term biologists use to describe the ever-possible potential for growth. Although life styles have a tendency to remain the same, under certain circumstances they can change. Therapeutic experiences do not have to occur solely in psychotherapy. Unlike Freud, Adlerians are not convinced of the effects of age upon a person's ability to change, a position analysts such as Kohut (1977) still held to even recently. Even old dogs can learn new tricks, and much the same young children, psychotics, addicts, sociopaths, and the like. Adler worked with all of them (Adler, 1956; Orgler, 1939/1963). People can modify how they think, and they can change the way they move toward their goals. Everybody can be better than he or she is currently. Such a statement does not mean that all people can be perfect, but they can be better than they are.

This brings us to the final point of this chapter. Cognitive dissonance is what occurs if people's conceptions do not meet reality (Festinger, 1957). How might this apply to life style?

Let us take an example or two. If I believe that there are no purple elephants, and I see one, one of two things must occur. Either my belief must change, or reality must. Either my conviction about elephants undergoes a modification ("Okay, there are purple elephants!") or I must deny reality ("No, I didn't see that!") or expose reality as false (such as by discovering the elephant has been painted for a circus performance). On a somewhat more realistic level, Jack believes that he is unlovable. Joan falls in love with him. Either his conviction about himself (his self-concept) must change, or he must alter reality (he provokes Joan into not loving him; he denies or ignores her feelings—"She's only saying that because she feels sorry for me"). If he accepts that she loves him, his view of himself must change. Life styles, if challenged, attempt to maintain equilibrium. They have a homeostatic function. Sometimes, people even attempt to change reality to suit their expectations. A poor map, a client recently said to us, is better than no map at all. Adlerian psychotherapy, in all its forms, is based upon this principle, and for the neurotic it is essential to help the patient develop a better map.

> This apperception-schema must always be traced and unmasked as being immature and untenable . . . .So long as he does not understand [his] error, so long as he regards his fictional world as the right one . . . he will

remain neurotic. If he can abandon his dream of world . . . he will begin to feel himself an equal among equals . . . and his reason and "common sense" will increase and gain control where heretofore he has been under the sway of his "private sense". . . . The cure or reorientation is brought about by a correction of the faulty picture of the world. (Adler, 1956, p. 333)

Adlerians confront patients with the patients' views of the world. As their life styles are challenged, they are tempted to resist or even leave therapy, but if the relationship is strong and the therapist and patient have established a trusting, cooperative atmosphere, then the patient's views are exposed, and change is likely.

☐ The Core Convictions of a Life Style: A Brief Analysis

The following is a brief example of the core convictions of Liz, the client who was discussed in Chapter 3, on development. Her convictions are the following:

> Self-concept: "I am at the mercy of others," "I can screw up," "I am a sensitive, caring person."
> Self-ideal: "In order to have a place, I should not make a mistake," "I must not lose control."
> *Weltbild:* "Life is a scary, punishing place," "Women can be emotional and overreact."
> Ethical convictions: "Honesty is important, even if it hurts," "If I lie, I will get punished."

The "subjective choice" to which Sartre referred in the opening quotation of this chapter is apparent: Liz feels at the mercy of others and has chosen not to be in that position again. Her ability to attempt to control herself, and hence her world, is the subjective choice around which she has built her life. For if she does not control herself and commits mistakes, she will be hurt. That is her reality. As a child, it was painful and "real." As an adult, it is feared and to be avoided. In many ways, it is as much a reality now as it was then. Her feelings of inferiority, inadequacy, and pain are real to her, and although "objectively" she no longer lives in that same, abusive household, phenomenologically she acts as if she does. Life has changed—her convictions have not. In constantly staying prepared for what might happen, she is living as if it will happen. In order to never again experience the abuse, she must always be prepared for it. That is her strength, and her problem: That which she seeks most to avoid, she lives with, in order to avoid it. The mind is its own place and "can make a heaven of hell, or hell of heaven."

☐ Summary

The life style is a creative, artistic production of the individual. It is a cognitive map that leads to the creation of goals in childhood. It is both flexible and adaptable to life and rigid and maladaptive to change. It is neither good or bad; it simply is. It leads us through life and brings us happiness and joy, pain and confusion. There are times when we would change it, but we have nothing that we can easily conceive of with which to replace it, or if we can conceive of such a thing, we may feel that we cannot actualize it. The life style is us, and we are it. We create it, we manage it, we fashion it, and we change it. We just may not see it, understand it, or know it needs to be changed. It is as unique as a fingerprint, but infinitely more complex and profound. We live our styles, for better or for worse.

The core convictions of the life style can and do cluster around common themes. Though the possible variations of convictions are mind boggling, the types of themes—although still enormous—are more manageable and easier to grasp. It is to these clusters of recognizable themes that we turn next. Though no two subjective choices are ever the same, some are strikingly similar.

☐ Points to Consider

The style of life is the individual's rule of rules. It is a set of attitudes and convictions about how to belong.

The life style does not necessarily contain instructions about exact behavior, for behavior can and does change depending upon the situation. It does lead to a prediction about probable behaviors.

For teaching purposes, the life style can be broken into its four component parts. The parts are the self-concept, self-ideal, *Weltbild*, and ethical convictions.

Adler spoke of socially useful and socially useless behaviors. Although he said that there were no "normal" life styles, he did note that they could be used in constructive or nonconstructive ways.

☐ . Questions

1. What is the difference between inferiority, inferiority feelings, and inferiority complex?
2. How is the self-ideal formed?
3. What is the difference between the self-concept and the self-ideal?
4. What types of convictions make up the *Weltbild?*
5. Discuss the process of cognitive dissonance. What is its relationship to life style convictions?
6. What are some of the core functions of the life style?
7. How is Adlerian psychology both a cognitive and a psychodynamic theory?

☐ Notes

[1]In the Li'l Abner comic strip he would often exclaim, "As any fool can plainly see. Ah sees it!"

[2]Rogers (1951) also pointed out the central role of empathy in helping the client in psychotherapy to change his or her self-concept.

[3]Such sentiments have been expressed by Carl Sandburg in his "Washington Monument by Night" ("Nothing happens unless first a dream"), Theodore Herzl ("If you will it, it is no dream"), and Senator Edward Kennedy, who in his eulogy of his brother quotes Bobby as saying, "Some men see things as they are and say why. I dream things that never were and say why not." Thoreau (1854/1991) writes, "If one advances confidently in the direction of his dreams and endeavors to live the life which he has imagined, he will meet with success unexpected in common hours."

CHAPTER

Typology

The first aspect, then, is teleonomic. Since behavior, I repeat, is action exerted upon the environment aiming from the moment of its initiation to produce results in the outside world, it cannot be compared to a random mutation generated quite independently of the environment . . . . Because this goal-directedness of behavior is essential to the organism's vital needs, and thus intrinsic to its overall dynamics, it requires from the outset detailed information about the environment toward which actions are to be oriented.

Jean Piaget (1976/1978)

. . . From this standpoint, social life appears to us a system of more or less deeply rooted habits, corresponding to the needs of the community.

Henri Bergson (1932/1956)

There are no two life styles that are identical. They are as different as fingerprints, as unique as snowflakes, and as varied as clouds in the sky. Adler (1956) stated that no two children grow up in the same family, for with the birth of each child, the family constellation changes, and hence new dynamics are created and maintained. As different as life styles are, so too are people. Yet people are not completely different in every way.

We do share aspects in common. As different as we are, we still have commonalities that are recognizable. As psychologists have attempted to do for more than a century, and philosophers and writers have tried for what seems forever, people predict other's behaviors. We make guesses about what will come next. Adler (1956) wrote that one of the key traits Adlerian psychologists must develop is the art of guessing (Dailey, 1966), and even late in his life, Adler, as we have seen, still credited Freud with having been the first to encourage this technique in clinical practice.

As Herold (1983) has documented, there are several attempts in Adlerian psychology to find common themes, or patterns, in life styles. Adler (1929c, 1935, 1956), Kefir and Corsini (1974), Kopp (1986), Manaster and Corsini (1982), and Mosak (1959, 1968, 1971a, 1973, 1979) have all presented, and elaborated upon, the issue of typology. A brief overview of each is in order.

Adler (1929b), in a work that has never been translated into English (Dutch, Spanish, Hebrew, yes, but not English), made an early attempt to form a typology. He discussed that some children preferred one sense modality over another, and he classified four primary "types:" motor, visual, auditory, and olfactory. Each modality had specific behavioral patterns and learning styles that would typically emerge. In another instance Adler (1933/1964f) speaks of the intellectual, emotional, and activity types. Similarly, some theorists consider that Adler's (1920/ 1983d) early work on birth order was a form of typology and speak of the "oldest born type," "middle type," or "youngest type" (Leman, 1985).

A more formal, and detailed, typology appeared in the first issue of the *International Journal of Individual Psychology,* in which Adler (1935) spoke of four types: the ideal, or socially interested, type; the getting type; the ruling type; and the avoiding type. These types could be categorized according to a four-fold system: degree of activity and amount of social interest. The ideal type was the only one discussed that could not be used in a destructive way. These people were interested in the welfare of others and worked cooperatively for the common good. They were characterized as having a high amount of social interest and a high degree of activity. The other three types could be used either constructively, nonconstructively, or destructively. "Getters" had low degrees of activity and social interest and were interested in getting as much as they could. Their primary orientation was to lean on others and put others into their service (this type is explored in greater detail subsequently). "Rulers" had a high degree of activity but a low amount of social interest, and they sought to dominate others and control them. "Avoiders," like the "getters," had low social interest and a low degree of activity, and they steered away from challenges and sought to distance themselves from demands.

Horney (1945, 1950), whose work is strikingly similar to Adler's in a number of ways (and is frequently required reading in many Adlerian training institutes), formulated her own typology, which bears noting. Horney (1945) originally conceived of three methods for dealing with "inner conflicts" that are aroused if individuals fail to live up to expectations they have for themselves. She defined these in terms of movement in relation to people. Individuals would either move toward, away from, or against people. In a later work (1950), she reconceptualized these movements as "solutions" and described them as self-effacement, resignation, and mastery. She acknowledges her indebtedness to Adler throughout her works (though often only briefly), but nowhere mentions his work on typology. A comparison might serve to clarify:

Adler	*Horney*
Getting type	Movement toward (self-effacing solution)
Ruling type	Movement against (appeal to mastery solution)
Avoiding type	Movement away (resignation/freedom as solution)

Examining Adler's types in relation to Horney's movement types and solution types, some parallels begin to emerge. What Adler described as "ruling," Horney described as "mastery" and "movement against." "Avoiding" types "move away" and seek "freedom" from responsibility and commitment, "resigning" themselves to their fate. "Getters" move "toward" others in order to be in a better position to receive and frequently adopt a "self-effacing" style, putting themselves down in order to keep those they perceive as more capable near them, so they can continue to "get." There are many such parallels in Horney's work.

Kefir and Corsini (1974) speak of dispositional sets. They claim that individuals have four primary methods that they use to solve challenges, and these four methods are neither good nor bad, but sole reliance upon any one at the expense of the others or too rigidly (i.e., without regard to the demands of the particular situation) results in maladaptive behavior. The four sets are accord, conflict, evasion, and neutral. Some people seek to find solutions through reaching an accord, that is, peaceful solutions. Others create conflict and increase tension. Still others sidestep and evade such issues; others remain neutral, and appear noncommitted, and in fact they may even be anonymous. For Kefir and Corsini, the flexible use of all four sets led to healthy adaptation.

Kefir (1972), Brown (1976), Dinkmeyer, Dinkmeyer, and Sperry (1987), and Manaster and Corsini (1982) discuss the issue of personal priorities. According to Kefir, who originally detailed this theory, individuals are exposed to an early situation that they cannot handle. This situation is called an impasse. Life styles are constructed in order to avoid this feared childhood situation from ever occurring again, and individuals develop priorities in order to avoid these impasses. The priorities, and what people with them seek to avoid, are as follows:

What is Sought	What is Avoided
Comfort	Stress/responsibility/expectations
Pleasing	Rejection
Control	Humiliation
Superiority	Meaninglessness

Someone with a priority of comfort, for example, strives to avoid too much stress or responsibility. For these people, Kefir hypothesized, life was too stressful, with expectations being too high for them, as children, and they grew up believing that the experience of stress is something to be avoided. Too much responsibility, therefore, and issues surrounding it, becomes an impasse for these people; it is something they have not learned to deal with, and because of their overemphasis upon seeking comfort, they still, as adults, do not learn to deal with it.

Finally, Manaster and Corsini (1982) have characterized people as types. They describe many such characterizations, with names such as Mack the Knife, St. Sebastian, and Dr. Doolittle. They briefly describe what each style is like (e.g., Dr. Doolittle is someone who prefers animals and objects to people and hence is a loner) and some possible background data on each. These are short-hand descriptions of typical life styles they have encountered in their clinical work.

Mosak (1959, 1968, 1971a, 1973, 1979) has written extensively on types. In examining the life styles of numerous individuals, he has found clusters of themes that can be described in brief, concise images. In an early work (Mosak, 1968), he related these common themes to diagnostic categories. For example, in addictive disorders, he has found two common themes, getting and excitement seeking. In depressive disorders, he has found themes of getting, controlling, and being good (Mosak, 1968, 1979). A more in-depth discussion of these themes, and types, is in order.

☐ Mosak's Typology: An Attempt at a Modern Theory of Types

Adler (1956) was opposed to classification. He did not believe in categorizing people according to specific diagnostic labels, for that violated the social, field theoretical perspective he felt was crucial for understanding individuals. However, for heuristic and teaching purposes, it became important to communicate to others. Although individual psychology is an idiographic discipline first and foremost, without nomothetic guidelines of some kind it would be impossible to teach it to others. His development of a theory of types (Adler, 1935) was an attempt to speak in generalities that could be used to describe some of the more common, central themes he found in life styles.

Mosak's work has had much the same motivation. He has written on 14 personality types (Mosak, 1971a) and provided in-depth descriptions of 2 of the 14 types (Mosak, 1959, 1973). The fourteen types are getters, controllers, victims, martyrs, drivers, those who need to be superior, inadequate ones, excitement seekers, babies, feeling avoiders, those who need to be good, those who need to be right, those who oppose ("aginners"), and those who need to be liked (pleasers). At the risk of oversimplification, these types are most easily identified by understanding their self-ideal statements, such as the getter believing that "in order to find my place, I should get."

The original manuscript for the book in which these types first appeared (Mosak, 1971a) was limited in the number of pages that could be used and, therefore, the number of types that could be examined. Other types that have been used by the authors include the observer, the measurer, the star, Annie Oakley, the survivor ("Rocky"), and the pole vaulter. These are just a few; there are more, as many more as there are people. Along a similar line, people are seldom of one type. Often, they are combinations of types, such as the controller-driver-superior combination that often produces what is now called a type A personality (Friedman, 1996; Williams, 1989)—someone who is especially vulnerable to heart disease and under considerable stress most of the time.

As Mosak (1979) has written, the types can be used in constructive, nonconstructive, or destructive ways, a point Kopp (1986) has detailed and expanded upon in his work. As we discuss subsequently, the issue is not what type one *is*, but rather how one *uses* that type. It is beyond the scope of this chapter to detail all 14 of the original types, and interested readers are referred to Mosak (1954, 1959, 1971a, 1973). Boldt (1994) also describes Mosak's types in her dissertation on characterological resistance, that is, resistance based upon life style, in psychotherapy. For present purposes, an examination of some of the other key types is in order.

Drivers

One of the most common, and most rewarded, types prevalent in our culture as we near the end of this century is what Mosak originally called the driver (Mosak, 1971a). Drivers are people who are typically classified as "workaholics," that is, they act as if they must have it all done—by yesterday. As Kopp (1986) has astutely pointed out, drivers have a goal of achievement. They measure themselves, and hence others, by what is accomplished, when, and how well it is done. He makes a distinction between strategies and tactics, which is helpful. Strategies have to do with convictions, what people believe about themselves, life, and others. Tactics are how such people get (i.e., move toward) what their cognitive map instructs them to be alert to. Mosak (1958) makes a similar distinction between the *modus vivendi* and the *modus operandi*, that is, between attitudinal set and behavior. For example, drivers typically have this strategy: Be productive in order to achieve! If used in a constructive way, these people's productivity often leads them to be helpful and supportive of others. The tactics they choose can be hard work, striving for accomplishment, and dedication. If they make mistakes, they tend to accept them, learn from them, and move on to other issues. Their self-esteem is usually not on the line.

In cases in which the drivers are using their style in destructive ways, their strategies are different. Although the overall goal of productivity and achievement remains the same, the life style convictions become somewhat more skewed: It is important to be number one! Given a cognitive map like this, their tactics tend to be more of the classic "workaholic" type, with strong trends toward compulsivity, ambition, and overly intense styles of interacting being prominent. They are often referred to as type A personalities (Friedman, 1996).

These people, as children, probably exhibited a high degree of activity. Achievement was perceived as important, and these children found their places through it. Within the early family constellation, drivers probably had an especially intense competition with a sibling (or siblings) and found that it was important to keep (at least) one step ahead of the competition and may have had the fear of falling behind. This was typically perceived as reinforced in school and with peers. Our culture does reward these types, and we do tend to pay the price for it if we push this style too hard: These individuals are prone to heart-related conditions, such as high blood pressure, heart attacks, strokes.

When drivers fall in love, like most other issues in their life, it can be perceived as something to be achieved. Such life "events" as courtship, marriage, family, and retirement are often perceived (possibly misperceived) as something that happens "on a time schedule." There is a time to be married, a time to have kids, this much needs to be done before the wedding, before the vacations, and so on. Sexuality, particularly during adolescence, can be viewed as another "achievement," and for those who maintain such a posture, "notches on bedposts" become the key criteria of a successful dating life.

One of the key "enemies" of drivers is not an enemy in the usual sense. This enemy is not encountered face-to-face, nor is it a person who can be killed off and forgotten about very easily. This enemy is free time. Too much time off without a book, worksheet, telephone nearby, or a mountain to climb can be very stressful. Drivers tend not to be excessively stressed by deadlines, meetings, and schedules, particularly if these are seen as part of the "job" requirements. Drivers are comfortable with them. They love mountains. Give them "busy work" or too much free time, and the end result is typically the same: They go crazy! They generally need to know that what they are doing will lead to something, something that they can look back upon and say, "I accomplished that." If they can, they do not experience subjective stress; they become tired, maybe even fatigued. Let them believe that what they are doing is for no particular good, and watch their fidgetiness increase. They can, and typically do, become irritable and restless at such times.

Drivers feel inferior if they cannot achieve. Time is something that they need to learn to live with, for time is their ultimate competitor. Will they die before they have accomplished what they want to accomplish? If they run the race too hard, they may hasten the arrival of the end—they tax their bodies and are forced to either slow down or die trying. If they are respectful of others, they enjoy the race; if they perceive them as threats, the race becomes exciting *and* taxing. The toll they pay is their wellness, their health, and strained interpersonal relations.

Babies

A point of clarification: Youngest born children are *not necessarily* babies! Babies can occur anywhere in the family constellation, and a frequent misconception is that if you are the youngest born, you must be a baby. "Youngest born" is a birth-order position. "Baby" is a type. They can, and admittedly often do, coexist, but no more so than drivers are necessarily oldest born. Many youngest-borns become drivers—they feel the most behind in the sibling array and try desperately to "catch up" the rest of their lives. Babies are entities unto themselves.

Babies have two complementary goals: support and play. They love attention and to be supported, and they frequently are quite good at giving attention and being supportive, but in playful, often emotional, ways. Babies love to have fun, to be carefree, and to play. These two goals, support and play, frequently intertwine. A closer examination sheds some light.

If approached constructively, the strategy of the baby is to have a good time, teach others to have fun, and show concern for the welfare of others in a good-natured, give-and-take way. For example, if you are laid up in the hospital, the baby will bring you games to play and play them with you. Babies may even jump up and stretch out in the bed with you. They mean no harm, and they can liven up a room and place things in perspective in just the right way. Their playfulness is warm, genuine, and elevating to those around them. Their tactics are humor, coyness, smiles, and a benign casualness, particularly when it comes to authority or convention. They receive their "strokes" through the playfulness given back to them. They want, at least temporarily, a playmate to support them in their revelry, and when it is time for business, they work, albeit with supervision, but they will get their chores done, so that they are then in a better position to go out and play. Other babies assume that work and responsibility was created for others. In terms of priorities theory, they seek comfort rather than responsibility.

A subtle, but crucial, distinction is made if the baby uses his or her style in a destructive way. The goals remain the same, but the strategy differs in a minute, but significant, aspect: Being cared for becomes being taken care of. They become masters at putting others into their service. The benign, playful give-and-take slides ever so gradually into a take-and-take. Rather than "let's play so we'll both feel better," it becomes "play with me. I'm bored," or "entertain me!" Their tactics become laziness, forgetfulness, helplessness, and incorrigibility. Temper tantrums and pouting are often seen. A whiny voice becomes almost a surgical tool for extracting what is needed.

As children, babies were the Peter Pans. They never wanted to grow up, and for many reasons their families were perceived as not wanting them to do so. Typically, babies realized that their families were too strict, too stodgy, and they were usually able to bring life to the crowd through their humor and playfulness. Parents can encourage this, especially in later- (or last-) born children, if they feel a sense of nostalgia about "letting go" of little Billy, Sherry, or Tommy (notice the "e" sound at the end of the names, names we refer to as diminutives). Babies perceive that they may have a place through maintaining that posture as adults. When they go out and find a job, it is not too surprising if it is boring, stodgy, and a bit too stuffy, until they arrive, that is.

Fun with others is constructive. Fun at the expense of others is not. Both of us making a mess together, and cleaning it up together, can be wonderfully liberating. Both of us making a mess, and you cleaning it up, can be a real pain—for you. Me making a mess and you cleaning it up is not fun at all for you; it can be downright abusive. Allow us to elaborate.

The subtlety of babies and their abuse of others, if they are using that style in a destructive manner, is a masterpiece. Those that they select to manipulate often feel guilty for challenging them (i.e., the babies) in the first place. After all, the babies frequently retort (in a whine, or pout), "What is the big deal? It's all in fun." And frequently, it is, and that is the crux of the problem. The fun does not stop. The same emotional playfulness can turn to temper tantrums, and people frequently "walk on eggshells" around them in order to avoid the fireworks.

Solitude is the biggest threat to babies. Although they are perfectly capable of being alone, they frequently feel lonely. With some social interest, they manage to rally the troops and everybody has a good time. Without it, it is not a matter of rallying the troops, it is a time to circle the wagons. They do not want to have fun; they want someone to create fun, and it is not going to be them. Similarly, babies may develop the skills to survive on their own; they just happen to prefer not to use them very often. Still, they can and do survive. On the more destructive side, they may not develop the requisite skills, and that typically means that someone has to do it for them. Let the games begin! They use their cuteness and manipulativeness to place others into their service, and as those who take care of them become increasingly more and more stressed and burned out, the babies continue to play.

Excitement Seekers

Excitement seekers are frequently similar to both drivers and babies. The crucial difference is one of emphasis. Whereas drivers often lead exciting lives, it is not the sensation that motivates them; it is the achievement. Babies can be wonderful at creating commotion, particularly during play time, but babies like to rest and be cuddled. For them, the interpersonal transactions become important; having fun is great, but having fun with others is better. Excitement seekers are stimulus junkies. It is the sensation they seek (Zuckerman, 1979). Our culture is a stimulus-bound culture. We have bright lights, loud music, busy roadways—not only with reference to traffic, but also when it comes to things along the sides of roads, such as billboards, signs, and so forth—and hundreds of television and radio stations. We print more books, newspapers, and journals than any one person could read in any one lifetime. A sign of the times is how many of us drive with the radio on, or sit with the television on, even if we are not watching it, simply for the "stimulation."

Excitement seekers typically have one dominant goal: to experience sensations. They think about stimulating topics, create wonderfully elaborate fantasies, do wild, exciting activities, and in general lead stimulating lives. On the useful, constructive side, their strategy is typically to lead creative, adventuresome lives. Their tactics involve exploration, discovery, creativity, risk, and novelty. They are active in their quest for something new, and will seek out adventure and work to create new possibilities.

Excitement seekers who use their style in destructive, noncooperative ways have a different strategy: to seek pleasure, excitement, and "highs" anyway one can. Their tactics are perhaps the most varied of the types discussed thus far. Creating fights, taking drugs, risky behaviors, thrill seeking (Farley, 1986), gambling, and putting their own and others' lives in danger are frequent tactics. "Live fast, die young, and have a good looking corpse," as Willard Motley (1989) wrote in his novel, *Knock on any Door.*

As children, excitement seekers probably exhibited high degrees of activity, similar to drivers (babies probably displayed both high and low degrees of activity, depending upon the situation). Neurodevelopmental data indicate that some individuals have higher stimulus thresholds than others (Miller, 1990). Such children are fussy and require more contact and stimulation than others, yet if they get it they typically are not satisfied. They reach satiation at higher levels than most, and they are typically extensive scanners of the perceptual field and prone to learn slowly from experience (Forgus & Shulman, 1979). In other words, they absorb a lot of data, process it slowly, and learn from their mistakes only after repeated trial and error (if then). Psychosocially, these children are actively engaged in everything—they want to see, do, and feel more, whatever more is. The more varied, the better, and these children are curious. Being safe is not as important as exploring, and they perceive the feedback from their caretakers more on the basis of its sensation value than its content. For example, little Suzy loves to watch Mom and Dad fight, not so much for what they say or do to each other, but for the tension and excitement it creates.

These individuals can be bold and innovative. They can seek out and explore new avenues and lead themselves and others into new insights. They can also get themselves into deep trouble. If the goal is to experience, it sometimes matters little what is experienced, as long as it is stimulating. Some become polydrug users. Significant others are often lost in the sensations of the moment; these people may be more in love with the feeling of love and passion than with the persons who provide the feelings. Hence, excitement seekers can make great dates but poor long-term partners, unless they learn to create excitement with those that they care about, rather than in spite of them.

Boredom is the challenge that excitement seekers fight most strongly. To be bored is to be "dead" in their lexicon, and to be dead is to stop feeling. There is so much to do, so much to try, to experience and taste, and

damned be those who get in their way. If their style is done constructively, they can be joys to be around, and if done destructively, it can frequently be tragic. Excitement seekers typically (but far from exclusively)
realize the dangers into which they are heading all the while that they
are heading into them. Those who care for excitement seekers sometimes become maddeningly frustrated as all they can do is sit and watch
(and cover their eyes) as the ones they love drive off into the sunset—at
120 miles per hour—or take that one extra "hit" of a drug. They love living on the edge—and often fall off. They dearly tax the ones they love
when they push "it" too far too fast. Farley (1986) and Zuckerman
(1979) describe similar types.

Pleasers

Pleasers are nice to be around, and one of their most endearing—and
perplexing—qualities, is that we seldom realize that we are around them
(Leman, 1987). Kopp (1986) has noted that these people can be very
diplomatic. In the mix of things, pleasers can be very accommodating
and quite facilitative of what transpires around them, without ever
really taking too strong a stand for themselves and their needs. As we
soon discover, their needs are very much tied not to the outcome of situations but to the process that accompanies it.

As both Kopp (1986) and Leman (1987) note, the overall goal of the
pleaser is to maintain peace and tranquility. Mosak (1971a) places the
emphasis upon being liked because they are so pleasing. Consequently
pleasers develop social skills that they trust will endear them to others.
Their paramount fear being not pleasing, they become hypersensitive to
criticism. To avoid possible criticism they become excellent "people readers." They behave like chameleons, "giving the customers what they
want" rather than stating their own opinions, taking a stand, or making
decisions of which others might disapprove. In doing so they frequently
lose their own sense of identity. As Aesop moralized in his fable, "The
Miller, His Son, and the Donkey," "He who tries to please everybody
pleases nobody." On the constructive side of life, the strategy is to help
resolve conflicts and bring about successful resolution of differing fac-
tions. The useful tactics include negotiation, mediation, arbitration, and
compromise. These individuals frequently keep us together and functioning as a team.

Pleasers encounter many perils (Hart, 1977). If their style is used in a
destructive manner, pleasers have a strategy that entails acquiescing to
others. They watch others and seek approval, and should they not get it
they feel devastated and rejected. It is difficult to negotiate for your best
interests if mine are too much on my mind. Therapists who do marital and

family counseling who are too oriented to pleasing have a hard time being confrontational and setting appropriate limits. They do not want to "rock the boat," so to speak, and risk having someone dislike them. They therefore become too preoccupied with how they are doing rather than with what they are doing. That kind of split in concentration, a manifestation of countertransference, tends to reduce performance, not enhance it.[1]

It is not uncommon to find pleasers who were family mediators even as children. Some of them are ACOAs (Adult Children of Alcoholics) (Kershaw-Bellemare & Mosak, 1993). These were compliant children who perceived their places in the family constellation as the ones who read the atmosphere and moods of the situation and people involved and *then* seemed to know just the right thing to say, or to ask for, which brought a smile to someone's face. Most children ask for what they want and *then* read the feedback about its possible achievement. Not so for these children. For pleasers, their "psychic" abilities are remarkable, if not occasionally outright amazing. They appear to know, before they are asked, what is the right thing to say or request, and they deliver it right on target. Frequently, they grow up alongside rather demanding siblings or parents, who model insensitivity or unpredictability. Keeping Father, with his temper and outbursts, in check, is felt to be their responsibility; or sister Karen, who could have a temper tantrum to end all temper tantrums, has to be kept appeased; otherwise Mother, who is already overtaxed, may become upset—if not depressed. These children find a way to comply, even if it is not their place to comply.

Pleasing is a burdensome responsibility. These people are typically nothing if not responsible, and if it is carried too far, they are too responsible, to the point of feeling guilty for having normal wants and needs. They often flagellate themselves for being "selfish" and overdo self-sacrifice. *Wanting* to not rock the boat becomes the prerequisite for *having* to not rock the boat.

Pleasers are wonderful lovers and caretakers. Those who love them frequently can end up feeling cheated, however, by a subtle "trick" that often goes undetected for years. As an example, Tom is married to Mary. Mary is the pleaser who carries her role a little too far. Tom, initially, is amazed at how responsive and "in tune" they are, especially because she seems to know what he wants without his having to ask. For months, they go out for sushi every weekend. Tom loves it. Mary appears to love it. Finally, typically during a fight, or overheard during a conversation Mary is having with an old friend, Tom discovers a rattling "truth:" Mary hates sushi. He confronts her, and she sheepishly admits it. He feels betrayed and, suddenly, rather foolish. Sometimes, the stakes are somewhat higher, such as having children, engaging in certain sexual practices, moving to certain locations in order to pursue "his career," and the like, and the nonpleasing spouse is left feeling dumbfounded. It is glorious to be pleased—it can feel belittling to be placated.

The diplomatic nature of pleasers can be a godsend. They can find the answers to difficult situations that many of us feel trapped in and lost. They listen to our troubles and settle our disputes. They help us to feel understood and appreciated. That can be their biggest challenge. They, too, want to be appreciated, but they seldom know how to come out and ask. Even if they know how, they fear to ask because they fear their overtures maybe rejected. For them, the process of human interaction is more important than the content—that is, they are typically more concerned with the feelings of those around them than with their own feelings. Is everybody happy? Yes? Then good! They must be too. Yet, something is missing from that equation. If they understand that, they can use their pleasing style in a useful, constructive manner and realize that they are not wrong for attempting openly to please themselves. Because one way in which to know that one has pleased is through receiving applause, many pleasers gravitate to the performing arts. Applause and compliment, their payoffs, are related to what they do rather than who they are, for they do not know who they are or what they want—beyond pleasing others.

☐ Typology: A Clinical Perspective

A brief excursion in the realm of psychopathology is in order, particularly as it relates to the topic of types. The early, classical Freudians felt that psychopathology could, and frequently did, develop parallel to character development. Hence, character neuroses were different than psychoneuroses, with the former generally having their roots in pre-oedipal (prior to 5 or 6 years of age) development. In those cases, psychopathology was "characterological" in nature. Psychopathology that had its roots in the oedipal or post-oedipal periods generally occurred despite having an intact character. Adler's notion of psychopathology, and therefore symptom formation, as being rooted in the life style of the individual (therefore, in the character, or personality) was not given much credence by the classical analysts. For Adler, all symptoms had to be understood on the basis of the life style, not independent of it.

Although Horney (1945, 1950) was an early proponent of Adler's view, mainstream psychoanalytic thinking was most clearly influenced by Shapiro, most noticeable by his work *Neurotic Styles* (1965). In that work, Shapiro argued that

> Styles or modes may be found that are capable of describing general aspects of function (such as cognition, emotional experience, and the like), modes that themselves will then be related and organized. Such consisten-

cies of individual functioning as those between symptom and adaptive traits may be conceived of as reflecting such general modes, giving shape alike to symptom and nonsymptom, to defense against impulse and adaptive expression of impulse. (p. 4)

With his work, it became "acceptable" to examine clients' "styles" and not simply symptoms. Paranoia became not simply a defense against what were then considered to be homosexual impulses, but, according to Shapiro, a clear and distinguishable style that affected symptoms and nonsymptomatic behavior alike.

Most recently, the work of Oldham and Morris (1990) has attempted to continue that tradition. They take the *Diagnostic and Statistical Manual of Mental Disorders* (American Psychiatric Association, 1994) personality disorders and present them in their "normal," nonpathological presentations. According to Oldham and Morris,

> Your personality style is your organizing principle. It propels you on your life path. It represents the orderly arrangement of all your attributes, thoughts, feelings, attitudes, behaviors, and coping mechanisms. It is the distinctive pattern of your psychological functioning—the way you think, feel, and behave—that makes you *definitely* you. (p. 15)

In this work, they attempt to show how some people are not typically "dependent personality disorders"; more likely, they have "devoted styles" that, under enough stress, decompensate into the pathological version. What each style perceives as stressful is dependent upon the style itself; for instance, a "dramatic style" is fine as long as he or she remains the life of the party or an actor. Pushed too far too often, that style can become the histrionic personality disorder.

Similar efforts have been made by Millon (1981). He felt that in order to understand psychopathology, one had to come to grips with the underlying personality pattern. He describes (giving credit to Adler) various patterns, such as the asocial pattern (schizoid personality disorder) and the aggressive pattern (antisocial personality disorder).

☐ Summary

Many theorists and clinicians are moving more and more toward Adler's (1935) stance, that certain themes, or patterns, emerge in the personalities of individuals that lead them to certain type of problems. The problems are not something that come over the style; rather, they are part and parcel of the style itself. Given certain themes, individuals will experience certain classifiable disorders if they decompensate (Mosak, 1968). It is how persons with these styles cope with life and its demands that we turn to next, for each style reacts in certain ways to the challenges of life.

☐ Points to Consider

Although no two life styles are identical, there are similarities that can be discussed. Those similarities form the basis of typological systems.

In Adlerian psychology, there have been numerous attempts to create typologies. Birth-order types, learning types, personal priorities, and Mosak's typology are some of the key ones.

Typologies can be important for several reasons. They help communicate to other clinicians, they facilitate prediction, and they are very helpful in conducting research.

☐ Questions

1. What is the difference between being a youngest born and developing the life style of a baby?
2. Karen Horney developed a system that stressed "solutions" to life's problems. How is her system similar to Adler's? How is it different?
3. What are some recent parallels in contemporary practice when it comes to typology?
4. What is stressful for a driver?
5. What were the four types Adler first identified in 1935?
6. Attempt to plot Adler's four life-style types on a graph, using degree of activity along the vertical axis and amount of social interest along the horizontal (baseline) axis. Where do each of the types fit?
7. What are the three ways in which types can be used?

☐ Note

[1]Pleasers, because they are excellent "people readers," often make excellent diagnosticians, but their function as therapists remains problematic.

CHAPTER

Inferiorities, Inferiority Feelings, and Inferiority Complexes

As a concept, self-esteem is extremely useful for those trying to understand why people act as they do. As a reality, the importance of high self-esteem simply cannot be overstated. It might be thought of as the sine qua non *of the healthy personality. It suggests a respect for and faith in ourselves that is not easily shaken, an abiding and deep-seated acceptance of our own worth. Ideally, self-esteem is not only high and unconditional; it does not depend on approval from others, and it does not crumble even when we do things that we later regret. It is a core, a foundation upon which a life is constructed.*

Alfie Kohn (1986)

It seems generally believed, that, as the eye cannot see itself, the mind has no faculties by which it can contemplate its own state, and that therefore we have not means of becoming acquainted with our real characters. . . . We are secretly conscious of defects and vices which we hope to conceal from the public eye, and please ourselves with innumerable impostures, by which, in reality, no body is deceived.

Samuel Johnson (1751/1973)

As we briefly touched upon in Chapter 4, people, by virtue of being human, experience incongruity between convictions. We all have "de-

78

fects and vices which we hope to conceal," but as Johnson noted almost 300 years ago, we are "secretly conscious" of our faults, our shortcomings. How do we become conscious of our shortcomings, our defects? Why should we be conscious of them? Would it not be better to either have no defects, as the perfectionist might assert, or at least not be aware of them? (The perfectionist would certainly consider that a wonderful state.) In order to be in a better position to answer such questions, and explore our all-too-human responses to such psychological and philosophical issues, we need to turn our attention to the concept of stress and its role in human functioning.

☐ Stress and Human Adaptation

Selye's (1974) work on stress and adaptation indicates that to exist without stress is impossible. He writes that

> *Stress is the nonspecific response of the body to any demand made upon it. . . it is immaterial whether the agent or situation we face is pleasant or unpleasant;* all that counts is the intensity of the demand for readjustment or adaptation. (pp. 14–15)

He notes, further on in his text, that "complete freedom from stress is death" (p. 20). Let us examine this in more detail.

Selye, a biologist first and foremost, like Adler before him was concerned with how living beings adapt to, compensate for, and cope with the stress life presents. Selye observed that different organisms react differently to the same stressors. For humans, prior learning and motivation become key factors in not only determining how they adapt to stress, but even in perceiving what will be considered stressful. For Selye (1974, p. 58), successful adaptation to stress requires "collaboration" and altruistic tendencies that overcome "selfishness" and "egotism" (p. 53) and better prepare the organism to adapt to life's stressors.

What does all this have to do with the purpose of this chapter, which explicates and details the role of inferiority feelings and complexes and differentiates them from actual inferiorities and our response to them? A great deal. Selye (1974) is accurately describing, from a biological viewpoint, how intercellular collaboration fosters healthy adaptation; and on a grander scale, how organisms that work collaboratively together are better adapted to struggle with and overcome environmental challenges. Excessive focus upon individual identity at the expense of the others leads to maladaptive coping mechanisms for dealing with life's challenges.

Ornstein and Sobel (1987) and Williams (1989) have written extensively on the role of useful, cooperative adaptation not only in preventing illness, but in fostering wellness. For all of these researchers, the key to wellness is cooperative, egalitarian stances toward others. The role of expectations in dealing with stress, and our bodies' reactions to it, helps determine our biological functioning.

The life style, with its constituent parts, holds the keys to the perceptual system, and therefore, to what the person perceives as distressful. Distress is harmful, unpleasant stress; it places the organism in potential danger. How we deal with that stress, and whether or not it becomes distressful and eventually harmful to survival, is a matter of how cooperatively and efficiently we adapt. The key, Selye maintained, was to experience "stress without distress."

An inferiority, as defined in Chapter 4, is objective and contextual. For the purposes of this chapter, it can be conceptualized as a stress, a challenge to the organism's adaptation. For example, in the fable of the fox and the sour grapes, I see some grapes I want, and as I reach for them, I realize I am too short to reach them. In this context, I am experiencing stress. It becomes distress if I feel inferior. The *feeling of inferiority,* as noted previously, is the evaluation we make of the objective situation. We need to adapt to that situation. If I shy away from the challenge of reaching for the grapes, *because I feel too inferior* and do not want others to perceive me as so, I am exhibiting an *inferiority complex.* Such a stance prevents me from using my creativity to devise a way to reach the grapes. I am more concerned with my appearance, my inferiorities, than with the demands of life. I am prestige-oriented,[1] rather than task-oriented. My ability to adapt, to survive and flourish, is impaired.

This prestige-oriented stance not only hampers my individual adaptation, it tends to impair my ability to effectively utilize my support system for assistance; in other words, I may not ask for help. Too much of an emphasis upon prestige and worth, and not enough upon the task, decreases my ability to function effectively. I may try to keep up appearances. I may hide out for fear of failure or humiliation. It limits my choices and options. This is maladaptive not only for myself but for those around me.

Inferiority feelings, as Adler (1927/1957) wrote, motivate us to "become" (Adler 1930/1963; Allport, 1955) and compel us to work together to overcome. They invite us to develop and expand our behavioral repertoire and to utilize creativity and imagination to project how things could be different in the future. Adler (1933/1964f, p. 73) writes, "To be a human being means the possession of a feeling of inferiority that is constantly pressing on its own conquest." Inferiority feelings encourage us to develop realistic *self-concepts* and simultaneously appropriate *self-ideals.* Biologically, our awareness of our inferiority has allowed us to adapt better and create societies and technologies that we would not have envisioned had we not felt inadequate to our current living conditions. Inferiority feelings encourage us to reexamine our situations and decide what we can do to change them. They allow us to grow, both individually, and as a species.

To sum up thus far, to be without stress is to be dead. To have no inferiorities is to be without movement, to be less than human, God-like. Because we do move, because we are alive, we encounter situations that require more of us than we are currently prepared to offer. Benign, ignorant indifference to such situations results in stagnation. We do not learn and we do not grow. Awareness of our inferiorities, via inferiority feelings, urges us to be both more astutely aware of what we are (self-concept) and what we need subjectively to want to be (self-ideal). How we deal with such an awareness determines how adaptive we are. If we display an inferiority complex, we withdraw from the challenge.

Before we more specifically examine how we cope with such challenges, either through coping mechanisms, safeguarding operations, excuses, aggression, or distance seeking, one additional dynamic requires consideration. What about those who apparently do not have inferiority complexes? In fact, they appear to have the opposite reaction, an overestimation and unrealistic appraisal of their abilities. Adler (1956) addressed such situations, and they require some elaboration.

☐ Superiority, Superiority Feelings, and Superiority Complexes

The dynamics of superiority need to be examined in light of two trends that individuals display. First, we explore them as part of a normal developmental process, and then as an overcompensation for the inferiority complex.

Some children are gifted and perceive themselves as such. Their self-concepts are something like "I am the best at . . ." By and large, they are the best at that particular item or class of items. Their feelings of superiority are focal, contextual, and "accurate." Jane is the best mathematics student in the school system. She has the awards to prove it. Developmentally, her sense of superiority in mathematics is appropriate. At this time, in this place or situation, she is objectively superior and may not feel superior as a person.

A second set of children is told they are superior. The messages they perceive feed into their developing self-ideals, and they begin to believe that they are superior as persons (cf. Muhammad Ali's "I am the greatest!"). Developmentally, they confuse their self-ideals with their self-concepts. They believe that because they should be superior, they are. They may be adapting to family dynamics. In some instances the quest for superiority may be compensatory for a parental inferiority complex.

In either of these cases, the notion of superiority complex, as Adler (1956) defined it, is not really at issue. Both cases are artifacts of learning and development and, to some degree, are more or less subjectively accurate appraisals of early childhood experiences.

These notions of superiority are to be differentiated from superiority complexes. Adler (1956, p. 260) stated unequivocally:

> The superiority complex is one of the ways which a person with an inferiority . . . complex may use as a method of escape from his difficulties. He assumes that he is superior when he is not, and this false success compensates him for the state of inferiority which he cannot bear. The normal person does not have a superiority complex, he does not even have a sense of superiority. He has the striving to be superior in the sense that we all have ambition to be successful.

The first two developmental situations we noted are indicative of what Adler referred to as "ambition to be successful." In the first scenario, the person attains his or her ambitions; in the second, the person, partly because of early feedback, believes he or she has been successful in attaining his or her ambitions. The superiority complex to which Adler refers is compensatory for inferiority feelings that are manifested as an inferiority complex.

The superiority complex is reactive; it occurs out of a form of psychological desperation and is an exaggerated attempt to act as if one were not feeling inferior and then acting that way. It is an attempt to act as if one were superior, even though one feels extremely far from it, without admitting it. As Johnson is quoted in the opening of this chapter, it is an "imposture," a curious blend of the words "impostor" and "posture." One assumes the posture of something one is not.

The superiority complex is nothing but a variation of the inferiority complex. These people are not more adaptive; they are just better actors. To return to our earlier example of the grapes, I act as if I can reach them, I boast or even lie about my having had them, and I attempt to convince others I can get them so very easily. Like its shadowy counterpart, it impairs adaptation and the necessary development of skills to actually attain what is needed. It too leads to further distress. The superiority complex is the vocal, prideful variation of the inferiority complex.

Given the fact that to be human means to experience some kind of inferiority feeling, how do we cope with such challenges? The first step is to perceive challenges as challenges, not problems. Life will challenge us—it is up to us whether or not we turn them into problems. Some challenges are greater than others. The stance we take toward those challenges determines our degree of adaptation.

In general, we can take two postures toward life and its stresses. We can see them as challenges and engage in what Adlerians call "coping behaviors"; or we can perceive them as problems and engage in what Adler (1956) and Credner (1936) called "safeguarding" behaviors, otherwise known as defense mechanisms.

☐ Coping Behaviors

Direct Problem Solving

The most obvious way to meet challenges is through direct problem solving. Attention is focused upon the task, and whatever resources are needed are mustered. If the examination needs to be passed, one studies; if the car is broken, one fixes it.

Compensation

Some situations are difficult to solve in a direct, straightforward manner. At those times, compensatory activities may be required in at least one of the following three ways: within the area, in another area, or overcompensation. A brief example of each clarifies.

Compensation within the area typically involves coping with the task despite what appear to be severe challenges. For example, if I break my arm, I learn to function with the cast; if I become blind, I learn to navigate my way around with a cane, a seeing-eye dog, and the like. Textbooks often cite Helen Keller, Teddy Roosevelt, and Demosthenes in this regard.

Compensation in another area entails working to build up one area if another is deficient. For instance, I may be poor in school, but I can become an excellent athlete.

An overcompensation occurs if people overexcel in an area despite having a setback. Specifically, someone who is deficient in one area works extra hard to become not only proficient but better than what would normally (typically) be expected from someone who started out without the deficiency. An example might be someone with a foot problem who becomes not only a "normal" walker but a great dancer. Thus, overcompensation, if directed toward constructive goals, may culminate in excellent achievements. Adler (1956, p. 28) writes, "When overcompensation attempts to assert itself in a cultural manner and in this effort enters into new, although difficult and often inhibited paths, the very great expressions of the psyche arise which we must attribute to genius."

What individuals do if they feel they cannot meet the tasks that life presents is the focus of the rest of this chapter. Life demands that we adapt to it, but all of us, to one degree or another, at times ask for a pardon, a dispensation, from life's demands. That only makes us "normal." As Lazarsfeld (1927/1991) has phrased it, we all need to develop the courage to be imperfect, or else we are always and forever seeking pardons. When these are used too often, or become the focus of one's life, is when we begin to move further and further away from common sense, and we begin to become less and less adaptive. State in movement Depression · Excuses

Safeguarding Behaviors

Adler (1956) considered safeguarding behaviors to originate as interpersonal phenomena, whereas the early Freudians (prior to the work of Anna Freud) considered defense mechanisms to be intrapsychic in nature. The difference is crucial. The Freudians see the ego as defending itself from the instincts. Adlerians see the *person* as protecting him- or herself against three threats to the self. The first is the threat to the physical self. We may get hurt, sick, and even die. The second involves social threat, that we may not look good in the eyes of others, that they may disapprove of us, humiliate us, or punish us. The third relates to the fear of loss of self-esteem, of not looking good in our own eyes. Contemporary psychoanalysts have since moved closer to Adler's position, emphasizing the role of defense mechanisms in protecting the ego (A. Freud, 1936/1946). What follows is a list of the six primary safeguarding operations Adler (1956) delineated throughout his writings (with appropriate subsections and elaborations). Generally speaking, all of these constitute what Adler (1956) used to call sideshows. Harkening back to his work with the sideshow performers, Adler observed that sideshows were effective means of distracting attention away from the main challenges of life (e.g., the tasks of life), and placing it upon other issues that were not constructive. Rather than deal with life, people created sideshows in order to distract themselves and others from the more important issues (Wolfe, 1932).

Symptoms

People who develop symptoms use them in order to evade some task, or challenge, for which they feel ill prepared. If I develop headaches, I may be too "ill" to study for the test. If I am too depressed, I may be able to get others to take care of me. If I become preoccupied with hearing voices commanding me to do things, I cannot meet the work task. The role of symptomatology in human functioning is explored in greater detail in Chapter 8, but for present purposes, suffice to say that symptoms are created to safeguard our self-esteem, exempt us from responsibility, and engage others.

Excuses

Excuses are typically conscious, whereas the aforementioned symptom formation is mostly unconscious. Individuals typically declare that "If it weren't for these . . . I'd be able to . . ." Adler (1931/1958) referred to this movement as "Yes-but" (cf. Berne's [1964] game, "Why don't you . . . ? Yes but . . ."). British Adlerians refer to it as "if only." For example, John has a handwashing compulsion. Placed into the language of the psychology of use, Adlerians would say John uses his handwashing in order to evade certain issues. More precisely, John's life style convictions are adhered to more rigidly than is beneficial, and he would rather cling to his beliefs than adapt to reality, what Adler (1956) called common sense. In order to at least appear to be meeting the challenges, he makes an excuse, such as, "If only I could just stop this damn handwashing compulsion, I'd be able to get back to working the way I used to." What he is doing is providing himself with an excuse and telling us what it is he fears incapable of doing—working at the level he once attained. Linden (1993) provides a detailed analysis of the role of excuses in everyday life. A more formal term for "making excuses" is rationalization. The rationalization permits the person to avoid feelings of deficiency and defeat, as in the fable of the fox and the sour grapes. Whenever one hears a "fox" uttering (or muttering), "Who cares?" one can assume that the fox cares more than he or she cares to admit. In this sense rationalization safeguards the person's pride system.

Aggression

Adler (1956) was the one who originally proposed the concept of aggression to Freud and the early psychoanalysts. Sicher and Mosak (1967) have explored the issue of human aggression in considerable detail. Briefly stated, Adler considered aggression to be a secondary phenomenon. It is a choice individuals make in order to move them toward their goals. If I value control and someone challenges me for it, I may become aggressive in order to regain control. The aggression is secondary to the conviction of being in control. Adler delineated three principle variations of aggression: depreciation, accusation, and self-accusation. In this delineation he anticipated attribution theory.

Depreciation is an actual putting down of others. If I feel inferior to you, I can work to elevate myself or I can bring you down. Two forms of depreciation are idealization and solicitude. With idealization, for example, we "measure thumbs down" to a "real person by an ideal" (Adler, 1956, p. 268). By maintaining that I am looking only for the "ideal woman," I secretly devalue most, if not all, of the women I meet—they are not good enough for me. If using the safeguarding operation of solicitude, individuals "act as if without their aid . . . others would be incapable of caring for themselves" (Adler, 1956, p. 269).[2] By assuming they need me so badly, I elevate myself at their expense. Teichman and Foa (1972) provide empirical support of Adler's views on the depreciation tendency.

Accusation as a form of aggression is relatively self-explanatory. Others are held responsible for our "defeats." The object of the accusation is typically the one who suffers the most because of the patient's symptoms. This is explored in greater detail in Chapter 9.

Self-accusation and guilt are the final forms of aggression Adler (1956) discusses. Adler noted that if people hurt themselves in order to hurt others, they are engaging in behaviors that are typical of children. He considered suicide the prime example of such a mechanism (K. Adler, 1961; Karon, 1964). It is the ultimate act of self-accusation aimed at hurting others. It should be noted that through self-condemnation one can also elevate oneself. "I may have done wrong but at least I have the decency to feel guilty" or, more transparently, the psychotic depressive's proclamation, "I'm the *worst* sinner God ever created."

Distance Seeking

Individuals typically display characteristic movements in relation to challenges. Whereas excuses are verbal, distance-seeking behaviors are related to movement; that is, they are indicative of what a person does. That person's rationale for such movement may be different than the movement itself, but as Adler often stated, "Trust only movement," for that tells one people's true intentions. Adler (1956) would quote Martin

Luther's aphorism "not to watch a person's mouth but his fists" and often advocated that if we want to understand a person, we have to close our ears. We have only to look. In this way we can see as in pantomime. He originally described four styles of distance seeking (Adler, 1914/ 1983e): backward, standing still, hesitation and back and forth, and creating obstacles. Mosak and Shulman (1977) have elaborated upon these, and their additions are mentioned here.

Backward movement entails moving away from a challenge. In the schizoid maneuver, one ignores "it" until it goes away. With the ostrich maneuver (denial), one buries one's head and acts as if the challenge did not exist. The unraveler, referred to by Mosak as "the Penelope maneuver," entails doing and then undoing in order to withdraw from the task. Penelope, in ancient Greek literature, was the wife of Ulysses. After he failed to return from his voyages (she waited 20 years), she began to be approached by suitors. Every day they would press her to marry, but she would hold them off by claiming to work on a burial shroud for Ulysses' father, Laertes. She informed the suitors that when she finished weaving the garment, she would marry one of them. Every day she would weave all day, and every night, after the suitors left, she would unravel it. Other types of backward movement include resignation (the half-hearted attempt) and the declaration of bankruptcy (totally giving up).

Standing still entails buying time. An example of such would be waiting for the "right" one to come along before one marries. It can be a long wait, especially if one really does not want to get married. Developmentally, an example of standing still might be if one acts as if one is still a late adolescent who drives fast cars, parties too much, has difficulty holding down a meaningful job, and continues to engage in short-term, noncommitted relationships even though one's peer group has reached adulthood. That person is standing still and refusing to "grow up."

Hesitation movements keep the person in place or taking "baby steps" in life. Procrastination is one form of hesitation. Running in place or marking time are others. In these cases people look like they are performing a lot of work, but they do not seem to be going anywhere. Adler (1914/1983e) characterizes the movement of the neurotic as "the hesitating attitude toward life." Back-and-forth movements involve taking several steps forward followed by several steps backward. The "cold feet syndrome" in the termination phase of therapy is an example of such movement. Adler (1956) considered a "Yes, but . . ." attitude to be another example. "*Yes*," the person says, "I know what I have to do, *but* you see I can't because . . ." Although Berne (1964) considered this the first "game" ever discovered in transactional analysis, Adler (1931/1958) had already discussed it in 1931. Another example of hesitating, or back-and-forth movement, is if couples get engaged, break it off, see other people, fall back in love, see each other again, break it off, see other people, and so on.

Finally, creating obstacles is another form of distance seeking. With this strategy, people move forward only after something is accomplished first. For instance, in creating hurdles, one cannot get to a task until one jumps through several hoops. A common example might be the person who cannot get a job until he settles his "emotional issues" first. As long as he does not want to work, he will never settle his emotional issues. If people make monsters or, to use Ellis's (1973) terms, "awfulize" and "catastrophize," they frighten themselves so badly that they cannot focus upon the task at hand. Choosing overwhelming tasks can be another way of creating obstacles. "I can't move on in life," she claims, "I'm just too far behind. After I get this mess sorted out, then I'll see." The mess, she later defines, is her entire life. Similarly, one can busy oneself with so many details that one never really gets to the heart of the matter. The compulsive neurotic engages in this mode of living. These are just some ways in which people create obstacles in order to not meet challenges.

Anxiety

Adler (1956) claimed that one way to avoid meeting challenges, and hence safeguard self-esteem, is to create anxiety. One can become so afraid of life, people, or tasks that one cannot function. Certain phobias, panic attacks, and what used to be termed "nervous conditions" all serve the function of allowing individuals to sidestep demands. People typically use the phrase "I'm afraid" in order to justify not accomplishing something. Anxiety, for Adler, was a safeguarding mechanism like many of the others mentioned in this section and had no particular relevance other than a means of evading challenges. For Adlerians, fear is no exemption. If it were, we would never learn to walk or cross the street.

Exclusion Tendency

Lastly, Adler (1956) discussed the exclusion tendency. With this, he referred to the dynamic of narrowing down one's approach to life. The more flexible one's life style convictions, the greater the ability to adapt to whatever life presents. Rigid, inflexible convictions either "break," that is, give in to the demands of life, in which case the person learns and grows, or they remain intact, which means that life has to change. Although one cannot readily change life, one can restrict, for example through denial, the number and types of experiences one has. For example, if I will only socialize with people who admire me, I have to limit my sphere of social interaction to those who fit my requirements. By narrowing down my approach to life, I exclude all those people or situations that do not meet my requirements.

Shulman (1964) has elaborated upon these safeguarding behaviors. His discussion revolves around what he terms defensive patterns, particularly seen in patients who are attempting to defend themselves against perceived threats from their doctors or therapists. He outlines 10 defensive patterns, and we briefly touch upon each.

☐ Defensive Patterns

According to Shulman (1964), patients have nine perceived dangers that they defend themselves against: being defective, being exposed, incurring disapproval, being ridiculed, being taken advantage of, getting necessary help, submitting to order, facing responsibility, and facing unpleasant consequences. If any one or more of these is perceived as likely to occur, patients engage in many of the following 10 defensive patterns.

Externalization

Patients tend to blame life or others for their problems. Rosenzweig (1944) refers to this as "extrapunitiveness." One version of that entails cynicism, in that "life is all garbage anyway, so what do you expect?" Externalization does not necessarily assign the blame to factors outside of the individual; it may also blame internal factors over which the person "has no control." We observe this in the legal defenses of insanity, diminished responsibility, and uncontrollable impulse. Other variations of externalization are proclamations of being a victim of sickness, of biochemical and genetic causes, of a bad background, or of being a victim of one's own impulses or even supernatural forces ("The devil made me do it!"), and consequently being unable to help oneself. Rebellion is another form of externalization. In rebelling, one can claim that because of "them" one had to do what one did; in other words, one blames parents, "authority," the Establishment, or "order" for one's behavior, and hence, one is justified in rebelling. Similarly, via projection, one can claim, "I'm not mad, you're the one being difficult," although all the while it is not the other, but oneself, who is mad. With projection, people "project" some internal motive onto others, and then hold them accountable for it.

Blind spots

Patients can choose not to see certain things. By developing blind spots, they can overlook issues that they do not want to see, and hence for which they do not want to accept responsibility.

Excessive Self-control

The ability to control one's emotions can be admirable. Carried to an extreme, one can behave like a robot and become a "feeling avoider" (Mosak, 1971a). Being overly controlled can be a way of not dealing with pain, or in some cases ecstasies.

Arbitrary Rightness

If people use this defensive pattern, they assume an "I'm right, you're wrong" stance that may have no grounding (or little basis) in fact. As one person declared, "I'm never wrong! I once thought I was, but I was wrong." Some individuals make up their minds and do not want to be confused by facts. They have their own opinions and do not want to hear otherwise. Their attitude is reminiscent of the bumper sticker that reads, "Don't confuse me with the facts. My mind's already made up."

Elusiveness and Confusion

To be confused means, "I'm not going to be pinned down" (Mosak & Gushurst, 1971), and if one cannot be pinned down, one cannot be wrong. If they do not remember, they cannot be held accountable. Those who use this pattern frequently speak much but say little. "Double talk" is common.

Retreat

For these people the motto might be "Nothing ventured, nothing lost." If retreating is used, patients simply may not come back. Given the opportunity, these people withdraw from demands. Adler (1914/l983e) provides many examples of what he calls distancing.

Contrition and Self-disparagement

Patients who use these techniques are pretending to blame themselves. A common example of this is a display of good intentions. By claiming, "I'm so sorry," they hope to gain forgiveness without being held too accountable (Beecher, 1950; Beecher & Beecher, 1971/1987; Bruck, 1950; Dreikurs, 1950b; Feichtinger, 1950; Geis, 1966; Rom, 1950; Sicher, 1950). They hope that the harder they beat themselves, the less others will do it.

Suffering

Suffering can be used for any of several purposes (Mosak, Brown, & Boldt, 1994). It can be a form of manipulation ("Look how much I hurt. See, I need special service") or a justification ("I deserve it. Look how I hurt when I'm deprived!"). Self-glorification can be yet another use for suffering ("Look how noble I am!").

Sideshows

This has been briefly mentioned previously, and Shulman (1964) partitions it out as a distinct defense mechanism in and of itself. It is a variant of creating obstacles. Instead of dealing with the "main tent" issues in life (Wolfe, 1932), patients can focus their attention (and others') upon less important, and at times trivial, matters. These sideshows allow them to evade the real issues.

Rationalization

Patients who use rationalization use "reasons" to actually excuse themselves from acknowledging defeat or deficiency or bad behavior. Wexberg (1947) speaks of "sour grapes" and "sweet lemon" rationalizations. In the former, the person assuages the pain of defeat by denying that she or he really wished to attain something. In the latter, the person soothes him- or herself by claiming that an undesirable outcome has positive aspects. If one's picnic has been rained out, one can always console oneself with rationalizations such as, "It's good for the farmers."

We conclude this chapter by adding to this set eight additional defense patterns, or safeguarding behaviors. We have used these in our teaching, supervision, and clinical work and have found them helpful.

Intellectualization

People using this defense mechanism keep others at a distance by talking in terms of abstract concepts and attempt to avoid feelings. If they are asked, "Have you ever been in love?" their answer likely is of the order, "Let's define our terms. What do you mean by love?"

Identification

If used constructively, the process of identification can help provide us with a sense of belonging and a foundation for the formation of our self-concept. We form our values and our gender guiding lines through identification. If used as a safeguarding device, identification can forestall action. Rather than going out and playing baseball, for instance, I can sit and watch my "heroes" play. I can gain self-esteem vicariously through other's activities and not engage in my own coping behaviors to raise my self-esteem.

Buying Double Insurance

With this tactic, I enter into a "win-win" situation. I behave in such a way as to ensure that no matter what the outcome, I land on my feet. For example, if I do not study for the test, and I pass, I am a "hero" because I did not crack a book. It must be because I am smart. If I fail, it is because I was either too lazy, or busy, or preoccupied, or so forth, not because I am dumb. Either way, I never really lose. I play it doubly safe.

Literalism

If I take everything very seriously, I can encourage others to behave carefully around me. If instructed to do something, I can act in such a way that I become obsessed with the letter, and not the spirit, of the law. For example, if Mother says to her son, "Put *all* your clothes in the laundry," and he puts everything in the laundry—shoes, jackets, ties, hat— he sends her a subtle message: "See what happens when you count on me or push me." She may stop asking him.

Literalism often makes good humor and comedy (Mosak, 1987b). At the end of each show, George Burns would request, "Say good night, Gracie," and Gracie Allen would respond, "Good night, Gracie." Abbott and Costello's routine, "Who's on First," is another such example. Clinically, literalism may disturb communication. In marriage counseling a man complains that his wife nags him 24 hours a day. Disgustedly his wife retorts, "You see what I have to put up with? Now tell the truth! Do I nag you when you're sleeping?"

Fantasy

Daydreaming can be fun and positive (Singer, 1975), but too much day-dreaming wastes time (cf. Walter Mitty). After all, there is an old expression: The first thing you have to do to make your dreams come true is wake up. Fantasy is engaged in if one cannot attain or accomplish something in actuality at the time. Three common themes of fantasy are the conquering hero, the suffering hero, and the lost prince or princess. In the first, only wonderful things happen. There is nothing the person cannot achieve or get. These fantasies provide a "high" for the day-dreamer. The suffering hero gains nobility as one imagines how tough life is, how overwhelming it can be, and how one must fight incredible odds and overcome outrageous fortune to simply survive. Life is full of travail and suffering. Suffering is the substitution of nobility for no ability (Mosak, 1987b). These fantasies help to confirm a pessimism about life and oneself and create a mood in the present. Prometheus is a case in point. When chained to a rock unto eternity with a raven nibbling at his liver, he cries out, "Ye gods! How I suffer!" The lost prince or princess fantasy emerges if children feel unloved or punished, but the fantasy may carry over into adulthood. It is based upon the assumption that parents who love their children do not ever punish them or disapprove of them. Because these "people" disapproved or punished them, they cannot be their real parents. And although these "parents" may "get points" for taking them in now, some day their "real" parents will return and rescue them from their current situation, and they will be loved ever after.

Displacement

With displacement, people tend to "kick the dog," when they really want to kick someone else. Transference is a form of displacement. For example, if Joe is aggravated with his boss, he is better served by speaking to his boss than by going home and taking it out on his wife and kids. Displacement allows individuals to evade dealing with tasks that they perceive as important, but they feel incapable of accomplishing. We feel, "You can't fight city hall!"

Doctrine of Balances

We sometimes attribute divine intervention to occurrences in order to safeguard our self-esteem. "If she is beautiful," we say, "she must be dumb." "Cold hands, warm heart." "Lucky at love, unlucky at cards." For every one thing a person is given, one is taken away, as if there were some greater force such as God or Providence maintaining a balance, assuring that despite one's deficiencies everyone gets something to counterbalance it. Thus, no one really is cheated in life. Although this feeling may provide consolation for some. evidence does not substantiate it.

Reaction Formation

Some Adlerians consider this a variation of compensation, and in many ways, it is. We assume an outward posture that is the opposite of what we really believe or feel. Children do this quite often, such as when little boys tease the girls they like best. As adults, we sometimes act as if we are opposed to certain topics or types of situations, when in fact we would secretly want to do them. For instance, Pete acts as if he would never want the kind of job Artie has. He really would but feels he could never have it, so he acts as if he does not want it.

☐ Summary

This chapter attempts to detail how people either meet or evade challenges that are placed before them. There are far more safeguarding mechanisms that we could describe, but space limitations preclude such an undertaking. At the root of all of these issues is the feeling of inferiority and how people choose to deal with such feelings. All of us, to some extent, meet some challenges some of the time; and all of us manage to sidestep some challenges sometimes, in an attempt to prevent us from exposing what we perceive to be our weaknesses and defects. We are, after all, human.

Until this point, we have written about challenges in general. Adlerians believe that there are certain challenges with which everyone must deal, either through direct problem solving, compensation, or safeguarding. These challenges are part and parcel of being human, and they require an answer from us, even if that answer is no. ("No," itself may be a defensive pattern.) These challenges, these tasks of life, are the focus of Chapter 7.

☐ **Points to Consider**

It is impossible to live without stress. For theorists such as Adler and Selye, successful adaptation requires collaboration and altruistic tendencies.

If people are task-oriented, they focus upon what needs to be done. If they are prestige-oriented, they focus upon how they are doing.

Everybody has inferiorities. The issue is how these are managed.

Just as some people have inferiority complexes, some have superiority complexes. Not all feelings of superiority are abnormal and compensatory for feelings of inferiority, however.

Generally speaking, people tend to either cope with situations as they arrive or engage in safeguarding mechanisms. Safeguarding mechanisms, more commonly known as defense mechanisms, limit the range of creativity and useful adaptation.

☐ **Questions**

1. Give some examples of "coping behaviors." How are these different from defense mechanisms?
2. What did Selye believe about stress? How could we most successfully deal with it?
3. What are some instances of people developing normal senses of their own superiority?
4. Give an example of buying double insurance.
5. What are some forms of distance seeking?
6. What are sideshows? How are they used and why?
7. In your conversations with family and friends, note how many safeguarding mechanisms you hear. Do you use any when you discuss some of your "issues?"

☐ **Notes**

[1]Usually this is termed "ego-oriented," but because Adlerians do not accept the Freudian topology of id, ego, and superego, we use "prestige-oriented" or "worth-oriented."

[2]Cf. Wylie's (1994) "smother complex."

The Tasks of Life

I assume . . . that a point was reached in the history of mankind when the obstacles to continuing in a state of Nature were stronger than the forces which each individual could employ to the end of continuing in it. . . . [S]ince men can by no means engender new powers, but can only unite and control those of which they already possessed, there is no way in which they can maintain themselves save by coming together and pooling their strength . . . and learn to act in concert.

Jean-Jacques Rousseau (1762/1947)

For Adlerian psychologists, understanding people is a two-sided issue. There is a social matrix, a context, in which people exist that cannot be ignored. The existential philosophers, in particular, have noted that people are "thrown" into a world, and that to attempt to conceive of people without taking into account the world in which they live limits our understanding of what being human means (e.g., Heidegger, 1927/ 1962). As we state in the chapter on the basic assumptions of individual psychology, Adlerians operate from a social-field theoretical perspective.

Like most theoreticians operating from a subjective, phenomenological perspective, Adler placed considerable emphasis upon understanding the private, personal world of the patients with whom he worked. The life style assessment, with its emphasis upon understanding the early childhood situation, family constellation, parental relationships, school and neighborhood environment, and early recollections (Powers & Griffith, 1987; Shulman & Mosak, 1988), attempts to access individuals' perceptions, impressions, and meanings they ascribe to life, themselves, and other people. Their maps, their blueprints about how to move through life, provide us with rich sources of information through which to understand them and, possibly, assist in changing them. That is half of the picture, however.

Although Adlerians place a great deal of emphasis upon the phenomenological, they also examine people's relationship to the world. It is this other half of the equation to which we now direct our attention. How do we understand the world? What do Adlerians mean by "world" and why should we pay attention to it at all? Is having a sound grasp of people's life styles not sufficient?

Adler (1956) stated that every life style is adaptable until life presents it with something for which the person is not adequately prepared. This is a crucial concept and requires closer examination.

Let us discuss, for instance, someone we call Bill. Bill has the life style of a getter (Adler, 1935; Mosak, 1959). He "arranges" life in such a way as to maximize his getting. As Mosak (1959) has explained, getters are more preoccupied with the act of acquisition than with the actual hoarding itself. Bill, for example, is more interested in the "hunt" (as he refers to it) than in the actual attaining of a romantic partner. He pursues vigorously, only to probably lose interest shortly after he has gotten what he wants, whatever that may be subjectively defined as. Given this style, his perceptual system is "biased" in favor of certain kinds of data. He views the world, life, other people, and circumstances from a vantage point that reinforces his expectations. He sets out to receive the kinds of responses that support him in that movement, even if he has to actively create situations that "give" him what he wants.

That is what Adler (1920/1983d, 1956) meant when he spoke of the "arrangement." We create feedback that supports our beliefs. Though we are frequently not aware of it, we do influence much of what we see around us. Let us elaborate on that point. If I construe life as being something that needs to be controlled, I will not only seek out situations that are in need of a "controller," I will probably create some of those same situations. I feel grounded, so to say, if I am controlling.

The problems arise—at least potentially—if life is not so accommodating. Controllers with nothing or no one to control can feel rather out of place. Mosak (1995a) has given them the "handle" of "St. George with no dragons to fight." How they find "security," or "belonging," is, in that situation, seriously called into question. Despite all efforts to control, life may not yield to the controller's demands.

Adler (1956) delineated three main challenges that individuals must confront. Regardless of our style, we have to take a stand on these issues. Work, social relations, and sex are three tasks of life to which we are obliged to respond. Later Adlerians have noted that he addressed two others in his writings, though he never fully articulated or discussed them in detail (Dreikurs & Mosak, 1966, 1967; Mosak & Dreikurs, 1967). These two additional tasks are self and spirituality. We believe, in line with Dinkmeyer et al. (1987), that parenting and family are another life task. Way (1950) and Wolfe (1932) have examined the life tasks and how they relate to life styles.

People attempt to meet the life tasks according to their life styles. Drivers typically storm their way through them and focus upon accomplishment. Those who need to be good do what is "right and proper." Excitement seekers solve the life tasks in as exciting a way as possible. To whatever extent feasible, most of us try to have life conform to our expectations. We bend life to our will.

Life and its responsibilities do not always accommodate to our demands. The more we push our styles, values, and expectations upon life, the more it may push back. In the end, we must adapt to it, for it will only accommodate us for so long. These five areas, work, social relations, sex, self, and spiritual, provide tests, what we called challenges in Chapter 6, that severely assess our ability to survive and thrive. Our cognitive maps need to be modified and reworked in order to navigate the new terrain life puts out before us. If we cling too tightly to our demands, beliefs, and convictions, we have trouble meeting the requirements of the situation. These tasks become potential stressors and potentially distressful if we are not flexible, open, and ready to meet them head on.

For some people, the issue becomes one of evading these tasks rather than meeting them. Their life styles, their maps, are not willing to accommodate the new terrain, and these people stubbornly refuse to admit that what they require of life is not what life is about. Their adaptations tend to become maladaptive, for it is not easy to have life bend to them on such a consistent basis. This topic, however, is explored in greater detail in Chapter 8. For present purposes, it is enough to be aware that, in the challenge to meet the life tasks, for these people a battle ensues, and it is a battle few individuals can "win" without considerable cost and suffering to themselves and those around them.

Adlerians attempt to learn how people adapt to their worlds. Their worlds, however, have these common tasks that are shared with others and their worlds. All of us are obliged to take a stand on the issues of work, social relations, sex, ourselves, our place in the cosmos (a subtask of spirituality), and what we are going to do about parenting and family, and all of us can be evaluated on how we fare in our efforts. The test of a life style is how it meets these challenges, these tasks. Each of these tasks has many components, and some of them tend to occur at certain developmental epochs of the life cycle. They provide nodal points of how the life style is doing, of how adaptable, flexible, and cooperative it can be. We all live in this world, and we tend to know about it most profoundly if we realize that it is not under our control, that the map we have of life is a fictional map, a map in which we have invested a great deal of time and energy, but whose correspondence to what is "actually out there" nonetheless may be fleeting, at best (Adler, 1956; Vaihinger, 1911/1965). It is at those times that we can measure ourselves and confront a most startling moment. Life may not be what we thought it was, what it appeared to be; what possibly, for a time, it seemed certain that it was; in the end, we only knew what we *thought* it was about. It is, and was, bigger than us and beyond our plan. It is at those times we become aware of our humanity.

☐ The Work Task

Regardless of what we do, we must do something with our time (Berne, 1964). Adler (1956) spoke of the work, or occupation, task. He wrote that

> The first tie sets the problem of occupation. We are living on the surface of this planet, with only the resources of this planet . . . . It has always been the task of mankind to find the right answer to the problem these conditions set us . . . . In every age, mankind has arrived at a certain level of solution, but it has always been necessary to strive for improvement and further accomplishments. (p. 131)

For Adlerians, people are tied to each other in their need to cooperate and build a community in which we can thrive and grow. By sharing the "work" required to survive, we can all function better. Very few of us, if any, could exist completely independently. The ability to make our own clothes, grow our own food, hunt, care for our own health, build our own shelters, and mate and raise a family is limited without support and constructive interdependence upon a community. As Wolfe (1932, p. 203) declares,

> We *must*[1] work, whether we wish to work or whether we prefer to be idle. The question of work is not a matter for us to decide according to our personal whim or fancy. The only choice that remains open to the individual

is the manner in which he or she makes his or her contribution to the commonweal (p. 203)

In general, there are six subtasks in the work task: occupational choice, occupational preparation, satisfaction, leadership, leisure, and sociovocational issues. Each is looked at more closely here.

Occupational Choice

"What do you want to be when you grow up?" That is a frequent question we ask of children. Defining an occupational niche is a difficult task for some people; for others, it is quite simple. In our culture, at this time, people are frequently defined by what they do. A popular phrase we have recently heard states that people used to work where they lived; now, they live where they work. We are a country that places great emphasis upon work, and how we define what we do usually plays a large part in determining who we are. Adlerians also stress the reverse: Who we are "determines" what we do. Our life styles help us define what we select as acceptable (Attarian, 1978). Controllers, for example, tend to pick occupations that allow them to exercise control.

Occupational Preparation

The training we receive, and eventually give to others, is the second subtask. As early as the elementary school years, children can be seen training themselves for certain occupations through preference for certain subjects. Parents and other family members model, encourage, and occasionally push, children into various areas. What we perceive as helpful in our movements toward our goal we do more of; that which we sense as having no or minimal use, we do less of.

Satisfaction

How satisfied are we with our work? Analogous to our discussion of private logic (Dreikurs, 1973), issues of satisfaction can be separated into two broad categories, daily and career. On a daily basis, the amount of job satisfaction we accept tends to run to either of two extremes. For some, daily satisfaction is of uppermost importance. They prefer to get paid every day, conceptualize their salaries in terms of hourly wages, and forego longer-term "career" goals. They like working days or nights, outdoors or indoors, regular or flexible hours, on salary or on commission.

For others, daily satisfaction is not the issue. If what they are doing is leading to some longer-range, "ultimate" career goal, they can tolerate a great deal of immediate, daily dissatisfaction. Their satisfaction comes with the attainment of their long-term goals. Many university students understand this concept all too well. The hours of studying, writing papers, doing research, taking examinations, and in general waiting to begin careers are rewarded when they begin their careers. Once again, issues of satisfaction are intimately tied to our life style goals.

Leadership

Determining whether we will be leaders or followers, who we perceive as leaders and followers, and how leadership is demonstrated will be yet another subtask. Children determine their place within their peer groups, at school, and eventually, on their jobs. At work, some feel more at ease leading (e.g., "I've got to be my own boss!"); others are noticeably more comfortable following. Some have difficulty "taking orders"; others are too willing to "follow" and lack initiative. Some are better leaders than others; still others lead brilliantly in certain situations, under the right conditions.

Leisure

What do we do when we are not working? For certain individuals, leisure time is not an issue, because they work virtually all the time. For others, the pursuit of leisure is a full-time job. Retirement issues are part of this subtask. Work is but one of five tasks that we must undertake. There needs to be time for other issues. Increasingly with the ageing of the population, the issue of retirement is another facet of this task.

Sociovocational Issues

The final subtask entails dealing with coworkers. Like many of the subtasks in this section, a considerable amount of training in this area can be seen in early-childhood school relationships. During family projects, how children relate to their siblings and parents plays a significant part as well. We encounter many people who are not our friends but to whom we are friendly. Coworkers play just such a role. Currently issues of sexual harassment are a prominent sociovocational problem.

☐ The Social Task

Wolfe (1932, p. 204) states:

> The second group of problems arises out of the specific human need for communal life. As individuals we are too weak to live alone, and nature has given us the human community as the best weapon against extinction. . . . The manner of his social adjustment admits of a tremendous variety of solutions, but the adjustment itself is fundamental to the good life and to human happiness. (p. 204)

We need to get along with each other. Without the community, without the support and cooperation of others, we would be extinct. For Wolfe and other Adlerians, the issue becomes not only a psychological one, but biological as well. As a species, humans need each other.

Adler (1956) stated that "we have always to reckon with others, to adapt ourselves to others, and to interest ourselves in them" (p. 132). He believed, like Sullivan (1953, 1964) years later, that psychology and psychiatry were social sciences, and more specifically interpersonal sciences. How we get along with each other is a basic question, for, as Sullivan noted, we react and develop in relation to other people, even if only in our minds and imaginations. The two main subtasks are how we belong and how we interact or, more precisely stated, the nature of our transactions with others.

Belonging

For Dreikurs (1933/1950a), the fundamental question of human nature was belonging. How do we choose to belong? It is not a question of whether or not we belong, but how. Even a hermit needs a town outside of which to live (K. Pancner, 1978). If I belong, the chances of my feeling inferior are minimal; and even if I do feel inferior, my withdrawing for too long is not very likely. Stated in the form of a ratio: Belonging = 1/inferiority feelings. This is an inverse proportion, by which the greater the sense of belonging, the less likely the feelings of inferiority and vice versa. How I found my place in childhood (typically, but not exclusively, in my family of origin) helped set the tone for my adult style of belonging. There is a good chance that if I felt that I belonged by being cute, helpless, and inadequate, the baby (Mosak, 1971a), I probably find my place in the social task through similar means. If other people accept me like that, I probably do not feel very inferior. If they do not, the challenge begins.

Transactions

Berne (1964, 1972) and subsequent transactional analysts have written extensively on this issue. Harris (1967) has outlined the basic positions that individuals take in reference to others. Massey (1989, 1990, 1993) has written on the relationship of Adler to Berne, as have Mozdzierz and Lottman (1973) and Wilson (1975). In fact, Berne (1972, p. 58) himself wrote that "of all those who preceded transactional analysis, Alfred Adler comes the closest to talking like a script analyst." The "I'm OK, you're OK" descriptions are strikingly similar to the Adlerian notion of inferiority feelings and superiority feelings. For example, "I'm not OK, you are" is, in transactional analytic terms, a statement of inferiority feelings. The "games people play" with each other, or the "ego states" (i.e., parent-adult-child) Berne uses, are ways in which individuals move toward their goals. People find their places with others, they gain a sense of belonging, through certain styles, using certain patterns or what Adler (1935/1964c) labeled complexes. In that paper, he spoke of (for instance) the redeemer complex, possessed by someone who sacrifices him- or herself for others.

☐ The Sexual Task

Humans come in two sexes. Adler (1978) disliked the phrase "opposite sex," for it implied an antithesis between the sexes that he felt was artificially produced by the culture and society at large. Horney (1926/1967, pp. 69–70), in a paper written in 1926, wrote that

> Owing to the hitherto purely masculine character of our civilization, it has been much harder for women to achieve any sublimation that would really satisfy their nature, for all the ordinary professionals have been filled by men. This again must have exercised an influence upon women's feelings of inferiority, for naturally they could not accomplish the same as men. . . . It seems to me impossible to judge to how great a degree the unconscious motives for the flight from womanhood are reinforced by the actual social subordination of women. One might conceive of the connection as an interaction of psychic and social factors.

Adler (1978, p. 8) might have written that same statement when he said that

> A serious result of this myth of the inferiority of everything female is a peculiar dichotomy of concepts. Masculine is simply identified with everything valuable, strong, and victorious, and feminine with obedient, servile,

and subordinated. This manner of thinking has become so deeply rooted in our culture that everything excellent has a male tint, whereas everything that is less valuable and objectionable is represented as feminine.

For Adler, and for Horney, a female is not the *opposite* sex, but the *other* sex. If we learn to cooperate, we better our existence. If we cannot cooperate, the species dies (Wexberg, 1929).

In general, the work task is the easiest to meet. It requires the least amount of cooperation and flexibility (Dreikurs & Mosak, 1966; Way, 1950). The social task, getting along with others in a sense of community and friendship, is the next easiest. It requires more cooperation and is a greater test of our adaptability. The sexual task requires the greatest amount of intimacy and, therefore, the most skill to fulfill on a consistent basis. It is the hardest task to meet. One of the biggest problems, though by no means the only one, is that men often view women as inferior, a fact reinforced by our culture. The sense that women are less than men is sometimes subtle and barely noticed, but it is still prevalent. Bieliauskas (1974) points out that the tendency of some women to view men as inferior does not solve the problem. Adlerians favor equality of, and cooperation between, the sexes. The ever-increasing divorce rate may be evidence of the difficulty people have in meeting this task.

There are four subtasks that need to be examined. They are the issues of sexual definition, sexual identification, development, and behavior.

Sexual Sex Role Definition

This subtask requires individuals to determine what it means to be a man or a woman. In the case of children, it involves the awareness of sex differences between boys and girls. Equality does not mean sameness, and although men and women are equal, they certainly are not the same. What those differences entail, as Adler and Horney noted in the passages in this section, is as much a social factor as it is a biological one.

Sexual Sex Role Identification

Once children have an awareness that a difference does exist between men and women (boys and girls), the issue rather rapidly becomes one of how closely they measure up to their conceptualization of masculine or feminine. The parental guiding lines are one obvious source of data, but so are siblings and peers, movies, television programs, and books. Children observe the differences and tend to overgeneralize, such as if they notice that Father does something differently than Mother and assume that the difference is not simply caused by the particulars of the family situation but is gender-related: "Men do . . ., but women do . . ." Issues of masculine and feminine protests can arise (Adler, 1910/1983a, 1939, 1956, 1978; Bieliauskas, 1974; Mosak & Schneider, 1977; Ronge, 1956).

The masculine protest is a frequently misunderstood concept. As Mosak and Schneider (1977) point out, it is an attempt to *attest* to the subjective "fact" that masculinity is prized and, as Adler (1978) and Horney (1926/1967) wrote, "superior" according to cultural standards. Individuals who display a masculine protest are attesting to the fact that they are overvaluing the issue of masculinity and are trying to appear superior. Both men and women may display masculine protests, because both may feel that it is more valuable to be men or "real men." As Ronge (1956) has pointed out, a feminine protest occurs as well, though admittedly with less frequency. That is the situation in which either men or women attest to the fact that it is better to act as if they were feminine, because they subjectively perceive that as being superior. This will probably become a more frequent phenomenon as society moves toward greater sexual equality. Although the masculine protest occurs in normal men and women, Adler (1930b) considered the masculine protest to be a common element in the development of all sexual deviations.

Sexual Development

There are certain developmental milestones, biological and social, with regards to sexual development through which individuals pass. Puberty, menstruation, developing secondary sex characteristics, masturbation, and successfully managing how they transmit to children their sexual identity are some of the typical milestones individuals encounter. Any of these issues can prove very challenging and can test the adaptability of the life style.

Sexual Behavior

Finally, there is the issue of sexual behavior itself. What is appropriate sexual behavior? How is intercourse performed? When do people begin acting upon their sexual feelings? Who are appropriate people with whom to engage with in sex? Is oral intercourse normal? Is this or that practice moral? These questions can prove quite perplexing, even to adults, and hard and fast rules are difficult, though not impossible, to derive. And currently there are the challenges related to AIDS and other sexually transmitted diseases. What about dating? How do we attain our sexual goals? Who is an appropriate dating partner?

☐ The Self Task

As Dreikurs and Mosak (1967) and Shulman (1965) discuss, Adler never fully delineated this as a task, but it is evident throughout his writings. The crucial question this task touches upon is: There is an "I" and a "me" (myself), and how does the I relate to myself (James, 1890)? People need to come to a conclusion about themselves, and that process and its outcome can greatly influence functioning in all of the other tasks. There are four main subtasks that we examine: survival, body image, opinion, and evaluation.

Survival

How our sense of self "survives" is a crucial question. Survival issues tend to center around three main areas: biological, psychological, and social. Biological survival entails my health: How healthy am I? Do I take care of myself, or do I not? What should I eat? How often do I exercise? Do I comply with medical advice? Do I regularly engage in dangerous activities? Do I take care of myself and my safety? Psychological survival is somewhat more familiar to most readers of this text. It revolves around self-esteem issues. Basically, psychological survival asks: Can I face myself in the mirror? If not, why not, and what am I willing to do about it? Can I live with myself? Social survival is similar to the issues defined under the social task, in particular, the subtask of belonging: Where do I fit in? How do I fit in? What do I have to change about me or develop in order to belong? More importantly, what will they think of me? Will they accept or reject me? Dare I risk this socially?

Body Image

My body may be just the kind of body I want—pretty, athletic, muscular, gorgeous eyes, the "right size" of breasts, "great legs," or graceful. On the other hand, it may not. The latter body image may keep plastic surgeons busy. In body-dysmorphic disorder it keeps both patients and surgeons busy.

The body I have may not always be the body I perceive. The greater the degree of congruence between the two, the better the chances of my doing something constructive about my perceptions, should I deem it necessary to do anything about it at all. For example, in case of anorexia nervosa, individuals perceive themselves as overweight when, for all practical purposes, they are underweight. Carried to an extreme, the disorder can be life-threatening. Until the perception of the body and the anorexic's actual body coincide, it is difficult to create positive change. If the actual body and the perception of it coincide, a person still has the issue of deciding whether or not she or he is comfortable with what she or he sees.

Opinion

What do I think of me? How do I relate to me? As James (1890) discussed, subjectively, individuals tend to make a distinction between the "I" and the "me," with the former being the subject and the latter, the object of experience. In practice, most of us place a blank space between the "I" and the "me:" "I _____ me." What goes in the blank space makes all the difference in the world. "Like," "hate," "love," "suspect," "appreciate," "ignore," and "focus too much upon" are some of the kinds of statements we frequently hear from clients when we ask them to "fill in the blank" during initial interviews. The opinion one has of oneself is a crucial component to one's life style and is a foundation to feelings of security, self-esteem, superiority, inferiority, and the like.

Evaluation

Sullivan (1953) has written considerably on this issue. He analyzes the difference between the "good me," the "bad me," and the "not me," tracing their origins back to the empathic bonding (or lack thereof) between mother and infant. For Sullivan, the good me develops if children receive a sense of warmth and compassion from their caretakers. The bad me develops if caretakers empathically communicate disapproval to their children. The not me develops if caretakers and children experience an empathic breakdown; the children, primarily because of overwhelming anxiety in the caregivers that moves them away from the children, receive no feedback about themselves at such times, and hence they do not accurately process information about themselves. Mosak (1973) describes the relationship between the good me and the bad me, and how such a relationship is maintained into adulthood in order to move toward a goal of controlling, particularly oneself. It is actually a spurious battle if one views it holistically, a battle of, "Who is stronger, me or me?"

☐ The Spiritual Task

Mosak and Dreikurs (1967) discuss that this task, like the self task, was mentioned throughout Adler's writings. Though he never fully articulated it, he often refers to it (Jahn & Adler, 1933/1964). There are five subtasks with which individuals deal: relationship to God, religion, the universe, immortality, and the meaning of life.

Relationship to God

What is my idea of God? Do I believe in a God or not? If I do, do I see God as unforgiving, punishing, loving, or indifferent? How should I relate to my perception of God (Armstrong, 1993; Miles, 1996)? Many of the dynamics of the life style can be seen clearly in how individuals perceive (or do not perceive) God. If there is no God, in what do I believe?

Religion

What do people do about religion? Do they run from it or toward it? Do they see it as a sanctuary or a place of punishment? Does it enrich their lives or cause them fear? Do they have religion? The stance individuals take toward religious practices is of interest as well. Do they practice rituals or not? Why do they practice some and not others? What is sin and, according to Menninger (1973), whatever happened to it? What does one do about guilt, atonement, and reconciliation (Mosak, 1987a)?

Relationship to the Universe

Some individuals see humans as simply another animal. Others see humans as the pinnacle of God's creation. Some conceptualize people as basically good; others see people as mostly bad. For some, humans can change; for others, existence is a matter of destiny or fate.

Metaphysical Issues

How do we view life and death? Some believe in reincarnation, and that they accrue karma, which determines as what species they will return.

Others believe that salvation is achieved through good deeds, and that rewards are given in an afterlife. Still others hold to the conviction that there is no sense of immortality, other than (perhaps) through good works that survive after one dies. Is there a soul? An immortal soul? Are there a heaven and a hell? Is there resurrection? Reincarnation? Not only can these issues reflect life style issues, they can prove to be stern tests to which life style convictions must adapt.

Meaning of Life

For some people, life has no meaning. For others (e.g., Frankl, 1925, 1963; Yalom, 1980), love provides meaning. Some, like the Epicureans of old, subscribe to a hedonistic philosophy, believing that the meaning of life is the attainment of pleasure; while others, especially some existentialists and some stoics, adopt a more pessimistic view, believing that the ultimate meaning of life is despair.

☐ The Parenting and Family Task

How do we relate to our families? Should we marry or cohabitate? How do we solve the issues of relating to our siblings, parents, grandparents, aunts and uncles, and children? This is similar to, but still different from, the social task. The bonds we have with family members can be much stronger, and much more intense, than with our friends. The issue of family dynamics has long been a focus of study and concern for Adlerians (Adler, 1930/1963, 1930/1970; Dreikurs, 1948a).

☐ The Life Style and the Tasks of Life

As has probably become increasingly evident throughout this chapter, individual psychology is a breadth psychology, as opposed to a depth psychology. We do not necessarily look to explore "deeper and deeper" layers of a personality and, hence, uncover the meaning of what causes "dis-ease" to people. We attempt to look across the personality, to show how wide and pervasive the life style is in people's functioning. The life tasks provide us with such an opportunity.

They are the points of contact between the person and the world. Too much emphasis upon either pole leaves the explorer with a distorted picture. Too much of an emphasis upon the subjective side presents a picture in which everything is relative; there is no basis for shared realities, common tasks, and mutual communication; and issues arise regarding the necessity of ethics and moral codes to guide conduct, for if life is completely a "matter of opinion," then anything goes. An overemphasis upon the objective pole results in the loss of personal freedom and responsibility as well. In that case, the environment and heredity play too crucial a role, and people become reactors to life, constantly attempting to adjust to it and not playing any part in creating it.

Adlerian psychology attempts to take both positions into account. It is not only the life style which is important; how the person adapts it to life's challenges—the life tasks—is crucial too. People need to face the challenge of work, but how they perceive it, train for it, define it, and feel about it is very much an interplay of what they bring to it (i.e., their styles of life and skills) and what it entails itself (e.g., the work task). Individuals do fall in love, and what they define as being suitable to do, with whom, for how long, and under what conditions encompasses both their unique style and the style of the other person set against the cultural norms and standards of the time. It is by walking both sides of this line that Adlerian psychotherapists and counselors come not only to understand but to help people to change.

Most of us can and do change on our own. To survive past infancy and early childhood means that we have had to adapt and find strategies that we found useful in getting us to our goals. To some degree or another, we do manage to meet the life tasks most of the time. Some individuals, however, meet them less frequently or in ways that most of us have difficulty comprehending.

What seems to characterize such individuals? At the risk of overstating the point, these people cling to their life styles more tightly, more desperately, more determinedly, than most. Their ability to bend to life is limited, sometimes for perfectly understandable reasons. For the most part, if any of us overstep our limits—if we attempt to do more, be more, and enforce our guidelines too stringently upon life—that is when we forget our place in the world. That is when we create solutions to the life tasks that lead us into ever-increasing difficulties, for as we attempt to articulate in Chapter 8, it is our solutions to life's challenges that lead us to problems, not the fact that life has challenged us. The irony is that it is typically not life that creates our problems; it is our solutions to life that create our problems. That is *the* irony, and what provides writers and artists with the opportunity to portray the human condition as both tragic and, just as significantly, optimistic.

☐ Summary

We have examined how the tasks of life are interwoven with our styles of life. This chapter is by necessity nothing but an overview. Literally, we could write volumes on the interactional effects between the styles people adapt to their perceptions of what is required of them and the life tasks. For now, this overview will have to do, for, being clinicians, we are interested in turning to a particular manner of addressing—or not addressing—the life tasks. That is the issue of maladjustment, or destructive functioning. In more common professional language, we now turn to the issue of psychopathology.

☐ Points to Consider

In order to understand people, Adlerians examine two key dynamics. The first is the life style, and the second is the situation in which the individual finds him- or herself.

Adler originally discussed three tasks of life. These are occupation, social relations, and love and sex.

Later Adlerians have identified three other tasks that Adler discussed but never clearly articulated. The three additional tasks are self, spirituality, and parenting and family.

☐ Questions

1. What are some of the subtasks involved in the occupation task?
2. Why do Adlerians emphasize understanding both the person (i.e., the style of life) and the situation (i.e., the tasks of life)? How did the existentialists describe this?
3. What are similarities between the work of Eric Berne and Alfred Adler? Between Harry Stack Sullivan and Alfred Adler?
4. Belonging = 1/Inferiority Feelings. What does this ratio mean?
5. What does Adler mean by the "masculine protest?"
6. What are some of the subtasks involved in the love and sex task?
7. How might atheism be an answer to the spiritual task?

☐ Note

[1]Although this may have been true during the Depression era when Wolfe made the statement, it is no longer true today.

CHAPTER

Psychopathology

Men at some time are masters of their fates;
The fault . . . is not in our stars,
But in ourselves . . .
    William Shakespeare (1599/1974)

Taken in context, the life style is intertwined with the tasks of life, and the tasks of life are the points at which people most commonly come to know about life. People are free, within limits, to select how to meet the tasks. This chapter focuses upon how they exercise that freedom in ways that are troublesome not only to themselves but to the community at large.

☐ Community Feeling and Social Interest: Theoretical Issues

Adler (1933/1964f) felt that social interest was an innate potential that had to be developed. As Ansbacher (1992b) has recently documented, although the phrase *social interest* has been used extensively in this country, it is not the best translation for what Adler (1956) called *Gemein-*

schaftsgefühl, and Ansbacher considers *community feeling* to be a more accurate, broader translation. Ansbacher states that

> the two terms rather than being synonyms represent indeed different, though related concepts—[community feeling] being the broader and more frequently used by Adler, and that particularly the English presentation of Adlerian psychology would gain if this difference were recognized and "community feeling" reinstated in its proper places, in addition to "social interest." (p. 402)

For Ansbacher, community feeling is the broader concept, incorporating the individual's sense of feeling at home in the world at large and responsible for the welfare of people in general. Adler (1933/1964f, pp. 275–276) wrote that

> [Community] feeling means above all a struggle for a communal form that must be thought of as eternally applicable, such as, say, could be thought of when humanity has attained its goal of perfection. It is not a question of any present-day community or society, or of political or religious forms. On the contrary, the goal that is best suited for perfection must be a goal that stands for an ideal society amongst all mankind, the ultimate fulfillment of evolution. . . . Our ideal of [community] feeling as the final form of humanity . . . is a regulative ideal, a goal that gives us our direction.

Social interest would be this principle as it applies to human interaction specifically. Ansbacher (1992b, p. 405) states that "Adler used 'social interest' in reference to the . . . life tasks. . . . For situations where other people are not directly involved, Adler retained 'community feeling.' " Some elaboration clarifies.

Community feeling is the empathic, emotional bond we have with each other and our world. As Adler (1933/1964f, 1956) writes, it is a *feeling.* Social interest is an *action* based upon the feeling of community, of a sense of belonging. If we have feeling for each other and our responsibility for not only ourselves at this time and in this place, we act so as to take into account the benefits of people who may not yet be alive. We have an obligation to people and life in general, and if our sense of community is strong, we take them into account in our actions and leave posterity a better world.

Mosak (1991a) refers to social interest as a construct. As a construct, people do not necessarily have it; they use it. Taking into account the principles of phenomenology, social-field theory, and psychology of use, Adlerians can say that people are using social interest if they display any of the following behaviors: courage, the courage to be imperfect, contribution to the common welfare, confidence, caring, compassion, creativity, closeness, cooperation, and commitment. There are not single, specific incidents that can forever and always be generalized into displaying social interest. At this time, in this situation, taking these kinds of issues into account, this particular behavior displays social interest. For example, in many situations, caring can be expressive of social interest (Kazan, 1978). There are some situations, however, in which caring may not be what the situation requires in order to move forward. At those times, courage (for instance) may be required, at others, creativity. To be more specific at this point requires data that we do not have. How does the individual perceive the situation? What are the demands of the moment? Knowing these kinds of questions, we can better guess what might be the requirements in order for us to use social interest.

A clinical example sheds some light. A client is crying because she has lost one of her children. The clinician who demonstrates caring at such a time might be using social interest. A similar, but different circumstance, would be a client who uses tears and manipulative behaviors to put others into her service. If she cries during a session, showing open caring for her might not be a display of social interest; a firm but kind commitment to the treatment plan, along with displaying confidence in her ability to solve the issue using her own resources, might be indicative of social interest. The same behavior, crying, would be responded to with two different behaviors, both of which are indicative of social interest, yet the behaviors (caring versus commitment) could not be too successfully interchanged without losing the meaning and overall goal, to encourage her to develop social interest in her.

This is the theory behind community feeling and social interest: If we feel a bonding, a sense of obligation and belonging to the general welfare of others and the future, we will probably use social interest in our interactions with others. I will probably recycle and will not litter *even if there is no one around when I do it* and there appears to be nobody who will immediately suffer because of my littering. I will take into account who may be around, on this planet, even after I am long gone. The feeling that we own this planet and are responsible for it not only now but in the future, after we are gone, is a part of community feeling. Deciding to recycle is a display of social interest. Fostering this feeling of interconnectedness, of belonging, is one of the key components of psychotherapy. How this relates to psychopathology is the focus of the next section.

☐ Community Feeling and Social Interest: Clinical Issues

For heuristic purposes, let us suppose that we could separate a life style from the tasks of life. Let us examine what happens in the (relatively) normal situation.

Another group, the first of the psychopathological group, responds with a different attitude. They respond with a "yes, but . . ." attitude. These used to be called psychoneurotics in older classificatory systems. Their attitude has two subdivisions, and we need to explore each in greater detail.

The first used to be found in those classified as the symptom neurotics. Their attitude declared, "Yes, but *I'm sick.*" This group moves along vertical planes and is "survival-oriented." They feel that to meet the task would jeopardize either their physical, social, or psychological survival. Instead of focusing primarily upon the task, they focus upon themselves, their inferiorities, and the risks of the undertaking. Rather than examine the challenge, evaluate options, and move ahead, they begin to safeguard themselves, seek distance, and make excuses. "Yes, I know I have to work, but I'm too nervous," is what Adler and his colleagues typically heard. Today, we might hear it called "anxiety" rather than "nervousness." Anxiety, depressive, somatoform, psychosexual, and adjustment disorders are the most common "neurotic" conditions listed in the *Diagnostic and Statistical Manual* (American Psychiatric Association, 1994; Sperry & Carlson, 1996). "I would marry, but I'm too depressed," and "Yes, I'd love to be more social, but I'm too afraid of speaking in front of people," are some of the more common variations we hear today.

The second subset used to be called the character neuroses and are now referred to as the personality disorders. The "yes, but . . ." attitude of these is "Yes, but *I'll do it my way.*" If life challenges them, they respond with their idiosyncratic approach, which they believe is a response to the task but somehow misses the mark (Sperry & Mosak, 1996). "Yes, I know I need to work, but I must be appreciated or else I won't be able to function," is what the narcissistic personality disorder typically believes (Sperry & Ansbacher, 1996). The paranoid, histrionic, borderline, and schizoid personality disorders are some of the more common presentations clinicians encounter.

Both these subsets, symptom neuroses and character neuroses, the "yes, but . . ." responses, are focused upon minimizing losses where the "yes" people attempt to maximize their gains. "Yes but" people see the proverbial glass as "half empty" and strive to prevent losing more. They already feel inferior, seek distance, safeguard themselves, and develop inferiority complexes. Their movement is vertical, and they are prestige-oriented. Rather than focus upon *what* they are doing, they look at *how* they are doing. Such a split in attentional processes typically impedes performance, creating a vicious circle: The more they focus upon themselves, the less they attend to the task; the less focused upon the task, the poorer they do and the worse they feel, thereby increasing their self-focus and perpetuating the cycle.

Thus far, we have the normals in this case, those who respond with a "yes, I can . . ." attitude and problem-solving approach to life's challenges, and the psychoneurotic, those who respond with a "yes, but . . ." attitude ("Yes, but I'm sick" in the case of symptom neuroses, and "Yes, but I'll do it my way" for the character neuroses). The final group are those who say no.

The attitude of "no" to life's challenges is typical of those who used to be classified as psychotic. The more common labels used currently are the schizophrenic, delusional, bipolar, and brief reactive psychosis disorders (Sperry & Carlson, 1996). These individuals not only refuse to meet life's challenges, they typically create nonconsensually validated tasks that they are wiling to meet—in other words, they refuse the "real" tasks and create in their delusions, hallucinations, and fantasies, tasks that they can meet in their own ways. Some examples clarify the issue.

Someone of the schizophrenic, paranoid type, might meet the spiritual task by creating the fiction that he or she is God, and others should bow and pray to him or her. The major depressive patient with psychotic features might meet the work task by declaring that life is over, the world is coming to an end, and therefore he or she does not have to confront such trivial issues as maintaining a job. Those with delusional disorder, erotomaniacal people, meet the sexual task by falling in love with someone famous and unattainable, thereby excluding all the rest that he or she encounters who would normally be more suitable.

People with all of the psychotic disorders, those with a "no" attitude to life, respond by either ignoring the consensually validated tasks or creating their own, out of their own private, idiosyncratic worlds. It is not necessary to say "No" to all of the tasks. "No" to a single task may be a psychotic evasion. The person may still seem "normal" in all other respects.

☐ Psychopathology: Structural and Dynamic Features

This text is not a book on psychopathology.[1] It is intended as an introductory text on Individual Psychology. Nonetheless, the general overview of Adlerian theory would be incomplete without a closer look at psychopathology from a more clinical perspective. With that as a goal, we briefly examine the previously mentioned categories (symptom neuroses, character neuroses, and psychoses) along two dimensions, their structural and dynamic features. Much of this work is derived from Dreikurs (1945, 1967), Mosak (1968, 1977b), and Shulman (1968/1984, 1973a).

Symptoms as Creations and Solutions

In general, symptoms are selected and chosen because they are perceived as facilitating movement towards the person's goal. Symptoms are not merely reactions; they are solutions. A symptom such as depression may serve many purposes, but by and large depression is conceptualized as an attempt to continue to move towards the goal the person has selected. For example, Pete may believe he has to get; he is of what Adler (1935, 1956; Mosak, 1959) called the getting type. If he feels that he is unable to continue getting, he may resort to using less active, more destructive ways of getting. By making himself depressed, he can place others into his service and have them help him get what he wants (K. Adler, 1961; Pancner & Jylland, 1996). Pete's life style refuses to bend to life; his self-concept/self-ideal convictions are structured so as to bias his perceptions: "I am small and need others." "I should get whatever I want." Given these two convictions, he may go to great lengths to get others to give to him. The key point is that his depression is not the "problem"; his manner of perceiving and interpreting life is. In other words, his life style, and his use of a depressive set of symptoms, allows him to maintain his convictions and have life meet him on his terms.

Organ Inferiority

Another reason, though far from the only one, that certain symptoms are selected is that there is an organ inferiority that predisposes individuals to "break down" at certain points. Adler (1956) wrote that "the organs most disturbed . . . are those which have been made susceptible by some inherited weakness" (p. 287). He means that under enough stress, we are likely to show the strain at our point of greatest physiological vulnerability (Griffith, 1984; Maniacci, 1996b). Most likely, as current research is demonstrating with increasing accuracy each decade, the physiological underpinnings of psychopathological disturbances play at least some role in symptom formation. However, as Adlerians, although we do not deny the existence of such factors, we see them as but one of several issues which need to be taken into account.

The Issue of Central Themes

As Mosak (1968) has delineated, life styles tend to have certain common patterns, or themes, that characterize them. If certain themes appear in clusters, individuals are more apt to develop (select) certain symptoms.

For example, if the themes of getting, opposing, and seeking excitement exist in the same life style, the chances are very high that such people will select certain behaviors that can be classically defined as sociopathic should their degree of activity be high and their amount of social interest or community feeling be low. What the *Diagnostic and Statistical Manual* (American Psychiatric Association, 1994) defines as antisocial personality disorder has many of the symptoms that cluster into these themes. We note in another chapter that the themes most commonly found in depression are getting, controlling, and wanting to appear or be good (Mosak, 1968, 1979). What actual behaviors are selected, and therefore what symptoms are used, depends upon the life styles of the individuals in question.

Emotions

Feelings, like symptoms, are also in service of the goal (Dreikurs, 1951). Adler (1927/1957) classified them into two broad categories: conjunctive and disjunctive. Conjunctive emotions are those that move us towards others. Disjunctive emotions are those that move us away from others, or create distance. The life style is the blueprint for movement through life; it is our guide and direction setter. Emotions "power" us to move. Without them, as Dreikurs (1951) has astutely pointed out, we would have trouble moving at all, for if we had to logically reason out everything we did, we could end up frozen in a logical abyss. Some bias is required in order to facilitate adaptation, and emotions provide us with the energy to move. Ellis (1973) holds similar views. With reference to psychopathology, emotions are no more a cause of our problems than life situations themselves. It is how we use our emotions that counts. As Dreikurs (1951, 1972) wrote, did you ever notice that we never get emotional when we are winning an argument? As soon as we are under the belief that we are losing, then we become emotional. The increased intensity provides us with a kind of "jump start" and allows us to move more intensely toward our goal.

As long as it suits my goal, I create emotions to move toward you. As soon as it no longer suits my goal, I create emotions that move me away from you. If my goal is to be right, if you validate that, I generate feelings that increase my contact with you, that move me toward you. Should you disagree, I am threatened, for my life style states that I should be right, and hence I generate feelings that move me away from you but allow me to subjectively continue moving toward my goal of being right. The popular sentiment, "I did it because I was angry," would not be quite correct, from the Adlerian perspective. We would tend to restate that as, "You mean you made yourself angry in order to do what you did."

Conscious and Unconscious Processes

For Adler (1956), the distinction between conscious and unconscious is not as relevant as it is for the more classically oriented analysts. Both are in service of the goal, and we see the unconscious as an extension of what is typically found in consciousness, only less clearly formulated. For Adlerians, individuals arrange to make themselves unaware of certain issues in order to facilitate movement. With regards to psychopathology, that means that we do not allow ourselves to focus upon certain issues, for to do so would only increase our sense of inferiority, and those who are displaying inferiority complexes are already all too aware of their shortcomings. Put succinctly, if I do not look at it, maybe I will not have to change it.

Adlerians prefer to speak of common sense and private logic (Adler, 1956; Ansbacher, 1965; Dreikurs, 1973). If using common sense, we know what the general opinion is and what the useful thing to do is; if using private logic, we follow our own biased, idiosyncratic thinking, which may not have much to do with common sense. As Mosak and Todd (l952) and Shulman (1985) have discussed, individuals construe their worlds through perceptual selectivity. This selectivity has elements that are unique to each person. The overlap between those common elements among people is considered common sense; it is high in social interest and community feeling. Such perceptions and attitudes share a common perspective and take into account others. Everyone, however, has his or her own biases. Private logic is the idiographic bias each person has that is unique to his or her life style. We all have private worlds,[2] and common worlds, we share with others; it is those private worlds, those thoughts, attitudes, beliefs, and convictions, that can cause us difficulty in adapting.

Dreikurs has outlined the structure of the relationship between common sense and private logic in the psychopathological disorders. In the symptom neuroses (e.g., anxiety, depression, psychosexual, adjustment, or somatoform disorders), the relationship is that the person has common sense but makes excuses in order to follow private logic. An example is, "Yes, I know I should work, but I can't because I'm too sleepy. If I don't get some sleep, how can I function?" Such a "yes, but I'm sick" attitude entails a couple of interesting dynamics. Such individuals know the "correct" thing to do—they have common sense, but they follow their private logic. In order to maintain their illusory attempt at common sense, they acknowledge the requirement but arrange to contradict it nonetheless. They become unaware of the purpose of their symptoms.

In the personality disorders (e.g., obsessive compulsive, borderline, antisocial, or dependent disorder), the "yes, but I'll do it my way" attitude is manifested structurally like this: The person has private logic, but acts as if that private logic was common sense. An example is, "Why shouldn't I steal? It's a dog-eat-dog world out there, and if I don't get it first, someone else will get it. Everybody knows that." These individuals act as if their private logic was common sense. They frequently do not see anything very wrong about their world views, and, in fact, they are amazed that others do not see life the way they do.

In the psychotic disorders (e.g., schizophrenia, bipolar), common sense is usually intact but, structurally, it looks like this: These people have common sense but ignore it, choosing instead to act as if their private logic were "real." An example is, "I am telling you, there are voices speaking to me! They are telling me to be on the lookout—the FBI has been bugging my teeth and can read my thoughts." These individuals, after their psychotic episode "quiets down," return to using some degree of common sense. In this bizarre but actual report from one of our patients, he acted "as if" he had very important information the FBI would want. Needless to say, his nonconsensually validated attempt at solving the self-task gave him a great deal of subjective importance. It also excused him from having to return to work and allowed him to stay on with his parents at home.

☐ Psychopathology and the Style of Life: Exogenous Factors

Let us return to where we began this chapter and reintegrate the life style into the life tasks. As Adler (1956) stated, every life style is adaptable until life presents it with a task for which it is ill prepared. Similarly, he believed that in every case of psychopathology the patient was partly right. By that, he meant that individuals developed their life styles as children in a context that to some degree supported, and may have even encouraged, the styles' development. If you grant the psychotic's initial assumptions about life and his or her place in it, everything that follows may make "sense." This is an important issue that needs to be considered in greater detail, for its implications can be rather far-reaching.

As we noted in Chapter 7, the life tasks provide the test upon which the adequacy of the life style is judged. Every life style may be adequate until it is put to the test. More specifically, there are certain issues that certain life styles have difficulty meeting. These issues, if one is speaking of psychopathology, are called exogenous factors. They provide the occasion for the onset of the disorders.

Whereas Freud spoke of trauma, Adler (1956, p. 295) spoke of "shock." For Freud, trauma was (generally speaking) objective and universal. There were certain issues that everybody had to meet, such as the Oedipal stage, and if these were not successfully negotiated, the trauma would result in neurotic suffering (typically symptom neuroses, most classically the hysterical conversion psychoneurotic reaction). Adler viewed shock as mostly—but not exclusively—subjective and a product of the life style. If the person's life style did not prepare him or her for some contingency, it could be experienced as a shock. Thus far, that makes us normal. We cannot be prepared for everything, and things are bound to be a shock to us sometimes, as if we step off the curb without looking and a car screeches to a halt a foot from us. We are not prepared to deal with certain issues. For example, controllers (Mosak, 1973) are poorly prepared to deal with three issues: death, physical disability, and mental disability. Any "hint" of these issues threatens them. For others who are not so preoccupied with control, these issues are not so threatening, though they may be discomforting.

With less community feeling, we are exposed to the greater testing of our private logic. The more idiosyncratic my thinking, the less common sense I display, the greater the potential for me to be shocked. Think about it: If I believe people should never leave me, the shock of someone actually dying will be much harder on me than on someone who does not have a similar conviction.

What characterizes individuals who develop psychopathology, according to Adler (1956, p. 295), is their "clinging to the shock effects." Anyone at anytime can be shocked by life. Some people are so shocked, they never let it go. They "nurse it, rehearse it," go over it in their minds again and again, and ruminate about it, as if they were enslaved by the thought. By clinging to the shock effects, they create an excuse for not moving on with life: "It was so bad, I can never allow that to happen again." With community feeling and social interest, these people learn from the event and the shock, engage in problem solving, utilize their support networks, and put it behind them (with time, of course). Others with less social interest withdraw further from the community, hence denying themselves the opportunity for support and growth. Rather than expose themselves with their inferiorities, as Adler (1927/1957) and Wolfe (1932) speculated that early humans did, and seek out each other in order to build stronger communities, these individuals withdraw in order to hide their inferiorities and maintain the semblance of superiority. Therefore, they do not learn as quickly, do not adapt as well, and put themselves at risk for yet another shock.

By clinging to the shock effects, such people allow themselves to use shock for safeguarding purposes: "I might have been happily married had it not been for . . ." The irony is that by clinging to the event, they evade the life tasks and simultaneously hold onto the very thing of which they are most afraid. That which they worked hardest to avoid, they cling to desperately. If I never want to be rejected, I can hold onto the one time I was and build my life around it, so as to never have to face it again. It is a tragic solution at worst, and a bitter one at best.

☐ A Case History

Following is a case history that highlights these factors. It is not intended to be an example of Adlerian psychotherapy. There are some published examples of such cases in the literature (e.g., Manaster & Corsini, 1982; Mosak & Maniacci, 1995; Peven & Shulman, 1986). Although this was a case in our private practice, and we discuss some of the tactics involved in the psychotherapy, we prefer to focus upon the life style dynamics, life situation, and selection of symptoms. The history is from a real case, but all identifying information has been disguised in order to protect the individual's identity.

Nick came for therapy after having seen one of the authors (MPM) do a life style assessment on a patient as part of a staff training session at a psychiatric hospital. Nick was employed as a master's level clinician and was working on his doctorate in counseling at the local university. He wanted to "have his life style done," as he put it, and he made the referral call himself. He was in his early 20s. He was seen for the initial interview by one clinician (MPM).

When he arrived for his initial interview, the presentation changed. He admitted that although the life style assessment was still his objective, he needed more than that. It seems he had been having some difficulty over the course of the past year or so. In fact, he had quite a bit of difficulty. In the past 11 months, he had had thirteen trips to local emergency rooms, each time for what he feared was a "heart attack." At each turn, he was given a clean bill of health, reassured, and discharged within hours. As the tolerance for his claims decreased with each repeat visit, he would take himself to a different emergency room with the subsequent "attack."

Nick stated that he had been married for 4 years to "a wonderful woman, the best thing" in his life. They loved each other very much, but these trips to the emergency room were "causing a lot of tension," and she had had "enough." She was an oldest-born who was 2 years older than Nick, a very responsible, "take charge" type of woman, he said, and she was running a daycare center for children. She was losing her patience. They had been trying to conceive a child for over a year, "with no luck," and this was a strain on her as well. With Nick not moving through his doctoral program as fast as he should (because of all of his "medical concerns"), and their increasing medical bills, she said he had to get some help immediately. Along with all this, he added that the couple lived in his parents' "summer home," rent-free, under the agreement that he and his wife "fix it up" and do some much-needed work around the house. He agreed to the deal because of the financial gain, but the extra workload was "killing him."

In the initial interview, Nick discussed that he came from a high-achieving family. His father had two master's degrees; his mother was completing her doctorate (in education); his one and only sibling, an older sister, was a lawyer who had set the state record for highest score on the bar examination; a maternal grandfather was a physician; and a maternal aunt had her doctorate in clinical psychology. Nick got along well with each of them, and they expected great things from him. He was "a genius," he reported. His IQ was actually in the genius range and he had very little trouble with school, when he could keep his mind focused, that is. With all that was happening, especially with his medical concerns, he just could not concentrate. When he was asked, "What would be different if we could do away with your worry about your health?" Nick replied that two things would be different: First, he would be able to finish his "damn degree," and second, maybe he could settle down his "nerves" and see what was going on about the couple's fertility issues.

Nick finished the interview with two additional points. One was that he still believed that all the "damn physicians were wrong," he did have an undiagnosed heart condition, and he would die from it; and another was that he had started smoking again, and that bothered him, for he knew that was not good for him, it was probably making things worse, and he knew he "should quit," as everybody kept telling him.

As is customary with many Adlerians, and our practice in particular, we gave Nick a tentative outline for how we would proceed. Because we practiced multiple psychotherapy, one of us (MPM) would be his primary therapist, with the other (HHM) sitting in every fourth session (or so) as a consultant. We would structure the next two sessions by gathering the data for a life style assessment. Nick agreed. Next, Nick was given a summary and feedback about what he had discussed. It seemed that there was a lot going on in his life. He seemed to be a man who pushed himself rather hard, had great expectations for himself, and spent little time relaxing or doing what he wanted. Nick was stunned; he never really thought about it. He was working nearly full time, working on his doctorate, fixing various rooms in the house, and maintaining a marriage and trying to get pregnant. He was told that perhaps he needed to be a little "sick," otherwise how else could he ever get time for himself? We even pondered whether he should take some time off from his school, because he could not concentrate anyway. At first, Nick strongly disagreed—he had to keep going, he had to "push himself." Remarkably quickly, however, he calmed down, smiled, and said, well, yes, he had thought he needed a break, but how could he explain it to his wife, his parents, his dean? Nick was told it was "doctor's orders" that he relax, and that we could write a letter for him to the dean of the department requesting a leave of absence. Nick was truly surprised and very grateful. We ended the interview by stating one last thing: Although yes, smoking is not good for him, maybe this was his only form of self-indulgence (he worked out regularly and was in excellent physical condition), and if for the short run he wanted to keep smoking, "What the hell, consider it a form of self-care."

Nick actually began to cry. When asked what was going on, how was he feeling, he replied that he could not explain it, but he felt so very relieved, as if someone "truly understood," and he never thought he would hear someone say to him it was alright not only to not go to school but to keep on smoking. He said he eagerly awaited the life style assessment.

Many of the aforementioned dynamics about psychoneurosis can be seen in this case. Nick knew what he wanted to do, but he felt compelled by what he "should" do. He was saying, "Yes, but I'm sick," to life. He never felt he had the right to pursue his own interests in life, but rather he had to keep up with a high-achieving family. When Nick was given permission to slow down, to relax, the purpose of his symptoms became apparent. He no longer needed them in order to "take a break," and he felt immediate relief. Someone had understood what he was saying with his symptoms, and now the process of trying to comprehend why he felt he needed the symptoms to excuse himself could begin. We started the life style assessment.

The family-constellation interview took about 45 minutes. Nick was the younger of two. His sister was 2 years older, very powerful, and very successful. She was a "straight A" student and the darling of the teachers. Not so with Nick. He was the "little devil," always in trouble, but extremely cute, endearing, and playful. He was tested in elementary school for what was believed to be Attention-Deficit Hyperactivity Disorder (ADHD), and that was when it was discovered that he was a genius. Nick was placed in accelerated classes, where he did better once he was allowed to work at his own rapid pace, but he still was a bit much to handle.

When asked what he wanted to be as a child, Nick said he had always wanted to be an actor, famous, with admiring fans all around him; when he told this to his mother, she said that no son of hers would be an actor (she was "teacher of the year" several times at the same elementary school that Nick attended) and that he had to be a doctor, like her father. Nick agreed, and remembers telling her that yes, he would be a doctor, but secretly, inside, he still longed for the spotlight.

Nick's mother was a "hypochondriac" who thought she was "dying" all the time. It had taken her over a decade to work on her doctorate, and in fact she was still working on it today. Any sniffle, sneeze, or soreness, and Nick said he and his sister were "whisked" off to Grandfather's office and then tucked into bed and given plenty of attention. He described his father as an honest man, hard working, who always worked himself too hard, put in overtime for his family, and got both his master's degrees nights and weekends. Mother, however, was the "boss." Whatever she said went, and everybody bowed to her will.

The data, though abbreviated here for convenience, highlight the key issues. Nick had wanted to play, have fun, as a child, but he felt pressured to "keep up," became discouraged, and used attention-getting mechanisms to keep others busy with him. Mother modeled sickness as an excuse for not achieving, and Father modeled achieving even if it meant working (sometimes) up to 65 hours per week. Nick tried to act as if he were Father, but he saw the benefits of acting as if he were like Mother. So he did both. If he felt he could achieve and outdistance his competitors, he would, but if he got "tired of the rat race," he would switch roles and act as if he were disabled. He acted it so well he even believed it.

His choice of a mate reflected this. Like his achieving sister, Nick's wife was an achieving oldest-born (who, incidentally, was raised with a handicapped little brother of her own) who was also 2 years older than Nick. He competed with her, tried to keep up with her, and sometimes got discouraged and switched to his "baby" mode, which elicited her caretaking style, and she (at least temporarily) took the pressure off of him. She was past the time she had established for herself to have children of her own. She wanted to be a parent more than anything she could imagine, and although she loved Nick very much, she was growing increasingly frustrated waiting.

In the next 45-minute interview, Nick gave nine early recollections, some of which are reproduced here:

Age 3: I was in my crib and it was early Saturday morning. I crawled out onto the dresser, down onto the floor, and ran into the playroom to watch cartoons. My parents came and got me, said I was not supposed to be up and in the room, and put me back in my crib. Feeling: Happy at first, and then sad I had to go back to my crib. Most vivid part: Being placed back in my crib.

Age 5: I went to work with [my other] grandfather. He drove a pie truck. I went to the back of the truck and said "What's in here?" and pointed to the empty row of pie tins. He said, "Go on, explore," and I did. Feeling: Wow, cool, he said I could look. Most vivid part: Just looking.

Age 8: I was being tested in school. This [female] psychologist was giving me an IQ test because they thought I was ADHD or something. I got every item correct except one! I couldn't figure that one question out. Feeling: Frustrated. Most vivid part: My parents were watching from behind a mirror and I knew I had to do my best.

Age 7: It was Christmas morning. Sister and I snuck out to peek at the gifts. There were hundreds of gifts under the tree, and mom and dad were setting up a video camera to tape our reactions when we came out. We realized we were going to spoil their surprise and disappoint them, so we snuck back into our rooms. When they called, we came out, and I acted so stunned, I grabbed my chest, yelled, and hit the floor as if I'd fainted. They loved it! Feeling: I made them happy. Most vivid part: The spotlight on me as I grabbed my chest.

Interpreted projectively, the themes become clear. Nick wanted to have fun, but he kept getting put back into his "crib." He would have loved for someone to give him permission to just relax and explore, even if his explorations led him to "nothing," but more often than not, he felt pressured (by women) to perform, as if the eyes and hopes of the family are on him, and he was frustrated by his inability to "know it all and live up to" his perfectionistic standards. In the end, the only escape—the only way to get all the goodies in life and not disappoint anybody—was to grab his chest, act as if he were dying, and get attention for it. The summary of these recollections (and the other five not reported here) was given to him. He was fascinated and felt the interpretations were "right on." He never made the connections of the significance of his current situation to his childhood history before. Out therapy began by teaching him to say no to his parents, his wife, and his own perfectionistic standards in a more prosocial, common-sense manner. He did, and after 18 months, he had no hospitalizations, no "heart attacks," and he dropped out of graduate school. Unfortunately, despite marriage counseling, Nick and his wife broke up. He began to admit that he really did not want kids, not for several years anyway, and that he wanted more time to "play." They broke up, peacefully, and within 2 years she remarried and now has two children.

Nick moved out of state. At 3- and 4-year follow-ups, he has been symptom-free. He remarried just this past year. He works as a master's level therapist during the day. Evenings and weekends he and his new wife run the local theater group in his community. He is the "lead actor." His mother has yet to finish her doctorate.

☐ Summary

For Adlerians, psychopathology is a combination of several factors, all intertwined: first, a low amount of community feeling and social interest; next, a rigid, inflexible life style that values its convictions over life and its demands (i.e., reality). A discouraged attitude toward life in which the person operates more prestige-oriented than task-oriented and moves not on a horizontal but a vertical plane is next. A predisposition to an organ inferiority that was most likely inherited and subjected to too much stress is yet another factor. Finally, life presents a challenge that becomes the exogenous factor for the onset of the psychopathology, a shock, which the individual clings to in order to safeguard self-esteem. Depending upon the amount of social interest, degree of activity, specific themes in the life style, structural relationship of common sense to private logic, and family history of organ inferiorities, certain symptoms appear and are used in the service of the individual's goal.

☐ Points to Consider

Community feeling, sometimes translated as social interest, is a key construct in Adlerian psychology. It is the empathic, emotional bond people have with each other.

Social interest keeps life styles operating on the useful side of life. Without some manifestation of it, people tend to develop disturbing behaviors.

Psychopathological conditions can be structurally described by examining the balance of common sense to private logic. The traditional categories of neurosis, psychosis, and personality disorders can be structurally differentiated using these two constructs.

Antithetical thinking, according to Adler, is a hallmark of potential rigidity and difficulty. Dividing the world into black and white, either/or categories only gets individuals into trouble.

Emotions are to be understood as motivators of behavior. They are not the cause of psychopathology.

☐ Questions

1. What is the difference between common sense and private logic? How is that important in differentiating types of psychopathology?
2. What role does biology play in symptom formation?
3. What might be some of the life style convictions of the antisocial personality disorder?
4. Freud wrote about trauma. What did Adler have to say about "trauma?"
5. What is meant by "clinging to the shock effects?"

☐ Notes

[1]See Sperry and Carlson (1996) for some recent conceptualizations of the *Diagnostic and Statistical Manual* (American Psychiatric Association, 1994) from an Adlerian perspective.

[2]Phyllis Bottome, a novelist who was highly influenced by Adler and was Adler's biographer (1957), published a novel, *Private Worlds* (1934), which Hollywood made into a movie.

Understanding a Person

. . . the world, the human heart and mind—
To understand these things must be our aim.

Goethe (1801/1949)

Some one might call me a fool . . . ; such a man measures temperance by
the . . . yard-stick of his own character. He must know that he is himself
what he calls me.

Euripides (circa 413 BC/1960)

In many ways, this is the point at which we began the book. As Aristotle
and an endless number of thinkers, dreamers, and other souls have pondered since the beginning of time, we *desire to know*. There is perhaps no
more compelling issue for us to know than ourselves. As Socrates and
the Delphian oracle declared in ancient Greece, "Know Thyself!" Philosophers, theologians, scientists—all of us—have struggled with that
dictum ever since (and probably even before Socrates declared it), and
the answers at which we have arrived have been as varied and as diverse
as the character of those who have asked. Goethe listed the world, heart,
and mind as the aim of our understanding, and it is no coincidence that
he wrote them in that order, poetic license notwithstanding. We seek to

know our world. That leads us, after a brief pause, to understand our hearts. Without a pause in his line, for there is no comma between heart or mind or break in the rhythm of the quote, Goethe states that our aim quickly comes to understanding the mind. The direction is not accidental—Goethe was a master of words and images. Understanding the world leads to understanding the heart, our passions, which invariably leads to the mind. The mind is the basis, the "last in the list," to paraphrase. They are intertwined, yes, but the order is not accidental. And then, there is Euripides.

Euripides, the author of *Medea* and *Electra* to mention but two of his tragedies, was the youngest of the classical "big three" playwrights of ancient Greece, the other two being Sophocles and Aeschylus, and one of the most prolific, having written more than 80 plays before his death. Like Shakespeare centuries later, Euripides was a master not only of tragedy but of comedy. It was an unusual combination, especially for his day, but, as critics have commented time and again, that may be one of the keys to both Shakespeare's and Euripides' brilliant insights into human nature. They could see the interconnectedness of both sides of humanity, for it is a fine line between what destroys us and uplifts us. It is ironic yet poignant that we speak of being driven "mad" with both connotations of "insanity" (i.e., losing one's senses) and "fury." In our quest to understand—"measure" in Euripides' language—others, we use the "yardstick" of our own "character." In one of his most insightful comments, the playwright declares that in our quest to measure others, we "must know" that we find in them what we are. But must we know? His comment is as ironic as it is incisive.

That is the trap we fall into in our quest to understand. We start out seeking to know life, the world, the nature of "things," and quickly find ourselves seeking to understand our passions and, therefore, our minds, our perceptions, and our thoughts and beliefs. But as physiologists have pointed out, the eye can see everything but itself. So we seek to know others, their passions, their minds, but we are what we call them. Behind every quest to know them, we find ourselves. To forget that, to not take that into account, leads to comedy, at best, and tragedy, at worst.

The balance of subject and object, the interrelatedness of what we study and what we are (what we seek or aim at), is becoming increasingly accepted, even in the "hard" sciences such as physics. Psychology can be amazingly oblivious to it, even after other disciplines have realized the influence we have upon what we see. When Adlerians attempt to understand a person, they strive to keep this balance in mind, to understand not only that person but how that person treats with others and with his or her world, our world, and the mutual effect we have upon each other. We follow Goethe's line of inquiry: To understand their world, we explore their hearts, and that entails knowing their minds, all the while trying to remain faithful to Euripides's principle: We are intimately tied to what we see in others, and we must not lose sight of that.

In a similar vein Ellis (1973) and Dreikurs (1951) agree that underlying every emotion there is a cognition. It is not that they ignore emotions; they merely have another approach to their understanding and treatment.[1]

☐ Diagnosis and Assessment

Adler (1956) made a distinction which is briefly examined here. The assessment process was a two-step matter for him. The clinician arrived first at the "General Diagnosis," then the "Special Diagnosis." One clarification is needed first.

Diagnosis generally differs from assessment, and although they are often used interchangeably, typically diagnosis entails understanding what is wrong, what makes the person "sick." Diagnosis is a medical model term. Assessment focuses upon what the person is, what makes the person "tick." It is diagnostic to know that people are in distress because they have a hand-washing compulsion; that tells us what is "wrong" with them. Knowing that they are controllers, people that only feel belonging if they are clean, organized, and "one step ahead" of life, tells us what they are about, what makes them "tick." The compulsive handwashers fear germs, which may place them out of control. They are the cleanest people, perhaps the only clean people in the world, and with their compulsions can look down on the rest of us dirty people. We examine both aspects.

The General Diagnosis examines individuals in their current situations. If people come into psychotherapy, the first task of the therapist is to understand how they are functioning in the here and now. Let us look at this process more closely.

☐ The General Diagnosis

Mosak and Maniacci (1995) have presented an example of an actual psychotherapy case, including portions of an initial interview that detail the process we are about to describe in general terms. Dreikurs (1954, 1967) has written about it as well. There are two basic parts to the General Diagnosis, understanding the subjective condition and the objective situation:

> In interviewing patients for the first time, we let them talk about their condition, their symptoms, their discomfort and dysfunctions. They give us then—as we call it—the "Subjective Condition." We know then how they feel what they experience within themselves, what they came for. (Dreikurs, 1967, p. 80)

This process can include a formal diagnosis (Sperry & Carlson, 1996; Sperry & Maniacci, 1992). After Adlerians have heard and understood what brought the patients to see them, they seek to understand how the patients function in meeting the tasks of life.

Adlerians then examine the "objective situations" of the patients. They want to know the fields in which the patients move, the conditions under which they live, how they actually function. Adler gave us a framework for such examination by pointing to the life tasks (Dreikurs & Mosak, 1966) which include all human actions and endeavors.

The general diagnosis is an attempt to understand individuals in their social worlds. Adlerians move back and forth between subjective and objective vantage points, in the process we explore in the chapter on the life tasks. Phenomenological comprehension entails seeing with their eyes, hearing with their ears, and, generally speaking, understanding what life is like for them from their vantage point (Adler, 1931/1958). That is the subjective part of the assessment. The objective part entails assessing how well they function in life. This is still, by and large, somewhat subjective, because Adlerians are still assessing how patients view the life tasks. It is relatively more objective, however, in that Adlerians are assessing how people function according to external criteria (see Chapter 7). Adlerians typically have varied styles for conducting assessments (Manaster & Corsini, 1982). Whereas psychoanalytic theory has undergone radical revision since Freud's time, the method of assessment and treatment has remained relatively consistent. This is not the case with Individual Psychology. Adler's theory has undergone very little revision, for, unlike Freud, who attempted to tie his system of psychology to the prevailing science of the day, Adler attempted to build his system based upon philosophy. Although science generally undergoes revision as new technologies lead to greater understanding, philosophy is much more stable in its assumptions. Unlike psychoanalysts, Adlerians have varied styles of conducting assessments and practicing psychotherapy. Although we share the basic philosophy and assumptions, there is a wide variety of therapeutic strategies from which we draw. Although working within the same system, Adlerians may do very different things. They are theoretic systematists and technical eclectics, although with respect to the latter, they are careful not to violate the basic assumptions of Individual Psychology. Overall, in initial clinical assessments, *if symptoms are involved,* there are two basic questions utilized in order to increase understanding, and we briefly examine them in order to provide readers with the flavor of what Adlerians do and how they work.

In investigating the subjective condition, Adlerians typically ask, "Who is most affected by your symptoms?" The answer to that question generally tells Adlerians against whom the symptoms may be directed. For example:

Therapist: So, who is most affected by your outbursts?
Client: I'm not sure what you mean.
Therapist: I mean, when you lose control, and throw things, who is most affected by it?
Client: Well, me, I guess.
Therapist: And then . . . ?
Client: And then? I guess now that you mention it, my wife. It drives her crazy. She hates it.

What the client has just told us, somewhat hesitatingly, is that his wife not only notices his outbursts, she is upset by them. What he originally believed to be *his* problem, an intrapsychic issue, was placed into a social-field theoretical and transactional perspective. Perhaps there is something in their marriage with which he is not happy, and through his outbursts he is attempting to communicate it. Perhaps he is punishing her or intimidating her or trying to push her away. These ideas can be explored.

In order to link the subjective condition and the objective situation, Adlerians use what is called "The Question" (Adler, 1929/1964d, 1956; Dreikurs, 1958, 1962; Mosak, 1995b). It tells for what purpose the symptoms are being used. To continue with the example:

Therapist: What would be different in your life if you didn't have these outbursts?
Client: Let me think . . . I guess I'd be happier.
Therapist: And if you were happier, then what?
Client: Then, I think I'd be better off, you know, I'd get along better with people.
Therapist: Like whom?
Client: My wife, my employees. They'd be more comfortable around me. I'd be more at ease too, not worrying about when I'm going to blow.

Once again, he has told us more than he realizes. He uses his outbursts in order to keep other people—and himself—on their toes. Without his outbursts, people would be more comfortable around him. Perhaps his goal is to keep them on edge so they can "jump" when he orders. Maybe he is a driver who will not tolerate anything but what he perceives to be excellence in pursuit of his becoming number one (Mosak, 1971a). This hypothesis and others can be more carefully assessed in subsequent interviews.

Another use for The Question is for differential diagnosis (Adler, 1956; Brown, 1995; Dreikurs, 1945, 1958, 1962; Mosak, 1977a). In trying to decide whether a somatic complaint is primarily functional or organic, clinicians can examine the response to The Question. If the client responds that, without the symptom, he or she would "feel better" and, with prompting, cannot come up with anything more specific, the probability of organic pathology underlying the symptom is great (Brown, 1995). If he or she says, "Well, then I'd be able to finish my schoolwork," for example, the purpose for having the symptom may be psychological or social and its origin *may* be functional. Notice we stress *may* be. More extensive medical or psychological work-up is usually advisable anytime a somatic complaint is the focus of treatment (Maniacci, 1996b). Even symptoms with a clear-cut organic pathology can be used for a psychological purpose. Maniacci has used the example of a broken leg. Its organic pathology is obvious, but a client can use it in order to get others to take care of him or her, and to put others into his or her service (cf. Berne's [1964] "wooden leg").

The solution-focused school of brief therapy has made extensive use of The Question (de Shazer, 1988; O'Hanlon & Weiner-Davis, 1989). They call it the miracle question:

> A framework for a whole series of questions (known collectively as "the miracle question") is used in almost every first session . . . to help client and therapist alike to describe what a solution might look like. . . . We have found this way of quickly looking into the future to be a most effective frame for helping clients set goals and thus describe how they will know when the problem is solved. (de Shazer, 1988, pp. 5–6)

They make no reference to Adler or Dreikurs but have documented how useful focusing upon goals can be, particularly if clients' symptoms are viewed as solutions to their problems.

This is an overview of what Adlerians do in their assessment of the general diagnosis. It puts them "in the ballpark." At the end of it, in the most general terms, Adlerians attempt to see where people fall in relation to their degree of activity and amount of social interest. They seek even more specificity, however, and for that purpose they turn to the special diagnosis.

☐ The Special Diagnosis

Whereas in the general diagnosis Adlerians attempt to understand people and how they function in the tasks of life, thus attaining a cross-section of their life styles in the here and now, present context, and to what they may be trying to avoid or say "yes, but . . ." (or "no"), in the special diagnosis they investigate the people in depth or, as we allude to elsewhere in this work, in breadth. They conduct what has been called an investigation of the life style.

Once again, some Adlerians never do a *formal* life style assessment. Others, particularly those who were trained by Dreikurs, Shulman, Mosak, or some others, do a formal assessment of the style of life (Dreikurs, 1956, 1958, 1967; Powers & Griffith, 1987; Shulman & Mosak, 1988). Manuals for the technique and process have been published, and for present purposes, only an overview of this complex but clinically rich process is explored.

There are two general parts of the life style assessment. First, clients are interviewed in order to assess their early childhood situation. After the data have been collected, their earliest childhood recollections are elicited. Summaries are provided of each, and lists of issues that need to be addressed are provided. Let us look at this process a bit more closely.

The Early Childhood Situation

Mosak (1972) and Shulman (1962) and Shulman and Mosak (1988) have written about this topic. Clients are interviewed in order to understand several factors from their childhood. How they got along with their siblings and found their place in their family of origin is explored. Also investigated is how they found their place in elementary school, with peers, and what they learned about their gender and sexual identity, how their health was, their body image, and what their parents and other significant adults were like during the clients' early life. This is then summarized in a brief statement that captures how clients grew up and viewed their early life situations. For an example, readers are directed to Dreikurs, Mosak, and Shulman (1984), Mosak (1995a), and Mosak and Maniacci (1995) for a transcription of a life style summary including a summary of the family constellation of a client (pp. 29–30).

Early Recollections

As Adler (1956) noted, there are no chance memories. What we remember from our early childhood is reflective of what we believe now. Mosak (1958, 1965) and Olson (1979) provide detailed descriptions of how to use early recollections in psychotherapy, and Powers and Griffith (1987) and Shulman and Mosak (1988) examine how to use them in the life style assessment process. Briefly, clients are asked to think back and describe the earliest incidents they remember. These memories should be from under the age of 10 years, be single, specific incidents, and include what is most vivid about the memory and how the client felt during it. For example, here is the memory of a 28-year-old woman:

> Age 3: I was with my mother. She was a school teacher and took me to school with her for parent-teacher conferences. I saw her talking to all these strange people, and I began to bawl really loudly. The feelings: Anger and frustration, I wanted her with me. The most vivid part: Crying.

We typically elicit between six and eight such memories. Similar to the early childhood situation, we then summarize them in order to provide a concise description of how clients currently see life. Once again, interested readers are referred to Mosak (1995a) and Mosak and Maniacci (1995) to see how the process can be applied with a client.

What this client is saying about herself is that she values people, and she wants them all to herself. When things do not go her way—and she is all too aware of what the "right" way is (her way)—she puts on an impressive display of what Adler (1956) called "water power," tears and a temper tantrum, in order to get what she wants. What she wants most is her way and people's attention. Of all the things she could remember from her childhood, why this one? Because it tells us how she views life now. She carries this around as a nonverbal lesson she learned prelinguistically (see the chapter on development for a more detailed discussion).

The special diagnosis, otherwise known as the life style assessment, helps to understand the client in particular, in his or her idiographic style. We then combine the knowledge from this portion of the assessment with what we learned in the general diagnosis to provide a picture of what this person is about, in his or her unique style (the special diagnosis), and how he or she is using it to adapt to life and its challenges (the general diagnosis). It is a brief step from this point to the psychotherapy itself, but that is addressed in greater detail in the next chapter.

☐ Dreams

Adler (1936, 1956), Dreikurs (1944), Gold (1979, 1981), Krausz (1959), and Shulman (1969) have written on dreams and dream interpretation. Bonime (1962) has written a manual on the clinical use of dreams that, as Shulman (1969) astutely notes, could have been written by Adlerians themselves. We view dreams as the extension of individuals' conscious processing; that it, we do not see dreams as emanating from *the* unconscious and, therefore, as attempts to disguise our true intentions from ourselves. They are a continuation of waking thought, but thought that is not bound by the constraints of logic and common sense. Dreams reflect our private logic most clearly. Whereas early recollections deal with long-term, personality goals (i.e., life style issues), dreams concern themselves with the more immediate, short-range goal of problem solving.

A client, a young man in his early 20s, provided the following dream:

> I was walking through a grocery store, by the produce section. I felt lost. The next thing I knew I was in a bathroom, standing at a urinal, when some guy comes in and starts shooting everybody with a machine gun. I pick him up, and without killing him, I slam him repeatedly into the wall and off the floor. As I walk away, I tell him he needs to get some religion in his life.

The client's associations to the dream were the following: The produce section—the healthy foods he should eat (fruits, vegetables, etc.); the bathroom—a place to relieve himself; the "shooter"—a famous athlete he admired in college. What is this client saying that can help us understand him?

He is driven by what Horney (1950, p. 64) called the "tyranny of the should." He is all too aware of what he "should do" in life. He should take better care of himself and take more responsibility for himself, as symbolized by being in the grocery store. It is there he feels lost. He knows he should, but he does not know how. Both his parents died of cancer at early ages, and his father was a physician. He watched as they died, and he felt helpless. When he feels lost, he focuses upon his own needs, but if he does, if he focuses too much upon relieving himself (and perhaps, his anger—symbolically stated by being at the urinal—and his being "pissed"), he is afraid he will get "shot down." What will shoot him down? His ambition. The famous athlete is how he would like to view himself. If he compares himself to others, he gets angry and wants to act out. He ends up "preaching," moralizing, and speaking about "higher things," and walks away feeling vindicated, at least for the moment.

The client is caught in a self-imposed trap, between what he should do and what he does. He wants to be angry, and if he is, it typically comes after he has felt lost about taking better care of himself. At those times, he feels competitive, but rather than too openly and directly expressing his anger, he assumes a moralistic, intellectual posture.

Dreams can be used to assess life style issues, and more immediate concerns. They can be used to check the progress of clients in psychotherapy. We generally create dreams in order to reinforce our movement in life, to rehearse future courses of actions, to problem solve, and to create a mood for the next day. There are many other functions they serve (Mosak, 1992; Shulman, 1969), and interested readers are referred to some of the articles noted at the beginning of this section for greater detail about dreams and their uses, particularly as they relate to the assessment process.

☐ Psychological Testing

As Mosak (1995a) has documented, older, European-trained Adlerians have eschewed testing, viewing it as too limiting and leading to categorization of individuals that loses the idiographic uniqueness that Individual Psychology stresses. Other Adlerians do recommend testing and use it quite often.

Bieliauskas (1972), Maniacci (1990), Mosak and Gushurst (1972), and Mosak and Maniacci (1993) have discussed how psychological tests such as the Rorschach, the Wechsler Intelligence Scale for Children, and drawing techniques (e.g., kinetic family drawings, Draw-A-Person Test), might be used from an Adlerian perspective. As long as the basic assumptions of Individual Psychology are not violated, tests can be quite beneficial to clinicians and clients.

For example, the Thematic Apperception Test (TAT) is a series of cards with black-and-white pictures depicting scenes or situations about which clients are asked to create stories. Schneider (1989) has recently published a children's version she calls the Children's Apperceptive Storytelling Test (CAST), which is based upon Adlerian principles and has the additional benefit of being standardized and normed. One of the cards in the TAT is of a boy, sitting at a table, looking at a violin. A client provided the following story to the card:

> This is a boy who is upset with himself. He sees the violin but he doesn't want to play it. He wants to be outside, playing with his friends. His parents are making him stay in and practice. He knows he should stand up to them, but he feels that will only get him in greater trouble. He doesn't know what he'll do, and he is sitting there, contemplating his options.

Adlerians interpret this in a manner analogous to the way we use dreams and early recollections. We look for what the client is saying about himself, how he views his role in life, other people, and his possible options for behavior. In other words, we examine his movement. He is saying, in this story, that he knows what he should do, but he is reluctant. He feels pressured by life and its demands, and he would rather be out "playing." In his imagination, he envisions how he would like to stand up to those who confine him, but his movement is hesitating—he "thinks a good game," but does not act upon it—and he ends up not moving at all. As he has constructed it, there are two options, fight or submit (antithetical modes of apperception). He does not move in either direction and creates a conflict, but a conflict with a purpose. As long as he does not move, he cannot be wrong and, hence, he "wins" (Mosak & LeFevre, 1976). This is an example of intellectualizing and thinking about what to do, rather than doing it (see Chapter 6, particularly the section on defensive patterns).

Many Adlerians, particularly Adlerians who are trained as clinical psychologists, use testing in order to gain glimpses of the style of life rather than to establish a nomenclature diagnosis. It is not the tests themselves that they emphasize, but their use. If used to elucidate the client's uniqueness, to understand his or her goals, intentions, and purposes, they can be extremely beneficial. In the Adlerian clinical psychologist's armamentarium are the conventional tests, the social history, the mental status examination, tests for organicity, role playing for assessment purposes, and a wide variety of techniques upon which clinicians rely.

☐ General Issues in Assessment

Lombardi (1973) has listed eight ways Adlerians assess individuals:

1. Case history data
2. Psychological interviewing
3. Expressive behavior
4. Psychological testing
5. Family constellation
6. Early recollections
7. Grouping
8. Symptoms

We have discussed numbers 2, 4, 5, and 6 already. Let us examine the others.

With the case history data, we do not have to interact with the client, but rather we review the case history in detail. Adler (1929a, 1931/ 1964a) presented two such cases, Miss R. and Mrs. A. With each, he listened to the detailed presentation of the case and interjected comments and interpretations along the way. This form of interlinear assessment characterizes the way Adlerians do assessment. They do not wait for all the data to be in before assessing. That is certainly not possible in psychotherapy—one cannot wait until "later" to assess. Assessment must be ongoing as the patient speaks. The Adlerian assessor generates hypotheses, accepts and rejects them, and generates alternative hypotheses, in an attempt to understand the immediate communication and to pattern the data to understand the total person.

By using expressive behavior, Individual Psychologists can take note of body language in order to infer what may be certain issues in the person's style of life (Mosak & Shulman, 1977; Peven, Mosak & Shulman, 1979). What are the body posture, sleep position, general manner of carrying oneself, and so forth that may provide clues to the person (Adler, 1929/1964d)? Adler felt that such issues, including handwriting, could be used to elucidate the style of life.

By grouping, Lombardi (1973) refers to interacting with individuals. If we do, we can see not only how individuals engage in transactions with others, but how they feel about them. Smithells (1983) has written on this as well. Dreikurs (1948a) and Grunwald and McAbee (1985) discuss how in the process of family counseling and understanding children, clinicians can use their own reactions to the children's behavior (specifically, their misbehavior) to detect children's goals (Dinkmeyer & McKay, 1973, 1982; Mosak & Maniacci, 1993). For example, if a young child's goal is to get attention from others, his or her parents frequently feel annoyed or amused. If the child's goal is power, others typically feel threatened and angry. This is discussed in greater detail in Chapter 10, in the section on Adlerian educational programs.

Finally, Adlerians can assess individuals by examining their symptomatic behavior. Shulman and Mosak (1967) have discussed the various purposes of symptoms and have divided them according to nine categories. Let us review each.

In the safety stratagem symptoms are designed in order to insure against failure, hurt, or loss of place. By developing certain symptoms, clients can assure themselves of not failing, such as if a man develops sexual impotence and uses that in order to evade ever failing at marriage. In the hero-martyr-saint stratagem, symptoms are created in order to show how strong, saintly, or noble individuals are. In the attention-service-love stratagem, symptoms are used to get something. Sometimes, what is gotten is love and attention. The power stratagem is designed to manipulate others or overwhelm others; the revenge and retribution stratagem is used as retaliation against someone or something. The face-saving stratagem is used to repair damaged self-esteem, such as if guilt feelings are used to excuse misdeeds (Dreikurs, 1950b; Mosak, 1987a). Creating excitement can be used as a stratagem if individuals create a furor and agitate others. In Berne's terms (1964), they "enjoy" playing "Uproar." The proof stratagem is designed to strengthen one's position, such as by creating rejection in order to "prove" one is right for not getting close to others. Finally, individuals can keep a symptom in reserve in order to bring it up and use whenever they need an excuse.

Symptoms for Adlerians are like dreams and early recollections. They are not repressive in function, but expressive. They provide clues to understanding with what life style issues individuals are attempting to deal.

☐ Theoretical and Philosophical Issues

In general, Adlerians attempt to understand people's goals and their movements toward them. The life style is the attitudinal posture people take to life and represents the core of the personality. The life style is concerned with the long-range movement of individuals. The immediate movement, specifically the behavior within the attitudinal posture (i.e., the life style), is also assessed. Although it can be, and frequently is, consonant with long-range, life style goals, it may not be. What I have for lunch may not be indicative of my life style. It could very well be a function of the context of the situation I am in, what I had for lunch yesterday, what is available, how much it costs, who is around, and so forth. Then again, it may have a great deal to do with my life style. We do not deny that possibility, we just caution against an immediate assumption that everything is indicative of the style of life. *Because it may be does not mean it has to be.* Similarly, in psychotherapy, clients may come in with life style issues, but they may come in for particular issues (or at certain times during sessions) with topics which are indicative of immediate concerns, what Adler (1956) sometimes referred to as subgoals. Kathy may be a getter, but that may not be an issue with how she deals with her coworkers every time she has a conflict with one of them. It could, and probably does, play a part much of the time, but certainly not every time.

Another theoretical issue concerns what Adlerians assess. Roughly, there are four guidelines that concern them. They are movement, purpose, meaning, and social usefulness.

By movement, they mean noting how people approach challenges. These are the "dance steps" to which we refer in Chapter 6. Some people move backward, others create obstacles, still others bury their heads in the sand. Adlerians look to see how they operate.

Next, Adlerians examine the purpose of the movement, symptom, or behavior. As we discuss in Chapter 2, they are interested in the final cause, the goal, of behavior. The purposes of symptoms, listed here as stratagems, are an example of this.

Adlerian therapists are concerned with understanding the meaning of behavior. Purpose and meaning in Adlerian psychology are closely related but are not identical. The purpose, for instance, of self-induced vomiting may be to avoid gaining weight; its meaning may be, "I can't stomach this." To carry this example further, the person who vomits, the bulimic, may be saying, "I can't stomach this," about a lot of issues, such as having to appear one way when feeling another. A life style might be constructed around such apparent duplicity. Look as if one does not eat too much, but secretly gorge oneself to the point of sickness. Openly appear obedient, but covertly rebel. "I want to have my cake and eat it too, but not appear as such," they could be communicating.

Lastly, Adlerians note the social usefulness of the behavior. Is it constructive, nonconstructive, or destructive? Does it entail a sense of community feeling, or not? If not, why not? Whenever possible, they look to encourage examples of community feeling and social interest and foster more of it.

☐ Summary

It is a difficult art to understand a person. We may find that the more we attempt to make it a science, the less we understand. Science has brought us great assets and has improved our lives immeasurably. Of that there is no doubt. Aristotle cautioned us centuries ago not to expect more precision from a topic than the topic could provide, and writers, poets, artists, and philosophers have studied human nature longer than science has existed. It is easy to write this chapter as if it were so neat, precise, and apparent. We know, all too well, it is far more challenging in practice. It is an art, and perhaps it needs to stay one. The methods of science can be used to verify our understandings, but when it comes to human nature, verification of what we know lags far behind the ability to theorize about it.

Understanding a person entails empathy, connectedness, and discipline. It is an art that one must practice and, yes, study. It leads us to know our world, a world that exists with people. Our assessments must be sensitive, compassionate, and disciplined, lest we forget that what we see in others is really an extension of ourselves. Perhaps Plato was correct, on some level at least, in his assumption that humans could only learn what they already know to begin with. In the process of understanding a person, we can often find in them what we have seen in us.

As is apparent, the process of assessment is already involved in the process of psychotherapy. More globally stated, once we understand something, we are well on the way to being able to change it. It is to this process we turn next, the topic of encouraging growth.

☐ Points to Consider

Adlerians attempt to understand individuals without violating the basic assumptions of Individual Psychology. Their assessments must therefore take into account holism, phenomenology, psychology of use, and social-field theory, to name but a few of the assumptions.

Whereas diagnosis attempts to understand what makes a person "sick," assessment tries to understand what makes a person "tick." Adlerians generally have two steps to their case formulations, the General Diagnosis and the Special Diagnosis.

The special diagnosis, for those Adlerians trained in the Dreikursian model, entails doing what is called a life style assessment. It is an investigation of the person's early childhood history and an examination of his or her earliest recollections.

"The Question" is a key diagnostic technique for Adlerians. Not only is it used for assessing what is avoided by clients, it can be used for differential diagnosis of somatic from psychogenic disturbances.

☐ Questions

1. What is "The Question?" How is it used by Adlerians?
2. What is the goal of the Adlerian in conducting the Special Diagnosis?
3. How do Adlerians use dreams in their assessments? What are some of their purposes?
4. What is an early recollection? How do Adlerians use them?
5. What is the Adlerian view of psychological testing?
6. Why do Adlerians ask, "Who is most affected by your symptoms?" Into what basic assumptions does that question tap?
7. What is meant by understanding the client's "expressive behavior?"
8. Discuss some of the various purposes of symptoms.

☐ Note

[1]This is a point Freud (1963) misunderstood when he accused Adler of having created a psychology without love. In 1908 Adler (1956) had already written on the child's need for affection.

CHAPTER

Encouraging Growth

Our Western tendency has been to believe that understanding follows technique; *if we get the right technique, then we can penetrate the riddle of the patient. . . . The existential approach holds the exact opposite—namely, that* technique follows understanding. *The central task and responsibility of the therapist is to seek to understand the patient as a being and as a being in his world. . . . This does not derogate disciplined technique. It rather puts it into perspective.*

Rollo May (1983)

Accustom yourself to give careful attention to what others are saying, and try your best to enter into the mind of the speaker. . . . To a man with jaundice, honey seems bitter; to one bitten by a mad dog, water is a thing of horror; to little children, a ball is a treasure of great price. . . . For can it be supposed that a man's erroneous thinking has any less effect on him than the bile in jaundice . . . ? To change your mind and to defer to correction is not to sacrifice your independence; for such an act is your own, in pursuance of your own impulse, your own judgment, and your own thinking.

Marcus Aurelius (circa 169/1964)

How do Adlerians encourage growth? As we discussed in Chapter 9, understanding is the key. Although it is not always necessary that patients understand the origin, nature, and dynamics of their problems, the psychotherapist should have some degree of insight into what is happening (Maniacci, 1991). We are guiding others—it does not seem too much to ask that we at least know where we are going (Mosak & Maniacci, 1998). As people have understood for centuries, we need to give careful attention to what others are saying, and enter their worlds. Techniques are of *secondary* importance (not of *no* importance) to understanding, empathy, and compassion. We cannot expect to foster community feeling in others if we do not feel it ourselves. Adlerians believe that social interest is contagious, that is, that acceptance of self and acceptance of and by others are interrelated (Berger, 1952; McIntyre, 1952).

Adlerians encourage growth in people and society along three dimensions. They use educational programs and techniques, counseling and psychotherapy, and social advocacy. Each is briefly examined.

Educational Programs and Techniques

Child Guidance and Parent Education

Adler (1917/1988b, 1926/1988a, 1930a, 1930b, 1930/1963, 1956); Adler and associates (1930); Dreikurs (1948a); Dreikurs, Corsini, Lowe, and Sonstegard (1959); Dreikurs, Grunwald, and Pepper (1982); Dreikurs and Soltz (1964); Holub (1928); and Loewy (1930) have been the strongest proponents of Adlerian child guidance and parent education. They wrote extensively on these topics and devoted a considerable amount of time disseminating parent and family education. Adler's work has been carried on by numerous Adlerians, most notably Beecher and Beecher (1955), Christensen and Schramski (1983), Corsini (1977), Corsini and Painter (1975), Dinkmeyer and McKay (1973, 1982), Dinkmeyer, McKay, and Dinkmeyer (1980), Grunwald and McAbee (1985), Walton and Powers (1974), and West (1986). Adlerian child guidance should not be confused with Adlerian child psychotherapy. The goal of the former is educational; the goal of the latter is therapeutic (Mosak & Maniacci, 1993).

Adler was a supporter of social reform and outreach programs (Ansbacher, 1992a; Hoffman, 1994). He worked often with troubled youth and their families, and with his coworkers established child guidance and marriage clinics for the lay public and teacher-education programs in the schools (Adler, 1956, 1978). At the time the Fascists assumed power in Austria in 1934 there were 28 child guidance clinics in operation. This outreach work has continued along three fronts: marital enrichment programs, parent and family education, and teacher education.

Although therapy was being conducted on a one-to-one basis, Adler's innovative contribution was what was later named "open forum counseling." Adler and his colleagues would counsel a family in sessions attended by other parents and teachers. In this manner other families and educators could benefit from the counselor's advice to the family being counseled. They received education in family constellation issues, sibling rivalry, encouragement, and communication techniques. Dreikurs, Gould, and Corsini (1974) later added the family council, a weekly meeting designed to foster family communication, family decision making, and a democratic family climate. The family council was also described by Barber (1972), Bartholow (1969), Catlin (1976), Phillips (1975), Poffenberger (1953), Rigney and Corsini (1970), and Weinhaus (1977). Dreikurs extended Adler's contributions to parent education in numerous publications. Sometimes this parent education was criticized as being directed to middle-class families; the criticism can be refuted in that several Adlerian family counseling centers were located in lower socioeconomic class neighborhoods (Hansen, 1944–45).

Three of the major components in Adler's childrearing methods were encouragement, the understanding of the four goals of children's misbehavior, and the use of natural and logical consequences.

Encouragement

Numerous factors exist that may invite people to become discouraged. Societally, such conditions as war and the threat thereof, poverty, famine, crime, and various forms of discrimination are givens to which people must respond with problem solving. At the family level childrearing practices; parental expectation, demand, and modeling; and sibling competition may serve, in noncausal fashion, to discourage children. The educational system may further discourage children. Given these discouraging influences, children, in Berne's terms (1972), may grow up as either "winners" ("princes" or "princesses") or "losers" ("frogs"). A winner is one who succeeds in what she or he attempts to accomplish; a loser does not. For Berne the goal is to convert frogs into princes or princesses. Berne and Adlerians share common descriptions of losers, often employing the same names, for example, "Sisyphus."

Adlerians describe the process of transforming frogs into princes as encouragement. The encouraged person demonstrates faith in self and life. Although not pollyanna-like or subscribing to the pursuit of perfection, the encouraged person is usually willing to rely on self to meet the tasks of life and is willing to rely on self in assuming risk if one either does not know the consequences or faces potentially negative consequences. The latter Individual Psychologists refer to as courage, etymologically related to the word *encouragement*. Adlerians see encouragement as a *sine qua non* in social relations (Dinkmeyer & Losoncy, 1996; Losoncy, 1977; Neuer, 1936), in education (Dinkmeyer & Dreikurs, 1963), and in the therapeutic process (Mosak, 1995).

Although Adlerians and Berne largely concur in their views of winners and losers, Adlerians place an additional "spin" on the topic. Although subjectively bank robbers may regard themselves as winners if the hold-up is successful, society does not view them as winners. In addition to merely being successful at what one attempts, in order for Adlerians to consider the person a winner, the goal must be on the useful side of life.

Adlerian psychology further distinguishes between losing (failing) and being a loser (a failure), between the deed and the doer, and in religious terms, between the sin and the sinner. Everyone fails at something every day. That does not make us failures. To illustrate, Paul Ehrlich won the Nobel prize in 1908 for discovering the first cure for syphilis. The drug, salversan, was informally known as 606 because the first 605 experimental drugs failed. A baseball player with a batting average of .300 can command a huge salary, yet he fails more than twice as many times as he hits safely. Failures, then, are those who believe that they are (the inferiority feeling) or behave as if they are (the inferiority complex).

There is reason to believe that the more we encourage others, the more we encourage ourselves. By helping others' transformation into princes and princesses we become princes and princesses ourselves. The implications for parents, educators, and therapists are transparent. Encouragement makes the practice of psychotherapy rewarding for both the patient and the therapist (Mosak, 1950).

The Four Goals of Misbehavior

According to Dreikurs (1948a), if children become discouraged in finding their places usefully, they attempt to pursue one of four goals of misbehavior:

Goal I.   Attention getting
Goal II.   Power seeking
Goal III. Revenge taking
Goal IV. Displaying inadequacy

Although in any single display of misbehavior a child may opt for any one of these goals, disturbed and disturbing children may characteristically select one goal as the most frequently pursued. These short-term, immediate goals can be detected in three ways:

1. By observing what happens when children misbehave; the response they receive may be what they are looking for through their behavior.
2. By the adults checking on how this misbehavior makes them feel. If the adult feels annoyed or feels it is "cute," the goal may be to obtain attention. Anger, on the part of the adult, is generally a response to an invitation to engage in a power struggle. Revenge typically evokes a sense of hurt in the adult. A display of inadequacy may leave the adult feeling discouraged, like giving up on the child or doing "it" for him or her. In other instances goal IV behaviors may evoke feelings in the adult of, "I have to redouble my efforts to conquer or eliminate the child's inadequacy."
3. By observing what happens if you attempt to naively correct him or her. For example, if one gives the attention-seeking child attention, he or she will stop briefly, only to begin again shortly thereafter. The understanding of which goal children (or adults, for that matter) are striving for facilitates the handling of the situation in which these feelings arise. The various educational programs provide detailed instructions on how to deal with such matters.

Natural and Logical Consequences

One widely used method introduced by Dreikurs (1948a), the use of consequences, may be used as illustration. Consequences take two forms—natural and logical. A natural consequence occurs through no active intervention by the adult; one simply allows the natural consequences of actions to take their course. If a person does not eat a meal, she or he may go hungry. If children do not wear gloves in wintry weather, the experience of discomfort generally teaches them the lesson better than reminding, coaxing, or scolding. If the natural consequence is too dangerous or not readily apparent (e.g., not eating vegetables may not have immediate natural consequences), logical consequences can be introduced. Whereas natural consequences teach the natural order of life, logical consequences teach the social order of life. For example, the logical consequence of not coming to meals on time can be that the child is not served that particular meal. Rather than employing punishment and reward as the prime means of discipline, Adlerians prefer to use consequences and encouragement.

In the educational programs, because the parent-child relationship is dyadic and bidirectional (Mosak, 1980), a wide variety of techniques for both parents and children is taught. The programs are designed to reach relatively well-functioning families who may profit from the instruction and eliminate the need for therapeutic intervention. However, many, if not all, of the techniques can be used in conjunction with psychotherapy (Mosak & Maniacci, 1993). Although Adlerians do focus upon reme-diation, they prefer prevention of negative behaviors and promoting growth in families and individuals.

Schools

Teacher-education Programs

These programs are designed to increase cooperation in the classroom. Teachers and school administrators attend these programs, which are conducted in the same manner as the parent and marital programs. Teachers learn how to better deal with children so as to increase teacher effectiveness in the classroom. Allen (1970), Corsini (1977), Dinkmeyer et al. (1980), Dreikurs et al. (1982), and Mosak (1971b) have developed these programs. Holmberg (1972) provides descriptions of how Adlerian methods have been introduced into schools. All of these programs are similar in structure and philosophy. The content differs according to the audience addressed.

Couple-enrichment Programs

Dreikurs (1946) and Dinkmeyer and Carlson (1984, 1989) have written marital education texts that have been used to conduct marital or cou-ple-enrichment programs. Couples meet in groups of 10 to 12 and, using one of these texts, discuss how to improve their marriages or relation-ships. The groups are typically led by counselors or paraprofessionals and run from an hour to an hour and a half in length. Exercises, video- or audiotapes, posterboards, and role playing are used to build relationship skills that strengthen couples (Sperry & Carlson, 1991).

Parent and Family Education Programs

Similar to the marital programs, these programs focus on how to build better family relationships. Beecher and Beecher (1955), Dreikurs (1948a), Dreikurs et al. (1974), Dreikurs and Soltz (1964), Dinkmeyer and McKay (1973, 1982), Popkin (1987), and West (1986) have written some of the more popular programs.

☐ Adlerian Counseling and Psychotherapy

We have noted that Adler and his associates ran 28 child guidance centers in pre–World War II Vienna, and because of this enterprise, many early textbooks mistakenly characterized Adlerian psychotherapy as only useful for children. During his Freudian period Adler treated adults and continued to do so throughout his lifetime (Manaster, Painter, Deutsch, & Overholt, 1977). Adlerian psychotherapy actually assumes numerous forms—individual, group, family, couple, and multiple—and the populations served range from the so-called normal through the spectrum of conditions listed in the *Diagnostic and Statistical Manual* (American Psychiatric Association, 1994). Older texts occasionally derided Adlerian psychotherapy as "superficial," an "ego psychology." Subsequent to the Freudian legitimization of ego psychology, these criticisms waned.

Adlerian psychology may be characterized as an analytic-behavioral-cognitive psychology. Let us examine some of the ways in which Adlerians function.

Adlerian Cognitive Therapy

Adlerians actively search for and confront cognitive distortions in their clients. As Shulman (1985; Forgus & Shulman, 1979) notes, Adler was the first cognitive therapist, a point Ellis (1973, p. 112) supports:

> Alfred Adler was certainly one of the main mentors in the formulation of RET (Rational-Emotive Therapy); and it is highly probable that without his pioneering work, the main elements of rational-emotive therapy might never have been developed. . . . Adler's view of emotion, and of its cognitive or reasoning correlates, was unusually incisive, perceptive and to my way of thinking correct.

As Freeman (1993, p. iv) notes:

> The seminal and groundbreaking work of Alfred Adler, Rudolf Dreikurs, and other Individual Psychologists has too often been given short shrift and only passing notice. . . . The theoretical orientation developed by Adlerians has been the basis for Frankl's logotherapy and the contemporary ego-analytic approach of the psychoanalysts and has been one of the major influences for the development of present day cognitive behavior therapy.

We have characterized Adlerian psychology as an analytic-behavioral-cognitive one. Adlerians are cognitive in their emphasis upon thinking and how belief systems affect motivation and emotion and behavior. As discussed previously, they also emphasize how that was learned, typically via psychogenetic reconstruction of early influences and the development of a cognitive structure, a system of beliefs and values Adlerians refer to as the life style. Although the term "cognitive restructuring" did not come into vogue until much later, this was Adler's aim. Adler (1923, 1934) at one point describes the goal of therapy as replacing large errors (in cognition) with smaller ones, "and to reduce these even further until they are no longer harmful" (Adler, 1923, p. 38). Ellis (1957) speaks of "depropagandizing" the patient. In 1997, the *Journal of Cognitive Psychotherapy* devoted an entire issue to exploring the Adlerian roots of cognitive therapy ("Adlerian and Cognitive Psychotherapies," 1997).

Adlerian Psychoanalysis

Having spun off from Freudian psychoanalysis, it is understandable that Adlerian psychoanalysis retains some of the methods Freud introduced. Although they reconstruct the past, Adlerians do not regard the past as causalistic. They explore motivations that are not always conscious, although Adlerians avoid reification and treat "conscious" and "unconscious" as adjectives rather than nouns. Both use dream analysis, the Freudians to resolve past conflicts, the Adlerians as immediate problem-solving behavior. Both explore the significance of the therapist-patient relationship (Mosak, 1965). They deal with the establishment of the relationship, resistance (Boldt, 1994), transference (although Adlerians define it differently than Freud and Jung) (Zborowski, 1997), and the termination of the relationship (Mosak, 1965, 1995a).

Adler (1912/1983b, 1929/1964d, 1956) described the Adlerian therapist's role in many ways. The therapist's role included the fostering of community feeling or social interest. What was consonant with social interest was also in the individual's self-interest. Although acknowledging that rational-emotive therapy possesses many similarities to Adlerian psychology, Ellis (1957, p. 4) expresses the opposite, that what is in the individual's self-interest is in the social interest:

> It is mainly, however, in the realm of his views on social interest that Adler would probably take serious issue with rational therapy. For the latter believes that rational human behavior *primarily* must be based on *self*-interest; and that, if it is so based, it will by logical necessity also have to be largely rooted in social interest. Adler seemed to believe the reverse; that only through a primary social interest could an individual achieve maximum self-love and happiness.

The therapist also closely observes the life style of the client and seeks to understand how the client interacts with the therapist. This interaction is to a large extent transferential and to some degree reality-based because the therapist does not adopt the role of the anonymous therapist. Because the client brings his or her life style to therapy, the relationship with the therapist may reflect the interaction of the client with others in his or her social milieu. These interactions are paramount within the Adlerian framework, so much so that Berne (1972) has hailed Adler as the first transactionalist.

Adler (1929/1964d) also characterized the therapist's role as assuming the belated function of the mother, that is, the one who encourages and corrects, a nurturer who teaches the client how to function more constructively in life. Rogers (1942, 1951), Maslow (1970), and Goldstein (1940/1963) refer to the latter as self-actualization and self-realization.

Adlerian Behavioral Therapy

Although in its psychoanalytic aspects Adlerian therapy aims at insight, insight does not consist merely of knowledge ("know thyself") or understanding. For the Adlerian there is no insight unless there is an action component. Mosak and Shulman (1967, p. 42) define insight as "a meaningful experience leading to perceptual change and leading to a change in the line of movement." Therefore, in addition to such media as psychoanalytic interpretation, resolving resistances, the transference, and cognitive restructuring, the Adlerian may conduct psychodrama or utilize music (Dreikurs, 1965; Dreikurs & Crocker, 1955; Greven, 1957), art (Cucher, 1976; Dreikurs & Shulman, 1969), or dance therapy (Espenak, 1981). The therapist may do task setting (assign "homework") (Mosak, 1995a; Peven & Shulman, 1986), encourage action (Dinkmeyer & Dreikurs, 1963; Dinkmeyer & Losoncy, 1996), and reinforce behaviors. Although these methods may be viewed as behavior modification, as Adlerians implement them they represent vehicles for motivation modification (Nystul, 1985).

Other Settings for Adlerian Psychotherapy

Adlerian Family Therapy

As Sherman and Dinkmeyer (1987) document, Adlerian family therapy is a systems theory that integrates many other theories. Foley (1989, p. 458) writes that:

Adlerian psychotherapeutic theory shares much with family therapy. Its emphasis on the family constellation is a major concept borrowed by family therapists. Adler's approach was holistic, as is family therapy. The use of paradox, a major weapon in family therapy, has its roots in Alfred Adler. . . . Likewise, an emphasis on the conscious and the present are Adlerian concepts. The freedom to improvise is a feature of family therapy and it, too, has its roots in Adler. . . . The basic concepts of family therapy are found in a latent state in Adler's thinking.

Adlerian family therapy can apply to many populations, from the "typical" family (Christensen & Schramski, 1983) to the family with severely disturbed members (Maniacci & Carlson, 1991).

Marriage and Couple Counseling

Procedurally Adlerians conduct marriage and couple counseling in various forms. All, however, are based upon the theoretical basic assumptions, and almost all are transactional in nature. Their approach is constructivist and systemic (Sperry & Carlson, 1991). Corsini (1967) has "invented" a "first-aid kit for marriage problems." It is designed for "the kind of problems too minor to require a specialist but too major to ignore" (p. 40). Deutsch (1967) and Papanek (1965b) utilized group therapy in the treatment of married couples. Pew and Pew (1972) rely on a rating method to trace the perception of self and spouse. Mozdzierz and Lottman (1973) utilize a transactional approach in examining the "games married people play." Following the lead of Dreikurs, Shulman and Mosak do life style matching to determine areas of compatibility and incompatibility, following this with a transactional approach to treatment unless the degree of psychopathology in one or both partners suggests that the partners should be seen separately for psychotherapy rather than engaging in marriage or couple counseling. Carlson and Sperry (1998) recommend a similar approach. Kern, Hawes, and Christensen (1989) also write about couple's work.

Adlerian Group Therapy

Dreikurs (1959) was the first therapist to introduce group therapy into private practice, the first of many Adlerians to practice group psychotherapy. Given the social-field theoretical assumption of Adlerian psychology, group therapy is a natural fit (Corsini, 1971, 1987; Papanek, 1965b; Shulman, 1973a). Adlerians, such as O'Connell (1975) and Starr (1977), have written texts on the Adlerian use of psychodrama, both in group and individual therapy, and Corsini (1966) wrote one of the early manuals on the use of role playing in psychotherapy.

Adlerian Individual Psychotherapy: General Guidelines

As Dreikurs (1956) discusses, Adlerian psychotherapy consists of four processes—relationship, investigation and understanding, interpretation, and reorientation and change. All of these processes are in motion throughout the entire course of the therapeutic encounter.

Relationship

Adlerians attempt, in terms of relationship, to establish the kind of atmosphere and relationship in which clients can feel comfortable divulging themselves, sharing feelings and cognitions with the therapist.[1] In spite of the efforts to keep the goals of the client and the therapist aligned, difficulties of various kinds, both on the part of the client and that of the therapist, occur, and the goals must be realigned in order for therapy to proceed. These resistances may be either situational or characterological (Boldt, 1994).

Because the life style is consistent, what people generally do outside of therapy they reprise, sooner or later, in therapy (Maniacci, 1996a). What the Freudians consider to be transference and working through, Adlerians (roughly) consider to be the dynamics of the life style and the process of reorientation. Like the Freudians of the Chicago Institute of Psychoanalysis (Alexander & French, 1946), the Adlerian therapist provides corrective emotional experiences.

Adler (1956, pp. 336–337), in describing transference, wrote,

> I expect from the patient again and again the same attitude which he has shown in accordance with his [life style] toward the persons of his former environment, and still earlier toward his family. At the moment of the introduction to the [therapist] and often earlier, the patient has the same feelings toward him as towards important persons in general. The assumption that the transference of such feelings or that resistance begins later is a mere deception. In such cases the [psychotherapist] only recognizes them later.

From this perspective, Adlerians do not wait for a transference neurosis to emerge; they can begin working on the cognitive distortions rapidly, as soon as they feel the relationship is sufficiently solidified to permit such restructuring (Maniacci, 1996a).

Finally there are the issues of termination, of dissolving the relationship. Many clients, for whatever personal reasons they may have, feel loath to relinquish therapy and may unconsciously wish to become "interminable patients" (Freud, 1937/1959).

In all of these relationship issues, the therapist must deal with the patient's motivations, expectations, demands, invitations, and tests.

Understanding and Investigation

Throughout the process the therapist engages in active listening to gain insight into the client's communication and behavior (Peven et al., 1979). She or he listens to tone, to volume, to emphasis, to accent, and for speech impediments (Mosak & Shulman, 1977). She or he listens to language, to metalanguage (Mosak & Gushurst, 1972), to regionalisms, to argot (Mosak, Mosak, & Mosak, 1979), to organ jargon (Griffith, 1984; Robb, 1932), and for verbal "pathology" such as parapraxes, neologisms, word salad, and aphasia (Mosak & Shulman, 1977). The therapist interprets in her or his own mind the meaning and the purpose of the client's communication. The therapist observes physical characteristics, carriage, dress, gesture, physical flaws, and impediments. Adler (1929/1964d), emphasizing the unity of the personality, comments that whatever a person does reflects the life style. Consequently, it is not too important that we have a specific format in therapy.[2] Adlerians can focus on past, present, or future. They can discuss current issues, current problems, fantasies, or dreams. They can give clients crayons and ask them to draw or they can invite them to create poetry. All of these communications may provide clues to the life style. Much Adlerian assessment is thus informal in nature in that the therapist constantly endeavors to understand (Peven et al., 1979).

Adlerians also perform formal assessment for the usual reasons and with the usual clinical instruments. They generally test for specific forms of information rather than administer complete batteries. The interpretation of these tests is based on Adlerian theory (Maniacci, 1990; Mele, 1993). For a more global approach the Adlerian aims for a life style summary in most instances. This is not necessarily true for such conditions as situational neuroses, toxic psychoses, and neurological conditions, but it is applicable to what previously were called psychoneuroses, personality disorders, and functional psychoses. In these instances one usually cannot do cognitive restructuring unless one knows the cognitive structure, namely the life style.

The knowledge of the life style only affords access to the person's long-range goals. Adlerians are also interested in the short-range goals of people. Early recollections, a projective instrument (Gushurst, 1971; Lieberman, 1957; Mosak, 1958; Munroe, 1955, Taylor, 1975), help therapists to understand the long-range goals; dreams, a problem-solving activity, inform about the short-range goals (Mosak, 1992). Because dreams are not seen as "the royal road to the unconscious," dreams do not constitute a *sine qua non* in Adlerian therapy, although they are widely used. Listening and observation may also give the therapist insight into both short- and long-term goals.

Interpretation

Although Adlerians are systematic theoretically, they are often technical eclectics. They feel free to intervene in any manner so long as the intervention does not violate the basic assumptions of Adlerian psychology and ethical standards. They use interpretation, reflection of feeling, paradoxical intention, humor, supportive techniques—a wide variety of therapeutic tactics (Mosak & Maniacci, 1998). They often teach social and communication skills.

Some use psychotropic medication and other somatic interventions. A division of opinion exists among Adlerians with regard to the prescription of medication in psychotherapy. Many medical-model practitioners (Pancner & Jylland, 1996; Sperry, 1990) are committed to prescribing medication, particularly with the chronically mentally ill (Maniacci, 1991); growth-model therapists are not. The former may use psychotropic medication as part of the therapy or for readying a patient for therapy; the latter group of Adlerians, viewing Adlerian psychotherapy as educational or reeducational, refrain from relying upon such medications. Mosak (1985, 1995b), in two papers, describes the treatment of depression and schizophrenia without medication.

Reorientation and Change

Therapeutic change is often considered to be the endpoint of therapy. Yet reorientation can commence as early as the telephone call to arrange the first appointment. Although the achievement of insight may be desirable, it may not always be necessary. People change every day without insight. Although insight often precedes behavior change, the order is frequently reversed. Doing something different, perhaps creative or innovative behavior change or problem solving, can *produce* insight. One observes this most transparently if one is working puzzles and finally arrives at the "aha response." Although Adlerians do not dismiss the role of insight, they are aware that how it is attained is not always so simple as is portrayed.

Every therapy has a specific theoretical goal. For example, the Freudian hopes that "where id was, there shall ego be." The Adlerian aims to remove inferiority feelings and promote social interest. However, for each therapy there are also practical goals, especially in an era of third-party payments and managed care. Among these practical goals are changes in behavior and feelings, symptomatic change, changes in outlook about the world (e.g., to become more optimistic), and changes in self-perception and self-esteem.

Various techniques, as well as encouragement, are employed to assist clients in their efforts to change. Many of these are discussed by Dinkmeyer et al. (1987), Mosak (1995a), Mosak & Maniacci (1989, 1995, 1998), and Mosak & Shulman (1967).

According to a survey conducted in 1972 and followed up in 1989, Adlerian therapy tends to be brief, typically lasting 4 to 6 months (16–24 sessions). Special issues of the *Journal of Individual Psychology* (Ansbacher, 1972) and of *Individual Psychology* (Sperry, 1989) contain papers devoted to brief therapy. Although Adlerians can and do engage in long-term therapy, by and large their work is brief (Maniacci, 1996a). As with taking one's car to the auto mechanic, some clients merely need to have their spark plugs cleaned; others require major overhauls.

Multiple Psychotherapy

Although multiple psychotherapy, or cotherapy as some refer to it, has been used sporadically and for specific purposes and populations since the beginning of the 20th century, it was midcentury before it was utilized as a regular vehicle for the conduct of psychotherapy (Dreikurs et al., 1984). Using two therapists, the method contains advantages for both therapists and patients. Multiple psychotherapy incorporates a flexibility not available in individual psychotherapy. If one therapist is not available because of illness or vacation, the patient still has access to another who knows the patient equally well. Patients have the benefit that "two heads are better than one." Therapists can apply correctives to each other and prevent the therapy from getting into a rut through facilitating dealing with transferential situations and meeting resistances. Multiple psychotherapy also provides an excellent method for training and supervision.

☐ Social Advocacy

Adler (1978) was politically active, especially during his early years (Ansbacher, 1992a). Ellenberger (1970) and Hoffman (1994) provide an overview of such matters. Adler was a proponent of women's rights, democratic reform, preventive medicine, community mental health, and educational reform, to name but a few of the issues he advocated (see our introduction). Dreikurs (1971) and many other Adlerians (e.g., Gottesfeld, 1966; Lerner, 1952) have continued that tradition, stressing the need to build better communities based upon egalitarian, democratic principles. Adlerians' work in parent and family education, open-forum family counseling, and teacher education and school reform continues in this tradition. Environmental concerns occupy the attention of other Adlerians (Heyligers-Gunning, 1970; Meiers, 1972).

☐ Summary

This chapter provides a brief overview of how Adlerians encourage growth in people. We gear our work not only to the "sick," or "disturbed" individuals, but to people, regardless of their age, status, or "diagnosis." Healthy, well-functioning individuals can benefit from our psychoeducational programs and psychotherapy, which can also do a great deal to serve as a preventative measure against future problems.

Our theory of counseling and psychotherapy takes into account many diverse perspectives and orientations, from psychoanalytic to cognitive, behavioral, existential, and family-systems viewpoints. Although Adlerians adhere to a consistent, unitary theory, they practice according to the needs of the situation and the dynamics of the case. In any one day, an Adlerian therapist might act like a cognitive therapist one session, a psychoanalyst the next, an existentialist the next, and a family therapist later. Even within the same session, such diversity might occur. All of this occurs within the framework of our basic assumptions listed at the beginning of this work.

We have come full circle. It is time to return our attention to where we started, and that is upon our theory itself. We know where it came from, who formulated it, how it developed, and how it operates. It is time to assess its usefulness, explore its limitations, and seek where else it needs to grow and expand. That is the focus of the next chapter, our last chapter, a critique of Individual Psychology. Like individuals themselves, if a theory is to remain healthy and vital, it needs to evolve, to adapt to changes and remain flexible enough to cope with whatever life presents. Let us assess and lay the groundwork for Adlerian psychology as it moves into the next century.

☐ Points to Consider

Adlerians operate in a number of ways to encourage growth. They use educational programs, counseling and psychotherapy, and social advocacy.

Through psychoeducation, Adlerians reach out to not only disturbed individuals, but to healthy people as well. They intervene not only with families and couples, but with schools and educational facilities as well.

With regards to counseling and psychotherapy, Adlerians are technically eclectic. That is, they use a wide variety of tactics in order to produce change. Adlerians use tactics that are cognitive, behavioral, and psychoanalytic. They work in individual, couple, family, and group formats, and in long-term and brief-therapy formats.

☐ Questions

1. What is the difference between logical and natural consequences?
2. What do Adlerians mean by encouragement?
3. What are some of the behavioral tactics Adlerians use with clients?
4. How do Adlerians define transference? How is it similar to and different from Freudian definitions?
5. What is multiple psychotherapy? Describe some of its advantages.
6. Adler described the Adlerian therapist's role as assuming the "belated function of the mother." What did he mean by that?
7. What are the four phases of Adlerian psychotherapy?

☐ Notes

[1]Adlerian psychology, like rational-emotive psychology, assumes that underlying every feeling a cognition exists (Dreikurs, 1951; Ellis, 1973).

[2]Currently some states and third-party providers demand treatment plans at the initiation of psychotherapy, creating a problem for Adlerian and person-centered therapists.

A Critique of the Theory of Individual Psychology

Giving good advice means the therapist assumes that people have rational control of what they are doing. To be successful in the therapy business it may be better to drop that idea.

Jay Haley (1976)

Common sense has its own necessity; it asserts its rights with the weapon particularly suitable to it, namely, appeal to the "obviousness" of its claims and considerations. However, philosophy can never refute common sense, for the latter is deaf to the language of philosophy. Nor may it even wish to do so, since common sense is blind to what philosophy sets before its essential vision.

Martin Heidegger (1943/1977)

Nothing is perfect. As we have attempted to detail throughout this work, striving to be perfect can be a neurotic goal that is unattainable and typically serves to alienate others. Individual Psychology is not perfect, and Adler himself, like all of us, made mistakes, not only as a person but as a theorist. What he created has stood the test of time remarkably well, but not without having been subjected to much criticism, not all of it unjustified. We will not concern ourselves with some of the more obvious points which Adler overstated, for we are more interested in the scope of his thought than the details. For example, as we briefly discuss in Chapter 9, Adler (1956) viewed dreams as problem-solving functions that were concerned with the future (i.e., where we are expecting to go or be in the immediate future), not as attempts to fulfil infantile wishes. In general, this is becoming increasingly accepted (e.g., French, 1952). However, he also commented that healthy individuals no longer dreamed because they had the courage to solve their problems during the day (Adler, 1929/1964b). That simply is not true. Adler overstated his case.

In attempting a critique of the theory of Individual Psychology, we examine 12 points that need to be examined. The first group are the "traditional" criticisms leveled against Adler and Adlerians. The second group are our thoughts about what we feel needs to be reexamined. We are not attempting to be comprehensive, for that would entail yet another entire manuscript. We are simply trying to be thought-provoking, not only for other Adlerians, but for any interested in psychological theory itself. We conclude with a look at how some of the basic Adlerian assumptions have become part of mainstream psychology, through the system known as cognitive constructionism.

☐ "Traditional" Criticisms

1. Story has it that during one of Adler's early lectures, a member of the audience stood up and proclaimed, "But Dr. Adler, all you speak is common sense!" Supposedly, Adler replied, "And what is wrong with that? I wish more psychiatrists did." Adlerians have traditionally been criticized for speaking "common sense."[1] Adlerians accept that criticism. It is a "valid criticism." Adlerians do speak common sense. Adler disliked technical jargon and wanted to base his system upon philosophy, not science, and he appealed to people who were not necessarily academically trained. He intentionally set out to make his system accessible to "common people." Like George Miller (1967), he wanted to give psychology away. Adler made it possible to train teachers, social workers, clergy, and even psychologists to work with people in trouble. Like Freud, he felt that one did not have to be medically trained to practice therapy. Once more, Adler also believed that people could help themselves ("The father of self-help," 1995), and he set out to explain his principles in such a way as to make them "user friendly."

2. "It is a superficial, ego psychology that overemphasizes rational processes." In about as many words, Freud attempted to dismiss Adler's

system. He also added that what Adler said was new was not true, and what Adler said was true was not new. As we note throughout the text, even psychoanalysis has become "ego-oriented" with the emergence of ego psychology, object relations theory, and self-psychology. The rise of cognitive therapy has been well documented. Adlerians do focus upon conscious operations, but they also examine what is not understood. Our concepts of the final, fictional goal and private logic are "beyond" rational, traditionally defined "ego" functions. But the emphasis is upon what people think, their perceptions, and expectations.

3. "It works only with normal people." Everything works with "normal" people. That is why they make such great clients. Adlerians have followed Adler's tradition and have worked with varied populations, including the psychotic, criminals, children, adolescents, families, and cross-culturally. Although the Freudians would not work with psychotic patients because the patients could not enter into a transference relationship, Adlerians, relatively unconcerned with transference, did treat them from the earliest times (Kramer, 1947; Seif, 1928; Trentzsch, 1928; Wexberg, 1928). A similar criticism is intended when Adlerians are "credited" with working with "children," but what they typically mean is that Adler's system works "only" with children. Yes, the principles work well with children, and Adler, Dreikurs, and other Adlerians have written extensively about child guidance. It is equally applicable to others (Hapworth et al., 1993).

4. "Its psychotherapy is manipulative." Every psychotherapy is manipulative (Dreikurs, 1960; Mosak & Maniacci, 1998). Even nondirective therapists "direct" their client by selectively reinforcing one type of comment over another (Greenspoon, 1955). "Um-hmm" is directive and rewarding; it tells the client to keep going into the area just raised. Adler gave therapists a direction, a guidepost, to direct their efforts—he called it community feeling and social interest. Adlerians do want to direct clients toward it, toward becoming useful, productive members of society and the community. They do not pride themselves in being value-neutral in that respect. They believe that people can learn, and they can change, and, with enough information, practice, patience, and encouragement, much can be accomplished. If that is manipulative, so be it.

5. "Everything is a matter of power, will to power, superiority strivings or inferiority, and compensation" (e.g., Murphy, 1947). One might form that impression by reading the Adlerian literature from the early part of the century. But it is certainly untrue of current theory. That criticism Adlerians do not accept as valid, except on a general, nomothetic level. We have discussed how Adlerians distinguish between the idiographic, specific case, and the general or nomothetic principle. Generally speaking, if we feel in the "minus position," that is when "trouble" is likely to

occur. The minus position depends upon the life style with which we are dealing. Insecurity, low self-esteem, lack of control, inadequacy, lack of mastery, "feeling down"—these are just some of the idiographic variations the feeling of inferiority can take.

These are the basic criticisms most Adlerians hear. There are gaps that exist in Adlerian psychology, and it is to those that we now turn our attention.

☐ "Gaps" in Individual Psychology

There are six main areas we believe Individual Psychology needs to address if it is to remain a viable, growing system. In no particular order of importance, we examine them, beginning with a point made by others that needs far more critical examination than has heretofore been accorded it.

1. "The life style is all. Everything comes down to the life style." No, it does not. Not everything a person does is a matter of life style. Although we need a cognitive map in order to get to our destination, that is, the goal, we also watch the other cars, take into account the road conditions, and look at the road signs. Despite what Adler has written and other Adlerians have detailed, there are many things that we do that have nothing to do with our style of life (Shulman, 1965). Dreams reflect our current activity and thoughts. We believe they seldom, if ever, have anything to do with our life style (though our style of solving the problems with which we are confronted in our dreams may be indicative of our style); yet some Adlerians disagree with this position (e.g., Gold, 1981) and believe that dreams are a part of our life style. Similarly, what I typically have for lunch has nothing to do with my life style. This requires elaboration.

Life style, as we are portraying it, develops in order to teach us, guide us, and instruct us about how to belong. Issues that pertain to how we bond, fit in, or find our place are matters that come under the direction of the life style. What color shirt I wear when I dress in the morning probably has nothing to do with such issues, unless appearance is crucial for my sense of belonging (Shulman, 1965). For many people, it is not an issue. There may be consistency to our behavior, even patterns, that are not life style issues, for they do not entail issues of how we belong. For example, we may have a fairly consistent preference for what we eat for lunch, yet that probably is not a decision that is based upon our life style convictions. What organizes these behaviors? Is it "the self?" Are there elements of "the self" that are not contained within the life style? These areas need to be explored in greater detail. For now we only have speculations, and much more theory and even research is needed to explore this topic. There are situational factors that interact with the life style, and more attention needs to be directed to these factors.

2. In general, Adlerians have not dealt with the issue of love in great detail. Freud (1963) accused Adler of having created a psychology without love. He wrote Oskar Pfister that Adler "forgets the saying of the apostle Paul . . . 'And I know that ye have not love in you.' He has created for himself a world without love and I am in the process of carrying out on him the revenge of the offended goddess of the libido" (p. 48). What is love? Is it merely one emotion among others? Is there something special to it? What about sexuality? How is that related to love? Are they similar, different, or only tangentially related? Adlerians, like other psychologists, are interested in the same questions raised by Jesus, Nietzsche, Schopenhauer, Fromm, Freud, and others (Ansbacher, 1966; Dreikurs, 1946).

3. For a theory and practice that deals with children to the extent Adlerians do, Adlerians do not have an adequate developmental (Mosak, 1991b) or learning theory (Croake & Robertshaw, 1987). When Adler was writing, there were no developmental theorists as we know them today (other than Freud's psychosexual stage theory). Erikson, Piaget, Sullivan, Mahler, Bowlby, Ainsworth, Gesell, and Stern came after Adler. Adlerians, except in a cursory manner, have not attempted to formulate a theory of development. By and large, they do not know what is "appropriate" for certain age groups and they do not attempt to take that into account in their work (with West's 1986 work being a notable exception).

4. Adlerians do not make enough of a distinction between the issues of responsibility and change. In many of Adler's original writings, he comes across as rather harsh and blaming towards patients. For example, although today "perversion" is a moral term, in Freud's and Adler's time it was a technical term. Because people can change does not mean that they will, nor does it explain how change occurs. They are responsible for changing themselves, but we do not detail how that process begins, maintains itself, and stops (see Mosak & Maniacci, 1998, for how this process operates in psychotherapy and counseling).

5. Along a similar line, Adlerians are more prescriptive rather than descriptive. Adlerians spend considerable time telling what to do without describing in any great detail what is going on. A clear, clinically rich exception to this is Shulman's (1968/1984) work on schizophrenia, in which he not only details what to do about someone who is using schizophrenic mechanisms but explores in great detail what the schizophrenic experience is like, describing it and tracing its course. Adlerians need more works like this, describing what is happening in detail.

6. Finally, Adlerians have existed as a school of psychotherapy since the second decade of this century, but they write little, if anything, about the process of psychotherapy except for assorted articles and chapters. An in-depth, detailed approach to Adlerian psychotherapy has yet to appear. They do function as system therapists, cognitive therapists, analysts, counselors, and so forth. When do they "shift hats," so to speak? How do they shift? Much more detail is needed if the art of Adlerian psychotherapy is to continue once the masters have stopped practicing.

☐ Adler's Continuing Influence

As we have noted throughout the text, Adler's system seems to be continually "rediscovered." As has been noted by Ellenberger (1970), it would be hard to find another theorist from whom so much has been taken without due credit being given. We have mentioned Adler's influence upon existentialism, family therapy, psychoanalysis (especially self-psychology and object relations), and cognitive-behavior therapy. We want to briefly turn to one of the latest trends in psychotherapy, constructionism, and highlight some of the remarkable similarities.

Cognitive Constructionism

Shulman (1985; Forgus & Shulman, 1979; Shulman & Watts, 1997) and Jones (1995) have presented the key works in this area, and the recent special issue of the *Journal of Cognitive Psychotherapy* ("Adlerian and Cognitive Psychotherapies," 1997) discusses the similarities between Adlerian and cognitive therapies, especially cognitive constructionism. We would like to address some of the similarities in order to highlight our thesis that Adler's ideas—if not his system—are becoming more and more "mainstream." The main texts we draw from in the cognitive constructionism literature are Guidano and Liotti (1983), Mahoney (1991), and Safran and Segal (1990), along with the aforementioned special issue of the *Journal of Cognitive Psychotherapy*.

Following are some of the important concepts in the cognitive constructionism literature. We examine each in turn:

1. Autopoiesis
2. Core ordering processes/personal-cognitive organization
3. Tacit-explicit knowledge
4. Feedforward mechanisms

5. Knowledge as self-knowledge
6. Attachment theory

Autopoiesis

This is the term many constructionists use to describe how individuals learn. From their perspective, individuals are active agents in their learning, that is, they are not merely passive receptors of data from their environment. Constructionists believe that individuals cocreate their worlds. This is hauntingly similar to Adler's concept of the creative self (Adler, 1956). Even the literal translation of the term "autopoiesis" gives "self-creative."

Core Ordering Processes/Personal-cognitive Organization

Either of these terms is used, depending upon what text is being read. Both mean the same thing: Individuals have a set, established way of construing their world, and this set determines how the individuals will interact with others. The personal-cognitive organization is the set of rules which underlies individuals' attempts at bonding. The counterpart in Individual Psychology is the concept of life style (Shulman & Mosak, 1988).

Tacit-explicit Knowledge

Constructionists write that knowledge is divided into two broad categories: tacit and explicit. Tacit knowledge is that which is barely understood, is usually learned prelinguistically, and exists nonverbally and without consensual validation. Explicit knowledge is that which is linguistically stored, consensually shared, and clearly understood. This is virtually identical to Adler's (1956) concepts of private logic and common sense.

Feedforward Mechanisms

In passive theories of the mind and brain, individuals are seen as mere receptors of the data coming in from the environment. Constructionists stress that although this is certainly true, the mind and brain are active as well in that we also send out signals that help produce the very feedback we receive. In other words, we may be sensitive to criticism, but our noticing such criticism in the first place is contingent upon us looking for it and being sensitive to it to begin with. We may even send out subtle cues that stimulate others to provide us with the feedback we receive. This is what we earlier referred to as the self-fulfilling prophecy, and another instance of what Adler (1956) called the creative self.

Knowledge as Self-knowledge

Constructionists note that since the personal-cognitive organization system controls all knowledge, whatever we know (basically) reflects something about who and what we are. This is most relevant when it comes to cognitive processes like memory. Constructionists believe that memory is not a passive faculty waiting to be retrieved. It is an active event that is created in order to justify current opinions and ideas about the self and others. Once again, this is almost identical to Adler's (1956) view of the importance of early recollections and biased apperceptions.

Attachment Theory

Constructionists believe that through early bonding interactions, individuals learn to encode and process information in such a way so as to feel secure. This becomes the basis of later attempts to bond with others; hence, if early attachment was disturbed or in any significant way disordered, as adults, we may continue the inappropriate attempts at bonding in much the same manner as we did as children. In fact, most constructionists believe that psychopathology is itself a disordered attempt at bonding. This is Adler's (1956) and Dreikurs' (1933/1950a, 1967) opinion as well. Adlerians believe that psychopathology is a discouraged attempt at belonging.

We discuss these points in order to make a point: As Adler predicted long ago, although his name might not be remembered, his concepts have become part of the mainstream. Although his name is seldom remembered in the constructionist literature, his ideas are certainly to be found. It is important for Adlerians to keep up with the literature, especially of new schools and of new developments in the "traditional" schools, or else we may continue to talk only to ourselves and fail to realize that we are much more mainstream than we realize. More dialogues like the one found in the *Journal of Cognitive Psychotherapy* need to take place.

The Future of Individual Psychology

Where does this leave Adlerians as the new millennium approaches? It is our belief that Adler's system is a living, viable system. As we point out repeatedly throughout the text, and Adler himself noted near the end of his life, Adler's ideas are becoming incorporated into the mainstream of clinical practice and theory. Through the ever-evolving theories of cognitive constructionism, cognitive behavior therapy, existentialism, and family therapy, and recent developments in psychoanalysis (especially object relations and self psychology), Adler's insights are becoming the basis for new generations of clinicians and academicians. Few may know his name, and even fewer seem to realize how similar their systems are to his, but, nonetheless, clinical psychology and psychiatry continues to move closer to the position adopted by individual psychologists. May this work help to build a bridge between these schools of thought and Adlerian psychology.

Dreikurs (1960, p. 3) once asked the question, "Are psychological schools of thought outdated?" He noted that it is impossible to not have a theory of human nature, and that even therapists who claimed they were eclectic still had a theory—eclecticism. The question became not whether or not one had a theory, but how well one understood the theory one had.

Regardless of the theory one holds, one should know it well, and one of the best ways to understand a theory is to learn it in relation to another system. Adlerian psychology is a good system to learn, especially if the goal is integration (Sherman & Dinkmeyer, 1987). By learning Adler's system, students and practitioners can better understand their current system. As we have repeatedly noted, because so many other systems have moved towards Adler's insights, Individual Psychology can provide a firm base from which to look at and examine other schools of thought.

The future of Individual Psychology? Who can say with certainty? As a movement and school of psychology, it may wax and wane. As a system and a coherent set of assumptions, it continues to grow and be validated.

☐ Summary

We hope these challenges are taken in the spirit they are intended. They need to be met. By providing a guideline, we hope to create a dialogue in which some of these issues, and others we have not addressed, are explored. We cannot answer the questions we have posed in this work, one reason being that they are beyond the scope of this work. One must learn to walk before one runs, the old saying goes, and Individual Psychology needed a new, introductory text that would describe and set forth its principles and applications. We hope to have done just that in this work.

☐ Questions

1. What is cognitive constructionism? What are some of its basic premises?
2. How are those premises similar to Adlerian psychology's basic assumptions?
3. How far should a theory be from "common sense"? If it is close to the "common sense," is that a problem?
4. What is the basic premise behind "feedforward mechanisms"? How does Adler describe such processes?
5. What would you see as some criticisms of Individual Psychology? How might an Adlerian address your concerns?
6. What similarities do you see between Adlerian psychology and other systems?

☐ Note

[1]Why this same criticism was not leveled against the eminent psychobiological therapist Adolf Meyer, whose collected papers were published as *The Common Sense Psychiatry of Dr. Adolf Meyer* (Lief, 1973) makes for interesting speculations.

☐ Annotated Bibliography

Adler, A. (1956). *The Individual Psychology of Alfred Adler* (H.L. Ansbacher & R.R. Ansbacher, Eds.). New York: Basic Books.
This is considered to be the primary text for understanding Adler. The Ansbachers have surveyed Adler's writings and come up with selections which provide readers with an overview of Adler's theory. It also has some very helpful commentaries.

Adler, A. (1964). *Superiority and social interest* (H.L. Ansbacher & R.R. Ansbacher, Eds.). Evanston, IL: Northwestern University Press.
This is a collection of Adler's later writings. As before, the Ansbachers have collected several writings from diverse sources, these mostly being from the last part of Adler's life. Once again, there are extremely useful commentaries throughout the text.

Adler, A. (1978). *Cooperation between the sexes: Writings on women, love and marriage, sexuality and its disorders* (H.L. Ansbacher & R.R. Ansbacher, Eds.). New York: Doubleday.
The last in the Ansbachers' trilogy, this volume examines Adler's early theoretical work, a period in which most of his writings had to do with love, sexuality, and gender dynamics. The commentaries, as usual, are excellent.

Dreikurs, R., & Soltz, V. (1964). *Children: The challenge.* New York: Duell, Sloan & Pearce.
This is one of the best books on parenting ever written. It is both theoretically sound and pragmatically helpful. It is Adlerian theory in practice, specifically as it applies to family dynamics.

Grunwald, B. B., & McAbee, H. (1985). *Guiding the family.* Muncie, IN: Accelerated Development.
These were students and coworkers of Dreikurs. In this book, clear, concise guidelines are presented for conducting family counseling from an Adlerian perspective with families from different backgrounds and with varied problems. Included are verbatim transcripts of what Adlerian family counselors actually do during sessions. A wonderful text for graduate students.

Hoffman, E. (1994). *The drive for self: Alfred Adler and the founding of Individual Psychology.* Reading, MA: Addison-Wesley.
This is probably the best biography of Alfred Adler available, or ever written. Hoffman examines, in detail, Adler's childhood influences, cultural and economic background, and theoretical development. A wonderful piece of scholarship that is very well written.

Mosak, H. H., & Maniacci, M.P. (1995). The case of Roger. In D. Wedding & R.J. Corsini (Eds.), *Case studies in psychotherapy* (2nd ed., pp.23–49). Itasca, IL: F. E. Peacock.
This is a transcript of brief psychotherapy (9 weeks) done before a live graduate student audience at an Adlerian training institute. The Adlerian tactics of life style assessment, interpretation, The Question, humor, encouragement, dream interpretation, and many others are demonstrated.

Mosak, H. H., & Maniacci, M.P. (1998). *Tactics in counseling and psychotherapy.* Itasca, IL: F. E. Peacock.
A useful manual designed to discuss what to do when therapists find themselves in various situations with certain clients. Over 100 tactics are described, almost all with actual case examples demonstrating their use.

Powers, R. L., & Griffith, J. (1987). *Understanding life-style: The psycho-clarity© process.* Chicago: Americas Institute of Adlerian Studies.
This a very good manual about how to conduct an initial interview and life style assessment interview. Included are forms needed to do the work, consent forms, billing agreements, and extremely useful transcripts detailing the "nuts and bolts" of how the process unfolds.

Sherman, R., & Dinkmeyer, D. (1987). *Systems of family therapy: An Adlerian integration.* New York: Brunner/Mazel.
This book examines Adlerian family therapy and describes its theoretical underpinnings and practical applications. Included is something unique: five chapters written by experts in family therapy who received training in both Adlerian family therapy and one other system, such as structural family therapy or strategic family therapy. This books demonstrates how Adlerian family therapy can be integrative and serve as a basis for mastering other systems of family therapy. A very good book.

Shulman, B. H., & Mosak, H.H. (1988). *Manual for life style assessment.* Muncie, IN: Accelerated Development.
This is *the* text for collecting, interpreting, and summarizing family constellation and early recollection material. It is written both as a theoretical textbook and a clinical manual.

Adlerian and cognitive therapies: Towards an integrative dialogue [special issue]. (1997). *Journal of Cognitive Psychotherapy, 11*(3).
In 1997, several theorists and clinicians from Adlerian, cognitive-behavioral, and constructionist backgrounds began a dialogue exploring the theoretical and clinical similarities and differences between Adlerian and cognitive psychotherapies. This special

issue explores their dialogue and points to future directions both Adlerians and cognitive therapists may want to explore.

Sperry, L., & Carlson, J. (Eds.). (1996). *Psychopathology and psychotherapy: From DSM-IV diagnosis to treatment* (2nd ed.). Washington, DC: Accelerated Development.
This edited book explores the *DSM-IV* from an Adlerian perspective. As noted often throughout this text and annotated bibliography, Adlerian psychology is extremely useful for theoretical integration. The editors have asked experts in the field to write about how Adlerian formulations can be used to both understand and develop a treatment plan that not only is theoretically solid but incorporates the *DSM-IV* model. A very helpful manual.

☐ Glossary

Behaviorism: A theory of personality and psychotherapy that stresses observable behavior and learning. The environmental influences upon the organism are emphasized, and therefore remediation is seen as directed to changing the environmental influences themselves through tactics such as reinforcement, punishment, and reward.

Cognitive therapy: A system of psychotherapy that assumes that individuals' dysfunctional behavior stems from their erroneous thinking about life, themselves, and the future. The focus of intervention is primarily directed to changing people's thoughts.

Community feeling: The more accurate translation of the German phrase *Gemeinschaftsgefühl*. A broader concept than the traditionally translated phrase, *social interest*, community feeling means a sense of commitment to and respect for the world at large, including but not limited to the social sphere of activity.

Compensation: The overcoming of deficit, physical or social through achievement, even excellence, in the area of the deficit or in another area. The deficit may be real, perceived, or imagined.

Consequences (natural and logical): A technique used by Adlerians, particularly those influenced by Dreikurs, in which individuals are allowed to experience the outcome of their actions or intentions. A natural consequence requires no active intervention and teaches the natural order of life; a logical consequence is established in advance by the parties involved and entails allowing people to experience the logically related outcomes of their actions, thereby teaching the social order of life.

Constructionism: A new trend in cognitive therapy. Individuals are not seen as passive receivers of stimulation from the environment, but rather as active agents who are constantly adapting to and influencing their environments. Therapists therefore do not question the accuracy of patients' thoughts (as in cognitive therapy) as much as they examine the consequences of having such beliefs.

Degree of activity: The amount of energy a person uses in solving the challenges of life. Though existing along a continuum, Adler generally spoke of people having either high or low degrees of activity.

Discouragement: In Adlerian psychology, the process by which individuals begin to doubt not only their place in their social world but their ability to usefully compensate for or cope with life's challenges.

Distancing: A safeguarding device by which people avoid a task or situation in order to protect their self-esteem.

Early recollections: Single, specific events remembered from under the age of 10 years. These events can be visually recalled and are used by Adlerians as a projective technique.

Encouragement: The inverse of discouragement. The individual believes in his or her effi-
cacy and feels optimistic about his or her place in the world.

Ethical convictions: One of the four component parts of the life style (the other three
being the self-concept, the self-ideal, and the *Weltbild*). Summarized as convictions
centering around "it is good to . . ." or "it is right to . . ." or "it is bad to . . ." or "it is
wrong to . . ." and so forth.

Existentialism: The system of psychotherapy and philosophy that examines the lived, experienced realities of humans. Generally speaking, existentialism accepts life's realities and attempts to look at how people cope with those givens of existence.

Family constellation: The early childhood social environment within the family. Generally
speaking, it entails the sibling array, parental guiding lines, and other role models and
alliances the child may have formed.

Fictional final goal: The end point of our striving. The point towards which we move in
order to assure our belonging, equivalent to the conviction in the life style called the
self-ideal.

General Diagnosis: The initial interview. The process by which Adlerians summarize the
current situation of the client as it is operating in the here and now.

Holism: The assumption in Adlerian psychology that people are different than the sum of
their parts. It entails looking at people as individuals, and not as parts or part-func-
tions (e.g., id, ego, drives, emotions).

Identification: The process by which people select others to model, imitate, or in general,
"be like."

Idiographic: The individual case. The single, specific dynamics of a particular situation.

Inferiority: An actual, observable function or system that falls short of some objective
standard. It is contextual and measurable, that is, it can change depending upon what
is measured.

Inferiority complex: A behavioral manifestation of a subjective feeling of inferiority. People with inferiority complexes avoid situations because they fear exposing their feelings of inferiority.

Inferiority feeling: A subjective evaluation; when the self-concept falls short of the self-
ideal or is not congruent with the self-ideal or ethical convictions.

Life style (*or* style of life): The attitudinal set of an individual. The set of convictions people develop that directs how they will belong. It is composed of four component parts:
self-concept, self-ideal, *Weltbild*, and ethical convictions.

Life style assessment: The method, pioneered by Dreikurs and furthered by others, that in-
vestigates the early childhood situation and early recollections of individuals in counseling or psychotherapy. The counselor's or therapist's formulations are then given
back to the individuals for their feedback and is used as a basis for treatment plan-
ning. Typically it is done as part of the Special Diagnosis.

Life tasks (*or* tasks of life): The challenges people must meet in order to function effectively. There are six tasks: occupation, social, love and sex, self, spiritual, and parenting and family.

Movement: This is akin to the concept of behavior. What an individual does in relation to
his or her goal.

Nomothetic: The general rule. The general dynamics of typical situations.

Organ inferiority: An organ or organ system that is deficient in form or structure. It is inherited and therefore subject to the law of compensation.

Phenomenology: A methodology in psychology and philosophy that examines the perceptions of the individual. It is a cornerstone of existentialism and Adlerian psychology.

Projection: The attribution of one's faults to others. It has a somewhat different meaning
when related to projective testing.

Psychology of use: The assumption that psychological processes are not static and therefore are more beneficially conceptualized as being used by individuals in order to further movement towards their goals. In the language of a psychology of use, for example, one would not say someone has a bad temper, but rather that he or she uses temper to move towards his or her goal.

Resistance: What occurs when the goals of two people, typically the patient and the psychotherapist, do not align.

Safeguarding: The process by which people evade challenges in order to defend their self-esteem. In other systems, this is known as a defense.

Self-concept: All of the convictions in the life style about what "I am . . ." or what "I am not . . ." One of the four component parts of the life style, the other three being the self-ideal, the ethical convictions, and the *Weltbild*.

Self-ideal: All of the convictions in the life style about what "I should be . . ." or what "I should not be . . ." in order to find my place and have significance. One of the four component parts of the life style, the other three being the self-concept, the ethical convictions, and the *Weltbild*. Equivalent to the final, fictional goal.

Shock: The reaction people have to situations for which they are unprepared. Similar to Freud's notion of trauma. Shock is both objective, in that something occurs that triggers the response, and relative, in that it is partially formed by the biases and subjective opinions of what is happening to the individual. In current clinical terminology, it is called "stress."

Sideshows: The evasions and detours individuals create in order to deflect attention away from their inadequacies and onto some matter of relative unimportance.

Social interest: An inadequate translation of the German phrase *"Gemeinschaftsgefuhl."* *Community feeling* would now be considered the more accurate translation. Roughly defined, it means an interest in the interest of others; the empathic bonding people feel for each other and the responsible actions and attitudes they take towards each other.

Special Diagnosis: The detailed, idiographic inquiry into the unique history of the individual. For contemporary Adlerians, it typically involves a life style assessment.

The Question: The assessment technique that asks patients the question, "What would be different in your life if you didn't have these symptoms?" or, "If I could wave a magic wand over your head and make your symptoms disappear, what would be different?" or, "If a miracle happened and you woke up and your problem no longer existed, what would be different?" Generally, it serves two purposes: to find out what the patient is avoiding and to aid in the differential diagnosis of somatic from psychogenic symptoms.

Teleology: Purposiveness in Adlerian psychology, the fictional final goal that organizes behavior.

Transference: In Adlerian psychology, the consistency of the life style as played out in therapy. The convictions about how to belong that operate outside of the psychotherapy eventually operate within the psychotherapy.

Weltbild: A German phrase that approximately translates to "picture of the world." One of the four component parts of the life style (the other three being the self-concept, the self-ideal, and the ethical convictions). All of the convictions about the "not me." The convictions that complete the phrases "life is . . ." or "people are . . ." or "men/women are . . ." and so forth.

REFERENCES

Adler, A. (1898). *Gesundheitsbuch für die Schneidergewerbe* [Healthbook for the tailor's trade]. Berlin: C. Heymanns.

Adler, A. (1908). Das Aggressionstrieb im Leben und in der Neurose [The aggression drive in life and in the neurosis]. *Fortschritte der Medizin, 26,* 577–584.

Adler, A. (1911). "Verdrängung" ünd "mannlichen Protest:" Ihre Rolle und Bedeutung für die neurotische Dynamik ["Repression" and "masculine protest": Their role and significance for the neurotic dynamic]. In A. Adler & C. Fürtmuller (Eds.), *Heilen und Bilden* (pp. 103–114). Munich: Ernst Reinhardt.

Adler, A. (1917). *Study of organ inferiority and its psychical compensation* (S.E. Jelliffe, Trans.). New York: Nervous and Mental Diseases Co. (Original work published 1907)

Adler, A. (1923). Psychische Kausalität [Psychic Causality]. *Internationale Zeitschrift für Individualpsychologie, 2*(6), 38.

Adler, A. (1924a). Training? *Internationale Zeitschrift für Individualpsychologie, 2*(6), 39.

Adler, A. (1924b). Über Weltanschauung. *Internationale Zeitschrift für Individualpsychologie, 2*(6), 38.

Adler, A. (1929a). *The case of Miss R.: The interpretation of a life story* (E. Jensen & F. Jensen, Trans.). New York: Greenberg.

Adler, A. (1929b). *Individualpsychologie in der Schule: Vorlesungen für Lehrer und Erzieher* [Individual Psychology in the school: lectures for teachers]. Frankfurt: Fisher Taschenbuch.

Adler, A. (1929c). *The science of living.* New York: Greenberg.

Adler, A. (1930a). *The pattern of life.* New York: Cosmopolitan.

Adler, A. (1930b). *Das Problem der Homosexualität: Erotisches Training und erotischer Rückzug* [The problem of homosexuality: Erotic training and erotic retreat]. Leipzig: S. Hirzel.

Adler, A. (1934). Lecture to the Medical Society of Individual Psychology, London, May 17, 1934. *Individual Psychology Medical Pamphlets, 13,* 11–24.

Adler, A. (1935). The fundamental views of Individual Psychology. *International Journal of Individual Psychology, 1*(1), 5–8.

Adler, A. (1936). On the interpretation of dreams. *International Journal of Individual Psychology, 2*(1), 3–16.

Adler, A. (1939). Sur la "protestation virile." [On the "masculine protest"]. *Courage, 2*(1), 8–10.

Adler, A. (1947). How I chose my career. *Individual Psychology Bulletin, 6,* 9–11.

Adler, A. (1950). Foreword. In R. Dreikurs, *Fundamentals of Adlerian psychology* (p. vii). New York: Greenberg. (Original work published 1933)

Adler, A. (1956). *The Individual Psychology of Alfred Adler* (H. L. Ansbacher & R. R. Ansbacher, Eds.). New York: Basic Books.

Adler, A. (1957). *Understanding human nature* (W. B. Wolfe, Trans.). Greenwich, CT: Premier Books. (Original work published 1927)

Adler, A. (1958). *What life should mean to you* (A. Porter, Ed.). New York: Prestige. (Original work published 1931)

Adler, A. (1963). *The problem child* (G. Daniels, Trans.). New York: Capricorn Books. (Original work published 1930)

Adler, A. (1964a). The case of Mrs. A. In H. L. Ansbacher & R. R. Ansbacher (Eds.), *Superiority and social interest* (pp. 159–190). Evanston, IL: Northwestern University Press. (Original work published 1931)

Adler, A. (1964b). The differences between Individual Psychology and psychoanalysis. In H. L. Ansbacher & R. R. Ansbacher (Eds.), *Superiority and social interest* (pp. 205–218). Evanston, IL: Northwestern University Press. (Original work published 1931)

Adler, A. (1964c). Complex compulsion as part of personality and neurosis. In H. L. Ansbacher & R. R. Ansbacher (Eds.), *Superiority and social interest* (pp. 71–80). Evanston, IL: Northwestern University Press. (Original work published 1935)

Adler, A. (1964d). *Problems of neurosis: A book of case histories* (P. Mairet, Ed.). New York: Harper & Row. (Original work published 1929)

Adler, A. (1964e). The progress of mankind. In H. L. Ansbacher & R. R. Ansbacher (Eds), *Superiority and social interest* (pp. 23–28). Evanston, IL: Northwestern University Press. (Original work published 1937)

Adler, A. (1964f). *Social interest: A challenge to mankind* (J. Linton & R. Vaughan, Trans.). New York: Capricorn. (Original work published 1933)

Adler, A. (1964g). *Superiority and social interest* (H. L. Ansbacher & R. R. Ansbacher, Eds.). Evanston, IL: Northwestern University Press.

Adler, A. (1970). *The education of children* (E. Jensen & F. Jensen, Trans.). South Bend, IN: Gateway Editions. (Original work published 1930)

Adler, A. (1978). *Cooperation between the sexes: Writings on women, love and marriage, sexuality and its disorders* (H. L. Ansbacher & R. R. Ansbacher, Eds.). New York: Doubleday.

Adler, A. (1983a). The masculine attitude in female neurotics. In *The practice and theory of individual psychology* (pp. 109–143). Totowa, NJ: Littlefield, Adams. (Original work published 1910)

Adler, A. (1983b). *The neurotic constitution* (B. Glueck & J. E. Lind, Trans.). Salem, NH: Ayer. (Original work published 1912)

Adler, A. (1983c). *The pattern of life.* Chicago: Alfred Adler Institute. (Original work published 1930)

Adler, A. (1983d). *The practice and theory of Individual Psychology* (P. Radin, Trans.). Totowa, NJ: Littlefield, Adams. (Original work published 1920)

Adler, A. (1983e). The problem of distance. In A. Adler (1983), *The practice and theory of Individual Psychology* (pp. 100–108). Totowa, NJ: Littlefield, Adams. (Original work published 1914)

Adler, A. (1988a). The child's inner life and a sense of community (L. Fleisher, Trans.). *Individual Psychology, 44,* 417–423. (Original work published 1917)

Adler, A. (1988b). Problem children (L. Fleisher, Trans.). *Individual Psychology, 44,* 406–416. (Original work published 1926)

Adler, A., & Associates. (1930). *Guiding the child* (B. Ginzburg, Trans.). London: Allen & Unwin.

Adler, K. A. (1961). Depression in the light of Individual Psychology. *Journal of Individual Psychology, 17,* 56–67.

Adler, K. A. (1963). Foreword. In *The problem child* (pp. vii–viii). New York: Capricorn Books.

Adler, K. A., & Deutsch, D. (Eds.) (1959). *Essays in Individual Psychology.* New York: Grove Press.

Adler, R. (1899, July–December). Sollen die Frauen sich den Studiuum der Medizin zuwenden? *Dokumente der Frauen* [Should women devote themselves to the study of medicine?]. 289–293.

Adlerian and cognitive psychotherapies: Towards an integrative dialogue [Special issue]. (1997). *Journal of Cognitive Psychotherapy, 11*(3).

Alexander, F. G., & French, T. M. (1946). *Psychoanalytic therapy.* New York: Ronald Press.

Allen, T. W. (1970, Summer). The evaluation of a program of special classes for "disruptive" children in an urban school system. *Community Mental Health.*

Allers, R. (1961). *Existentialism and psychiatry.* Springfield, IL: Charles C. Thomas.

Allport, G. W. (1955). *Becoming.* New Haven, CT: Yale University Press.

Allred, G. H. (1974). *On the level: With self, family, society.* Provo, UT: Brigham Young Univesity Press.

American Psychiatric Association. (1994). *Diagnostic and statistical manual of mental disorders* (4th ed., rev.). Washington, DC: Author.

Ansbacher, H. L. (1951). Causality and indeterminism according to Alfred Adler and some current American personality theories. *Individual Psychology Bulletin, 9,* 96–107.

Ansbacher, H. L. (1959a). A key to existence. *Journal of Individual Psychology, 15,* 141–142.

Ansbacher, H. L. (1959b). The significance of the socio-economic status of the patients of Freud and Adler. *American Journal of Psychotherapy, 13,* 376–382.

Ansbacher, H. L. (1962). Was Adler a disciple of Freud? A reply. *Journal of Individual Psychology, 18,* 126–135.

Ansbacher, H. L. (1964). Introduction to the Torchbook edition. In A. Adler (1964), *Problems of neurosis: A book of case histories* (pp. ix–xxx). New York: Harper & Row.

Ansbacher, H. L. (1965). *Sensus privatus versus sensus communis. Journal of Individual Psychology, 21,* 48–50.

Ansbacher, H. L. (1966). Love and violence in the view of Adler. *Humanitas, 2,* 109–127.

Ansbacher, H. L. (1967). Life style: A historical and systematic review. *Journal of Individual Psychology, 23,* 191–212.

Ansbacher, H. L. (1968). The concept of social interest. *Journal of Individual Psychology, 24,* 131–141.

Ansbacher, H. L. (Ed.). (1972). Adlerian techniques of psychotherapy: Proceedings of the Fourth Brief Psychotherapy Conference [Special issue]. *Journal of Individual Psychology, 28*(2), 121–122.

Ansbacher, H. L. (1992a). Alfred Adler, pioneer in prevention of mental disorders. *Individual Psychology, 48,* 3–34.

Ansbacher, H. L. (1992b). Alfred Adler's concepts of community feeling and of social interest and the relevance of community feeling for old age. *Individual Psychology, 48,* 402–412.

Ansbacher, H. L., & Ansbacher, R. R. (Eds.). (1978). *Cooperation between the sexes.* Garden City, NY: Doubleday.

Arciniega, M., & Newlon, B. J. (1983). Cross-cultural family counseling. In O. C. Christensen & T. G. Schramski (Eds.), *Adlerian family counseling: A manual for counselor, educator and psychotherapist* (pp. 279–292). Minneapolis, MN: Educational Media.

Aristotle. (1941). *Metaphysica* [The Metaphysics](W. D. Ross, Trans.). In R. McKeon (Ed.), *The basic works of Aristotle* (pp. 689–926). New York: Random House. (Original work published circa 350 BC)

Armstrong, K. (1993). *A history of God.* New York: Ballantine Books.

Attarian, P. (1978). Early recollections: Predictors of vocational choice. *Journal of Individual Psychology, 34*(1), 56–62.

Aubry, W. E. (1972). Life style analysis in marriage counseling. *Marriage and Family Counseling Quarterly, 8*(1), 39–46.

Aurelius, M. (1964). *Meditations* (M. Staniforth, Trans.). New York: Penguin. (Original work published 169)

Barber, K. E. (1972, December). *The family council* (Pacific Northwest Cooperative Extension Bulletin #127).

Bartholow, R. (1969). How to hold a family council. *Oregon Society of Individual Psychology Newsletter, 10*(2), 9–ll.

Basch, M. F. (1988). *Understanding psychotherapy.* New York: Basic Books.

Beck, A. T. (1976). *Cognitive therapy and the emotional disorders.* New York: International Universities Press.

Beecher, W. (1950). Guilt feelings: Masters of our fate, or our servants? *Individual Psychology Bulletin, 8,* 22–31.

Beecher, W., & Beecher, M. (1951). What makes an Adlerian? *Individual Psychology Bulletin, 9,* 146–148.

Beecher, W., & Beecher, M. (1955). *Parents on the run.* Marina Del Ray, CA: Devorss.

Beecher, W., & Beecher, M. (1987). *The mark of Cain: An anatomy of jealousy.* Richardson, TX: Willard & Marguerite Beecher Foundation. (Original work published 1971)

Berger, E. M. (1952). The relation between acceptance of self and expressed acceptance of others. *Journal of Abnormal and Social Psychology, 47,* 778–782.

Bergson, H. (1956). *The two sources of morality and religion* (R. A. Brereton, Trans., with assistance from W. H. Carter). Garden City, NY: Doubleday Anchor. (Original work published 1932)

Berne, E. (1964). *Games people play.* New York: Grove Press.

Berne, E. (1972). *What do you say after you say hello?* New York: Grove Press.

Bertallanfy, L. v. (1968). *General systems theory.* New York: Braziller.

Bieliauskas, V. J. (1972). *The House-Tree-Person (H-T-P) research review.* Beverly Hills, CA: Western Psychological Services.

Bieliauskas, V. J. (1974). A new look at "masculine protest." *Journal of Individual Psychology, 30*(1), 92–97.

Birnbaum, F. (1935). The Individual Psychological Experimental School in Vienna. *American Journal of Individual Psychology, 12,* 1–11.

Birnbaum, F. (1961). Frankl's existential psychology from the viewpoint of Individual Psychology. *Journal of Individual Psychology, 17,* 162–166.

Boldt, R. (1994). *Lifestyle types and therapeutic resistance: An Adlerian model for prediction and intervention of characterological resistance in therapy.* Unpublished doctoral dissertation, Adler School of Professional Psychology, Chicago.

Bonime, W. (1962). *The clinical use of dreams.* New York: Basic Books.

Bottome, P. (1934). *Private worlds.* Boston: Houghton Mifflin.

Bottome, P. (1957). *Alfred Adler: A portrait from life.* New York: Vanguard Press.

Bowlby, J. (1983). *Attachment* (2nd ed.). New York: Basic Books.

Brown, J. F. (1976). *Practical applications of the personality priorities.* Clinton, MD: B. & F. Associates.

Brown, P. (1995). *The reliability and validity of "The Question" in the differential diagnosis of somatogenic and psychogenic disorders.* Unpublished doctoral dissertation, Adler School of Professional Psychology, Chicago.

Bruck, A. (1950). Do we need the concept of guilt feelings? *Individual Psychology Bulletin, 8,* 44–48.

Carlson, J., & Sperry, L. (1998). *The disordered couple.* Bristol, PA: Brunner/Mazel.

Catlin, N. (1976). The family council. In J. W. Croake, H. O. Protinsky & N. Catlin (Eds.), *Adolescence: Developmentally* (pp. 86–90). Bremerton, WA: Economy Printing.

Christensen, O. C., & Schramski, T. G. (Eds.). (1983). *Adlerian family counseling: A manual for counselor, educator, and psychotherapist.* Minneapolis, MN: Educational Media.

Clance, P. R. (1986). *The impost phenomenon: Overcoming the fear that haunts your success.* New York: Bantam.

Colby, K. M. (1951). On the disagreement between Freud and Adler. *American Imago, 8,* 229–238.

Colby, K. M. (1956). Discussion of Adler's ideas by Freud and others. In A. Adler, *The Individual Psychology of Alfred Adler* (H. L. Ansbacher & R. R. Ansbacher, Eds.) (pp. 69–75). New York: Basic Books.

Corsini, R. J. (1966). *Roleplaying in psychotherapy: A manual.* Chicago: Aldine.

Corsini, R. J. (1967). Let's invent a first-aid kit for marriage problems. *Consultant, 7,* 40.

Corsini, R. J. (1971). Group psychotherapy. In A. G. Nikelly (Ed.), *Techniques for behavior change* (pp. 111–115). Springfield, IL: Charles C. Thomas.

Corsini, R. J. (1977). Individual Education. *Journal of Individual Psychology, 33,* 21–29.

Corsini, R. J. (1987). Adlerian groups. In S. Long (Ed.), *Six group therapies* (pp. 1–47). New York: Plenum.

Corsini, R. J., & Painter, G. (1975). *The practical parent.* New York: Harper & Row.

Credner, L. (1936). Safeguards. *International Journal of Individual Psychology, 2*(3), 95–102.

Croake, J. W., & Robertshaw, D. (1987). *Toward an Adlerian theory of learning.* Seattle, WA: Seattle Institute of Adlerian Studies.

Cucher, L. M. (1976). The art of Adlerian art therapy. *Individual Psychologist, 13*(2), 37–43.

Dailey, C. A. (1966). The experimental study of clinical guessing. *Journal of Individual Psychology, 22,* 65–76.

Davis, A., & Havighurst, R. J. (1947). *Father of the man.* Boston: Houghton Mifflin.

de Shazer, S. (1988). *Clues: Investigating solutions in brief therapy.* New York: W. W. Norton.

Deutsch, D. (1967). Group psychotherapy with married couples. *Individual Psychologist, 4*(2), 56–62.

Dewey, E. (1971). Family atmosphere. In A. G. Nikelly (Ed.), *Techniques for behavior change* (pp. 41–47). Springfield, IL: Charles C. Thomas.

Dinkmeyer, D., & Carlson, J. (1984). *Time for a better marriage.* Circle Pines, MN: American Guidance Service.

Dinkmeyer, D., & Carlson, J. (1989). *Taking time for love.* New York: Prentice Hall.

Dinkmeyer, D. C., Dinkmeyer, D. C., Jr., & Sperry, L. (1987). *Adlerian counseling and psychotherapy* (2nd ed.). Columbus, OH: Merrill.

Dinkmeyer, D. C., & Dreikurs, R. (1963). *Encouraging children to learn.* Englewood Cliffs, NJ: Prentice-Hall.

Dinkmeyer, D. C., & Losoncy, L. (1996). *The skills of encouragement.* Delray Beach, FL: St. Lucie Press.

Dinkmeyer, D., & McKay, G. D. (1973). *Raising a responsible child.* New York: Simon & Schuster.

Dinkmeyer, D., & McKay, G. D. (1982). *The parent's handbook: Systematic training for effective parenting (STEP).* Circle Pines, MN: American Guidance Service.

Dinkmeyer, D., Sr., McKay, G. D., & Dinkmeyer, D., Jr. (1980). *STET: Systematic training for effective teaching.* Circle Pines, MN: American Guidance Service.

Dreikurs, R. (1944). The meaning of dreams. *Chicago Medical School Quarterly, 5*(3), 4–6, 25–26.

Dreikurs, R. (1945). Psychological differentiation of psychopathological disorders. *Individual Psychology Bulletin, 4,* 35–48.

Dreikurs, R. (1946). *The challenge of marriage.* New York: Duell, Sloan and Pearce.

Dreikurs, R. (1948a). *The challenge of parenthood.* New York: Hawthorn.

Dreikurs, R. (1948b). The socio-psychological dynamics of physical disability. *Journal of Social Issues, 4,* 39–54.

Dreikurs, R. (1950a). *Fundamentals of Adlerian psychology.* New York: Greenberg. (Original work published 1933)

Dreikurs, R. (1950b). Guilt feelings as an excuse. *Individual Psychology Bulletin, 8,* 12–21.

Dreikurs, R. (1951). The function of emotions. *Christian Register, 130,* 11–14, 24.

Dreikurs, R. (1954). The psychological interview in medicine. *American Journal of Individual Psychology, 10,* 99–122.

Dreikurs, R. (1956). Adlerian psychotherapy. In F. Fromm-Reichmann & J. L. Moreno (Eds.), *Progress in psychotherapy* (pp. 111–118). New York: Grune & Stratton.

Dreikurs, R. (1958). A reliable differential diagnosis of psychological or somatic disturbances. *International Record of Medicine, 171,* 238–242.

Dreikurs, R. (1959). Early experiments with group psychotherapy. *American Journal of Psychotherapy, 13,* 882–891.

Dreikurs, R. (1960). Are psychological schools of thought outdated? *Journal of Individual Psychology, 16,* 3–10.

Dreikurs, R. (1962). Can you be sure the disease is functional? *Consultant.*

Dreikurs, R. (1965). Music therapy. In N. J. Long, W. C. Morse, & R. G. Neuman (Eds.), *Conflict in the classroom: The education of emotionally disturbed children* (pp. 199–202). Belmont, CA: Wadsworth.

Dreikurs, R. (1967). *Psychodynamics, psychotherapy and counseling.* Chicago: Alfred Adler Institute.

Dreikurs, R. (1971). *Social equality: The challenge of today.* Chicago: Alfred Adler Institute.

Dreikurs, R. (1972). Dreikurs' sayings. *Individual Psychologist, 9*(2), 38–45.

Dreikurs, R. (1973). The private logic. In H. H. Mosak (Ed.), *Alfred Adler: His influence on psychology today* (pp. 19–32). Park Ridge, NJ: Noyes Press.

Dreikurs, R., Corsini, R., Lowe, R., & Sonstegard, M. (Eds.). (1959). *Adlerian family counseling.* Eugene, OR: University of Oregon.

Dreikurs, R., & Crocker, D. (1955). Music therapy with psychotic children. *Music therapy, 5,* 62–73.

Dreikurs, R., Gould, S., & Corsini, R. J. (1974). *Family council.* Chicago: Henry Regnery.

Dreikurs, R., Grunwald, B. B., & Pepper, F. C. (1982). *Maintaining sanity in the classroom* (2nd ed.). New York: Harper & Row.

Dreikurs, R., & Mosak, H. H. (1966). The tasks of life I: Adler's three tasks. *Individual Psychologist, 4,* 18–22.

Dreikurs, R., & Mosak, H. H. (1967). The tasks of life II: The fourth life task. *Individual Psychologist, 4,* 51–55.

Dreikurs, R., Mosak, H. H., & Shulman, B. H. (1984). *Multiple psychotherapy.* Chicago: Alfred Adler Institute.

Dreikurs, R., & Soltz, V. (1964). *Children: The challenge.* New York: Duell, Sloan & Pearce.

Dreikurs, S., & Shulman, B. H. (1969). Art therapy for psychiatric patients. *Perspectives in Psychiatric Care, 7*(3), 134–143.

Dubelle, S. (1997, September). Part two: Excerpts from an interview with Heinz Ansbacher, Ph.D. *The Quarterly: Publication of the Adlerian Psychology Association of British Columbia,* 5–7.

Ellenberger, H. F. (1970). *The discovery of the unconscious.* New York: Basic Books.

Ellis, A. (1957). Rational psychotherapy and Individual Psychology. *Journal of Individual Psychology, 13*(1), 38–44.

Ellis, A. (1973). *Humanistic psychotherapy.* New York: McGraw-Hill.

Ellis, A. (1990). *Reason and emotion in psychotherapy.* New York: Citadel Press.

Espenak, L. (1981). *Dance therapy.* Springfield, IL: Charles C. Thomas.

Euripides. (1960). *Electra.* (M. Hadas & J. McLean, Trans). In *Ten plays by Euripides* (pp. 205–239). New York: Bantam. (Original work published 413 BC)

Farau, A. (1964). Individual Psychology and existentialism. *Individual Psychologist, 2*(1), 1–8.

Farley, F. (1986, May). The big T in personality. *Psychology Today,* 45–52.

The father of self-help. (1995, May/June). *Psychology Today.*

Feichtinger, F. (1950). The psychology of guilt feelings. *Individual Psychology Bulletin, 8,* 39–43.

Feldmann, E. (1972). Thirty days with Alfred Adler. *Journal of Individual Psychology, 28,* 81–89.

Festinger, L. (1957). *A theory of cognitive dissonance.* Palo Alto, CA: Stanford University.

Foley, V. D. (1989). Family therapy. In R. J. Corsini & D. Wedding (Eds.), *Current psychotherapies* (4th ed., pp. 455–500). Itasca, IL: F. E. Peacock.

Ford, D. H., & Urban, H. B. (1963). *Systems of psychotherapy: A comparative study.* New York: John Wiley & Sons.

Forgus, R., & Shulman, B. H. (1979). *Personality: A cognitive view.* Englewood Cliffs, NJ: Prentice-Hall.

Frankl, V. E. (1925). Psychotherapie und Weltanschauung. *Internationale Zeitschrift für Individualpsychologie* [Psychotherapy and philosophy of life]. *3,* 250–252.

Frankl, V. E. (1963). *Man's search for meaning.* Boston: Beacon Press.

Frankl, V. E. (1983). *The doctor and the soul.* New York: Vintage Books.

Freeman, A. (1993). Foreword. In L. Sperry & J. Carlson (Eds.), *Psychopathology and psychotherapy from diagnosis to treatment* (pp. iii–vi). Muncie, IN: Accelerated Development.

French, T. M. (1952). *The integration of behavior* (Vol. 2). Chicago: University of Chicago Press.

Freud, A. (1946). *The ego and the mechanisms of defense* (rev. ed.). London: Hogarth. (Original work published 1936)

Freud, S. (1950). *The question of lay analysis.* New York: W. W. Norton.

Freud, S. (1959). Analysis terminable and interminable. In *Collected papers* (vol. 5, pp. 316–357). New York: Basic Books. (Original work published 1937)

Freud, S. (1963). *Psychoanalysis and faith.* New York: Basic Books.

Freud, S. (1965). *The interpretation of dreams* (J. Strachey, Trans.). New York: Avon Books. (Original work published 1900)

Freund, H. (1928). Über Training [On training]. *Internationale Zeitschrift für Individualpsychologie, 6,* 370–373.

Friedman, M. (1996). *Type A behavior.* New York: Plenum.

Fromm, E. (1941). *Escape from freedom.* New York: Farrar & Reinhart.

Fromm, E. (1961). *Marx's concept of man.* New York: Frederick Ungar.

Furtmüller, C. (1964). Alfred Adler: A biographical essay. In A. Adler (1964), *Superiority and social interest* (pp. 309–393). Evanston, IL: Northwestern University Press.

Gazzaniga, M. S. (1985). *The social brain.* New York: Basic Books.

Geis, H. J. (1966). Guilt feelings and inferiority feelings: An experimental comparison. *Dissertation Abstracts, 13,* 8515.

Goethe, J. W. (1949). *Faust* (part one) (P. Wayne, Trans.). Baltimore: Penguin Books. (Original work published 1801)

Gold, L. (1979). Adler's theory of dreams: An holistic approach to interpretation. In B. Wolman (Ed.), *Handbook of dreams* (pp. 319–341). New York: Van Nostrand Reinhold.

Gold, L. (1981). Life style and dreams. In L. Baruth & D. Eckstein (Eds.), *Life style: Theory, practice and research* (2nd ed., pp. 24–30). Dubuque, IA: Kendall/Hunt.

Goldstein, K. (1963). *Human nature in the light of psychopathology.* New York: Schocken Books. (Original work published 1940)

Gottesfeld, H. (1966). Changes in feelings of powerlessness in a community action program. *Psychological Reports, 19,* 978.

Greenspoon, J. (1955). The reinforcing effect of two spoken sounds on the frequency of two responses. *American Journal of Psychology, 68,* 408–416.

Greven, G. M. (1957). Music as a tool in psychotherapy for children. *Music Therapy, 7,* 105–108.

Griffith, J. (1984). Adler's organ jargon. *Individual Psychology, 40,* 437–444.

Grunwald, B. B., & McAbee, H. (1985). *Guiding the family.* Muncie, IN: Accelerated Development.

Guidano, V. F., & Liotti, G. (1983). *Cognitive processes and emotional disorders.* New York: Guilford Press.

Gushurst, R. S. (1971). *The reliability and concurrent validity of an idiographic approach to early recollections.* Unpublished doctoral dissertation, University of Chicago.

Haley, J. (1976). *Problem-solving therapy.* New York: Harper Torchbooks.

Hansen, E. (1944–45). The child guidance clinic of Abraham Lincoln Center. *Individual Psychology Bulletin, 4,* 49–58.

Hapworth, W., Hapworth, M., & Heilman, J. R. (1993). *"Mom loved you best."* New York: Smithmark.

Harlow, H. (1958). The nature of love. *American Psychologist, 13,* 673–685.

Harris, T. A. (1967). *I'm OK—you're OK.* New York: Harper & Row.

Hart, J. L. (1977). The perils of the pleaser. In J. P. Madden (Ed.), *Loneliness: Issues of living in an age of stress for clergy and religion* (pp. 41–55). Whitinsville, MA: Affirmation Books.

Harvey, J. C., & Katz, C. (1986). *If I'm so successful, why do I feel like a fake? The imposter phenomenon.* New York: St. Martin's Press.

Heidegger, M. (1962). *Being and time.* (J. Macquarrie & E. Robinson, Trans.). New York: Harper & Row. (Original work published 1927)

Heidegger, M. (1977). On the essence of truth. In D. F. Krell (Ed. and Trans.), *Basic writings* (pp. 113–141). New York: Harper & Row. (Original work published 1943)

Herold, P. (1983). *Adlerian approaches to typology.* Unpublished master's thesis, Alfred Adler Institute, Chicago.

Heyligers-Gunning, C. I. (1970). Alles kan ook anders over de vervuiling [Everything can also be otherwise with respect to pollution]. *Mededelingenblad von de Nederlandse Werkgemeenschap voor Individualpsychologie, 19*(2), 4–8.

Hoffman, E. (1994). *The drive for self: Alfred Adler and the founding of Individual Psychology.* Reading, MA: Addison-Wesley.

Holmberg, J. (1972). *"We love to learn."* Rockford, IL: Rockford Public Schools.

Holt, H. (1967). Existential analysis, Freud and Adler. *Journal of Existentialism, 8,* 203–222.

Holub, M. (1928). *Geschwisterkampf* [Sibling rivalry]. Vienna: Moritz Perles.

Horney, K. (1945). *Our inner conflicts.* New York: W. W. Norton.

Horney, K. (1950). *Neurosis and human growth.* New York: W. W. Norton.

Horney, K. (1967). The flight from womanhood. In *Feminine psychology* (H. Kelman, Ed.) (pp. 54–70). New York: W. W. Norton. (Original work published 1926)

Husserl, E. (1962). *Ideas: General introduction to pure phenomenology.* (W. R. B. Gibson, Trans.). New York: Collier. (Original work published 1913)

Jahn, E., & Adler, A. (1964). Religion and Individual Psychology. In A. Adler (1964), *Superiority and social interest* (pp. 271–308). Evanston, IL: Northwestern University Press. (Original work published 1933)

James, W. (1890). *The principles of psychology.* New York: Holt.

Janet, P. (1924). *Principles of psychotherapy.* New York: Macmillan.

Johnson, E. L. (1966). Existential trends toward Individual Psychology. *Individual Psychologist, 3*(2), 11–13.

Johnson, S. (1973). On self-love and indolence. In A. M. Eastman et al. (Eds.), *The Norton reader* (3rd ed., pp. 579–583). New York: Norton. (Original work published 1751)

Jones, E. (1953, 1955, 1957). *The life and work of Sigmund Freud* (3 vols.). New York: Basic Books.

Jones, J. V., Jr. (1995). Constructivisim and Individual Psychology: Common ground for dialogue. *Individual Psychology, 51,* 231–243.

Karon, B. (1964). Suicidal tendency as the wish to hurt someone else, and resulting treatment technique. *Journal of Individual Psychology, 20,* 206–212.

Kazan, S. (1978). Adler's *Gemeinschaftsgefuhl* and Meyeroff's caring. *Journal of Individual Psychology, 34*(1), 3–10.

Kefir, N. (1972). *Priorities.* Unpublished manuscript.

Kefir, N., & Corsini, R. (1974). Dispositional sets: A contribution to typology. *Journal of Individual Psychology, 30,* 163–178.

Kelly, G. A. (1955). *A theory of personality.* New York: W. W. Norton.

Kern, R. M., Hawes, E. C., & Christensen, O. C. (Eds.) (1989). *Couples therapy: An Adlerian perspective.* Minneapolis, MN: Educational Media.

Kernberg, O. F. (1975). *Borderline conditions and pathological narcissism.* New York: Jason Aronson.

Kershaw-Bellemare, R., & Mosak, H. H. (1993). Adult children of alcoholics: An Adlerian perspective. *Journal of Alcohol & Drug Education, 38,*(3), 105–119.

Kohn, A. (1986). *No contest.* Boston: Houghton Mifflin.

Kohut, H. (1971). *The analysis of the self.* New York: International Universities Press.

Kohut, H. (1977). *The restoration of the self.* Madison, CT: International Universities Press.

Kopp, R. R. (1986). Styles of striving for significance with and without social interest: An Adlerian typology. *Individual Psychology, 42,* 17–25.

Kramer, H. C. (1947). Haufigkeit und Bedeutung von Minderwertigkeitsgefuhl in Psychose [Frequency and significance of inferiority feeling in psychosis]. *Internationale Zeitschrift fur Individualpsychologie, 16*(2), 65–74.

Krausz, E. O. (1959). The homeostatic function of dreams. *Individual Psychology News Letter, 9,* 48.

Krausz, E. O. (1973). Neurotic versus normal reaction categories. In H. H. Mosak (Ed.), *Alfred Adler: His influence on psychology today* (pp. 53–57). Park Ridge, NJ: Noyes Press.

Lazarsfeld, S. (1991). The courage for imperfection. *Individual Psychology, 47,* 93–96. (Original work published 1927)

Leman, K. (1985). *The birth order book.* New York: Dell.

Leman, K. (1987). *The pleasers.* Old Tappan, NJ: Fleming H. Revell.

Lerner, H. H. (1952). Methodological convergence and social action. *Journal of Social Issues, 8,* 75–80.

Lieberman, M. G. (1957). Childhood memories as a projective technique. *Journal of Projective Techniques, 21,* 32–36.

Lief, A. (Ed.) (1973). *The commonsense psychiatry of Dr. Alfred Meyer.* North Stratford, NH: Ayer.

Linden, G. W. (1993). Excuses, excuses! *Individual Psychology, 49,* 1–12.

Loewy, I. (1930). Small children in guidance clinics. In A. Adler & Associates, *Guiding the child* (pp. 157–165). New York: Greenberg.

Lombardi, D. N. (1973). Eight avenues of life style consistency. *Individual Psychologist, 10,* 5–9.

Losoncy, L. (1977). *Turning people on: How to be an encouraging person.* Englewood Cliffs, NJ: Prentice-Hall.

Mahoney, M. J. (1991). *Human change processes.* New York: Basic Books.

Maimonides, M. (1944). *Mishne Torah (Ha-yad ha-chazakah).*[Mishne Torah (The strong hand)]. New York: Hevro. (Original work published 1180)

Manaster, G. J. (1973). Cultural patterns of coping. In R. F. Peck et al. (Eds.), *Coping styles and achievement: A cross-national study of children* (Rep. Proj. HRD-167-55, OE-5-85-063). Austin, TX: University of Texas.

Manaster, G. J., & Corsini, R. J. (1982). *Individual Psychology: Theory and practice.* Itasca, IL: F.E. Peacock.

Manaster, G. J., Painter, G., Deutsch, J., & Overholt, B. (Eds.). (1977). *Alfred Adler: As we remember him.* Chicago: North American Society of Adlerian Psychology.

Mandell, S. (1942). An only girl among brothers. *Individual Psychology Bulletin, 2,* 25–30.

Maniacci, M. P. (1990). *An Adlerian interpretation of the Comprehensive System of the Rorschach inkblot test.* Unpublished doctoral dissertation, Alfred Adler Institute, Chicago.

Maniacci, M. P. (1991). Guidelines for developing social interest with clients in psychiatric day hospitals. *Individual Psychology, 47,* 177–188.

Maniacci, M. P. (1993). A primer of Individual Psychology. In L. Sperry & J. Carlson (Eds.), *Psychopathology and psychotherapy from diagnosis to treatment* (pp. 599–611). Muncie, IN: Accelerated Development.

Maniacci, M. P. (1996a). An introduction to brief therapy of the personality disorders. *Individual Psychology, 52,* 158–168.

Maniacci, M. P. (1996b). Mental disorders due to a general medical condition and other cognitive disorders. In L. Sperry & J. Carlson (Eds.), *Psychopathology and psychotherapy: From DSM-IV diagnosis to treatment* (2nd ed., pp. 51–75). Muncie, IN: Accelerated Development.

Maniacci, M. P., & Carlson, J. (1991). A model for Adlerian family interventions with the chronically mentally ill. *American Journal of Family Therapy, 19,* 237–249.

Maslow, A. H. (1962). Was Adler a disciple of Freud? *Journal of Individual Psychology, 18,* 125.

Maslow, A. H. (1970). *Motivation and personality.* New York: Harper & Row.

Massey, R. F. (1989). The philosophical compatibility of Adler and Berne. *Individual Psychology, 45,* 323–334.

Massey, R. F. (1990). Berne's transactional analysis as a neo-Freudian/neo-Adlerian perspective. *Transactional Analysis Journal, 10,* 173–186.

Massey, R. F. (1993). Neo-Adlerian constructs in Berne's transactional analysis. *Individual Psychology, 49,* 13–35.

May, R. (1983). *The discovery of being.* New York: W. W. Norton.

McIntyre, C. J. (1952). Acceptance by others and its relation to acceptance of self and others. *Journal of Abnormal and Social Psychology, 47,* 624–625.

Meiers, J. (1972). Protection environmentale [Environmental protection]. *Bulletin, Société Française de Psychologie Adlérienne, 14,* 47–49.

Mele, E. (1993). *A framework for an Adlerian interpretation of Thematic Apperception Test profiles associated with program completion.* Unpublished doctoral dissertation, Adler School of Professional Psychology, Chicago, IL.

Menninger, K. (1973). *Whatever became of sin?* New York: Hawthorn.

Miles, J. (1996). *God: A biography.* New York: Vintage Books.

Miller, G. (1967). On turning psychology over to the unwashed. *Psychology Today, 3*(7), 53–54.

Miller, L. (1990). *Inner natures.* New York: Ballantine.

Millon, T. (1981). *Disorders of personality.* New York: John Wiley & Sons.

Milton, J. (1957). *Paradise lost.* In M. Y. Hughes (Ed.), *John Milton: Complete poems and major prose* (pp. 173–469). Indianapolis: Odyssey Press. (Original work published 1674)

Minuchin, S. (1974). *Families and family therapy.* New York: Basic Books.

Mosak, H. H. (1950). *Evaluation in psychotherapy: A study of some current measures.* Unpublished doctoral dissertation, University of Chicago.

Mosak, H. H. (1954). The psychological attitude in rehabilitation. *American Archives of Rehabilitation Therapy, 2,* 9–10.

Mosak, H. H. (1958). Early recollections as a projective technique. *Journal of Projective Techniques, 22,* 302–311.

Mosak, H. H. (1959). The getting type, a parsimonious social interpretation of the oral character. *Journal of Individual Psychology, 15,* 193–198.

Mosak, H. H. (1965). Predicting the relationship to the psychotherapist from early recollections. *Journal of Individual Psychology, 21,* 77–81.

Mosak, H. H. (1968). The interrelatedness of the neuroses through central themes. *Journal of Individual Psychology, 24,* 67–70.

Mosak, H. H. (1971a). Lifestyle. In A. G. Nikelly (Ed.), *Techniques for behavior change* (pp. 77–81). Springfield, IL: Charles C. Thomas.

Mosak, H. H. (1971b). Strategies for behavior change in schools: Consultation strategies. *The Counseling Psychologist, 3*(1), 58–62.

Mosak, H. H. (1972). Life style assessment: A demonstration focused upon family constellation. *Journal of Individual Psychology, 28,* 232–247.

Mosak, H. H. (1973). The controller: A social interpretation of the anal character. In H. H. Mosak (Ed.), *Alfred Adler: His influence upon psychology today* (pp. 43–52). Park Ridge, NJ: Noyes Press.

Mosak, H. H. (1977a). Does a "TMJ" personality exist? In H. Gelb (Ed.), *Clinical management of head, neck, and TMJ pain and dysfunction* (pp. 195–205). Philadelphia: W. B. Saunders.

Mosak, H. H. (1977b). *On purpose.* Chicago: Alfred Adler Institute.

Mosak, H. H. (1979). Mosak's typology: An update. *Journal of Individual Psychology, 35,* 192–195.

Mosak, H. H. (1980). *A child's guide to parent rearing.* Chicago: Alfred Adler Institute.

Mosak, H. H. (1985). Interrupting a depression: The pushbutton technique. *Individual Psychology, 41,* 210–214.

Mosak, H. H. (1987a). Guilt, guilt feelings, regret and repentance. *Individual Psychology, 43,* 288–295.

Mosak, H. H. (1987b). *Ha ha and aha: The role of humor in psychotherapy.* Muncie, IN: Accelerated Development.

Mosak, H. H. (1991a). "I don't *have* social interest:" Social interest as construct. *Individual Psychology, 47,* 309–320.

Mosak, H. H. (1991b). Where have all the normal people gone? *Individual Psychology, 47,* 309–320.

Mosak, H. H. (1992). The "traffic cop" function of dreams and early recollections. *Individual Psychology, 48,* 319–323.

Mosak, H. H. (1995a). Adlerian psychotherapy. In R. J. Corsini & D. Wedding (Eds.), *Current psychotherapies* (5th ed., pp.51–84). Itasca, IL: F.E. Peacock.

Mosak, H. H. (1995b). Drugless psychotherapy of schizophrenia. *Individual Psychology, 51,* 61–66.

Mosak, H. H., Brown, P. R., & Boldt, R. M. (1994). Various purposes of suffering. *Individual Psychology, 50,* 142–148.

Mosak, H. H., & Dreikurs, R. (1967). The life tasks III: The fifth life task. *Individual Psychology, 5,* 16–22.

Mosak, H. H., & Gushurst, R. S. (1971). What patients say and what they mean. *American Journal of Psychotherapy, 25,* 428–436.

Mosak, H. H., & Gushurst, R. S. (1972). Some therapeutic uses of psychologic testing. *American Journal of Psychotherapy, 26,* 539–546.

Mosak, H. H., & Kopp, R. R. (1973). The early recollections of Adler, Freud, and Jung. *Journal of Individual Psychology, 29,* 157–166.

Mosak, H. H., & LeFevre, C. (1976). The resolution of "intrapersonal conflict." *Journal of Individual Psychology, 32,* 19–26.

Mosak, H. H., & Maniacci, M. P. (1989). An approach to the understanding of "schizophrenese." *Individual Psychology, 45,* 465–472.

Mosak, H. H., & Maniacci, M. P. (1993). Adlerian child psychotherapy. In T. R. Kratochwill & R. J. Morris (Eds.), *Handbook of psychotherapy with children and adolescents* (pp. 162–184). Boston: Allyn & Bacon.

Mosak, H. H., & Maniacci, M. P. (1995). The case of Roger. In D. Wedding & R. J. Corsini (Eds.), *Case studies in psychotherapy* (2nd ed., pp. 23–49). Itasca, IL: F. E. Peacock.

Mosak, H. H., & Maniacci, M. P. (1998). *Tactics in counseling and psychotherapy.* Itasca, IL: F. E. Peacock.

Mosak, H. H., Mosak, L. E., & Mosak, N. S. (1979). *The argot of the drug culture.* Chicago: Alfred Adler Institute.

Mosak, H. H., & Schneider, S. (1977). Masculine protest, penis envy, women's liberation and sexual equality. *Journal of Individual Psychology, 33,* 193–201.

Mosak, H. H., & Shulman, B. H. (1967). *Introductory Individual Psychology: A syllabus.* Chicago: Alfred Adler Institute.

Mosak, H. H., & Shulman, B. H. (1977). *Clinical assessment: A syllabus.* Chicago: Alfred Adler Institute.

Mosak, H. H., & Todd, F. J. (1952). Selective perception in the interpretation of symbols. *Journal of Abnormal and Social Psychology, 47,* 255–256.

Motley, W. (1989). *Knock on any door.* De Kalb, IL: Northern Illinois University Press.

Mozdzierz, G. J., & Lottman, T. J. (1973). Games married couples play: An Adlerian view. *Journal of Individual Psychology, 29,* 182–194.

Munroe, R. L. (1955). *Schools of psychoanalytic thought.* New York: Dryden Press.

Murphy, G. (1947). *Personality: A biosocial interpretation.* New York: Harper.

Neuer, A. (1936). Courage and discouragement. *International Journal of Individual Psychology, 2*(2), 30–50.

Nietzsche, F. (1967). *The will to power* (W. Kaufman & R. J. Hollingdale, Trans.; W. Kaufman, Ed.). New York: Vintage. (Original work published 1888)

Norcross, J. C., & Goldfried, M. R. (Eds.). (1992). *Handbook of psychotherapy integration.* New York: Basic Books.

Nunberg, H., & Federn, E. (Eds.). (1962). *Minutes of the Vienna Psychoanalytic Society.* New York: International Universities Press.

Nystul, M. S. (1985). The use of motivation modification techniques in Adlerian psychotherapy. *Individual Psychology, 41,* 489–495.

O'Connell, W. E. (1965). Humanistic identification: A new translation for *Gemeinschaftsgefühl. Journal of Individual Psychology, 21,* 44–47.

O'Connell, W. E. (1975). *Action therapy and Adlerian theory.* Chicago: Alfred Adler Institute.

O'Connell, W. E. (1976). The friends of Adler phenomenon. *Journal of Individual Psychology, 32,* 5–17.

O'Hanlon, W. H., & Weiner-Davis, M. (1987). *In search of solutions.* New York: W. W. Norton.

Oldham, J. M., & Morris, L. B. (1990). *The personality self-portrait.* New York: Bantam.

Olson, H. A. (Ed.). (1979). *Early recollections: Their use in diagnosis and psychotherapy.* Springfield, IL: Charles C. Thomas.

Orgler, H. (1963). *Alfred Adler: The man and his work.* New York: Mentor Books. (Original work published 1939)

Ornstein, R., & Sobel, D. (1987). *The healing brain.* New York: Simon & Schuster.

Pancner, K. (1978). The use of parables and fables in Adlerian psychotherapy. *Individual Psychologist, 15*(4), 19–29.

Pancner, R. J., & Jylland, C. W. (1996). Depressive disorders. In L. Sperry & J. Carlson (Eds.), *Psychopathology and psychotherapy: From DSM-IV diagnosis to treatment* (2nd ed., pp. 115–157). Washington, DC: Accelerated Development.

Papanek, H. (1965a). Adler's concepts in community psychiatry. *Journal of Individual Psychology, 21,* 117–126.

Papanek, H. (1965b). Group psychotherapy with married couples. In J. H. Masserman (Ed.), *Current psychiatric therapies* (pp. 157–163). New York: Grune & Stratton.

Peven, D. E., Mosak, H. H., & Shulman, B. H. (1979). *Interviewing: A syllabus.* Chicago: Alfred Adler Institute.

Peven, D. E., & Shulman, B. H. (1986). Adlerian psychotherapy. In I. L. Kutash & A. Wolf (Eds.), *Psychotherapist's casebook* (pp. 101–123). San Francisco: Jossey-Bass.

Pew, M., & Pew, W. L. (1972). Adlerian marriage counseling. *Journal of Individual Psychology, 28,* 192–202.

Phillips, D. (1975). The family council: A segment of adolescent treatment. *Journal of Behavior Therapy, and Experimental Psychiatry, 6,* 283–287.

Piaget, J. (1978). *Behavior and evolution* (D. Nicholson-Smith, Trans). New York: Pantheon. (Original work published 1976)

Poffenberger, T. (1953). *The family council . . . kids can confer.* Corvallis, OR: Oregon State College.

Popkin, M. (1987). *Active parenting: Teaching cooperation, courage, and responsibility.* San Francisco: Harper & Row.

Powers, R. L., & Griffith, J. (1987). *Understanding life-style: The psycho-clarity© process.* Chicago: Americas Institute of Adlerian Studies.

Radl, L. (1959). Existentialism and Individual Psychology. In K. A. Adler & Danica Deutsch (Eds.), *Essays in Individual Psychology* (pp. 157–167). New York: Grove Press.

Rigney, K. B., & Corsini, R. J. (1970). *The family council.* Chicago: Family Education Association.

Robb, M. (1932). Organ jargon. *Individual Psychology Medical Pamphlets, 4,* 61–68.

Rogers, C. R. (1942). *Counseling and psychotherapy.* Boston: Houghton Mifflin.

Rogers, C. R. (1951). *Client-centered therapy.* Boston: Houghton Mifflin.

Rom, P. (1950). These feelings of guilt. *Individual Psychology Bulletin, 8,* 32–38.

Ronge, P. H. (1956). The "feminine protest." *American Journal of Individual Psychology, 12,* 112–115.

Rosenzweig, S. (1944). *Rosenzweig Picture-Frustration Study.* St. Louis, MO: Author.

Rousseau, J. J. (1947). The social contract or, principles of political right. In E. Barker (Ed.), *Social contract* (pp. 167–307). New York: Oxford University Press. (Original work published 1762)

Safran, J. D., & Segal, Z. V. (1990). *Interpersonal process in cognitive therapy.* New York: Basic Books.

Sartre, J. P. (1956). Existential psychoanalysis. In *Being and nothingness* (H. E. Barnes, Trans.) (pp. 712–734). New York: Washington Square Press. (Original work published 1943)

Schaffer, H. (1974). Existentialisme Sartrien et psychologie Adlerienne [Sartre's existentialism and Adlerian psychology]. *Bulletin, Société Française de Psychologie Adlérienne, 20,* 1–7.

Schaffer, H. (1976). Existentialisme Sartrien et psychologie d'Adler [Sartre's existentialism and Adler's psychology]. *Bulletin, Société Française de Psychologie Adlérienne, 26,* 1–9.

Scheibe, K. E. (1970). *Beliefs and values.* New York: Holt, Rinehart & Winston.

Schneider, M. F. (1989). *CAST: Children's Apperceptive Storytelling Test.* Austin, TX: Pro-Ed.

Seif, L. (1928). Zur Problem der Psychosen [The problem of the psychoses]. *Internationale Zeitschrift für Individualpsychologie, 6,* 273–279.

Seif, L., & Zilahi, L. (Eds.). (1930). *Selbsterziehung des Charakters* [Self-education of character]. Leipzig: S. Hirzel.

Selye, H. (1974). *Stress without distress.* New York: Signet.

Shakespeare, W. (1974). *The tragedy of Julius Caesar.* In C. B. Evans (Ed.), *The Riverside Shakespeare* (pp. 1105–1134). Boston: Houghton Mifflin. (Original work published 1599)

Shapiro, D. (1965). *Neurotic styles.* New York: Basic Books.

Sherman, R., & Dinkmeyer, D. (1987). *Systems of family therapy: An Adlerian integration.* New York: Brunner/Mazel.

Shulman, B. H. (1962). The family constellation in personality diagnosis. *Journal of Individual Psychology, 18,* 35–47.

Shulman, B. H. (1964). Psychological disturbances which interfere with the patient's cooperation. *Psychosomatics, 5,* 213–220.

Shulman, B. H. (1965). A comparison of Allport's and the Adlerian concepts of life style: Contributions to a psychology of the self. *Individual Psychologist, 3,* 14–21.

Shulman, B. H. (1969). The Adlerian theory of dreams. In M. Kramer (Ed.), *Dream psychology and the new biology of dreaming* (pp. 117–137). Springfield, IL: Charles C. Thomas.

Shulman, B. H. (1973a). *Contributions to Individual Psychology.* Chicago: Alfred Adler Institute.

Shulman, B. H. (1973b). What is the life style? In B. H. Shulman, *Contributions to Individual Psychology* (pp. 16–44). Chicago: Alfred Adler Institute.

Shulman, B. H. (1984). *Essays in schizophrenia* (2nd ed.). Chicago: Alfred Adler Institute. (Original work published 1968)

Shulman, B. H. (1985). Cognitive therapy and the Individual Psychology of Alfred Adler. In M. J. Mahoney & A. Freeman (Eds.), *Cognition and psychotherapy* (pp. 243–258). New York: Plenum.

Shulman, B. H., & Mosak, H. H. (1967). Various purposes of symptoms. *Journal of Individual Psychology, 23,* 79–87.

Shulman, B. H., & Mosak, H. H. (1988). *Manual for life style assessment.* Muncie, IN: Accelerated Development.

Shulman, B. H., & Watts, R. E. (1997). Adlerian and constructivist psychotherapies: An Adlerian perspective. *Journal of Cognitive Psychotherapy, 11,* 181–193.

Sicher, L. (1950). Guilt and guilt feelings. *Individual Psychology Bulletin, 8,* 4–11.

Sicher, L. (1955). Education for freedom. *American Journal of Individual Psychology, 11,* 97–103.

Sicher, L., & Mosak, H. H. (1967). Aggression as a secondary phenomenon. *Journal of Individual Psychology, 23,* 232–235.

Singer, J. (1975). *The inner world of daydreaming.* New York: Harper & Row.

Skolnick, A. S. (1986). *The psychology of human development.* Chicago: Harcourt Brace Jovanovich.

Smithells, T. A. (1983). Working with children: Observation, interpretation and psychological disclosure. In O. C. Christensen & T. G. Schramski (Eds.), *Adlerian family counseling: A manual for counselor, educator and psychotherapist* (pp. 117–136). Minneapolis: Educational Media.

Smuts, J. C. (1961). *Holism and evolution.* New York: Viking Press. (Original work published 1926)

Snygg, D., & Combs, A. W. (1959). *Individual behavior.* New York: Harper.

Sperry, L. (Ed.). (1989). Varieties of brief therapy [Special issue]. *Individual Psychology, 45* (1 & 2).

Sperry, L. (1990). Personality disorders: Biopsychosocial descriptions and dynamics. *Individual Psychology, 46,* 193–202.

Sperry, L., & Ansbacher, H. L. (1996). The concept of narcissism and the narcissistic personality disorder. In L. Sperry & J. Carlson (Eds.), *Psychopathology and psychotherapy: From DSM-IV diagnosis to treatment* (2nd ed., pp. 337–351). Washington, DC: Accelerated Development.

Sperry, L., & Carlson, J. (1991). *Marital therapy.* Denver: Love.

Sperry, L., & Carlson, J. (Eds.). (1996). *Psychopathology and psychotherapy: From DSM-IV diagnosis to treatment* (2nd ed.). Washington, DC: Accelerated Development.

Sperry, L., & Maniacci, M. P. (1992). An integration of DSM-III-R diagnoses and Adlerian case formulations. *Individual Psychology, 48,* 175–181.

Sperry, L., & Mosak, H. H. (1996). Personality disorders. In L. Sperry & J. Carlson (Eds.), *Psychopathology and psychotherapy: From DSM-IV diagnosis to treatment* (2nd ed., 279–335). Washington, DC: Accelerated Development.

Spiel, O. (1956). The Individual Psychological Experimental School in Vienna. *American Journal of Individual Psychology, 12,* 1–11.

Starr, A. (1977). *Rehearsal for living: Psychodrama.* Chicago: Nelson-Hall.

Stepansky, P. (1983). *In Freud's shadow: Adler in context.* Hillside, NJ: Analytic Press.

Stern, A. (1958). Existential analysis and Individual Psychology. *Journal of Individual Psychology, 14,* 38–50.

Stern, D. N. (1985). *The interpersonal world of the infant.* New York: Basic Books.

Stone, I. (1971). *Passions of the mind.* New York: New American Library.

Sullivan, H. S. (1953). *The interpersonal theory of psychiatry.* New York: W. W. Norton.

Sullivan, H. S. (1964). *The fusion of psychiatry and social science.* New York: W. W. Norton.

Taylor, J. A. (1975). Early recollections as a projective technique: A review of some recent validation studies. *Journal of Individual Psychology, 31,* 213–218.

Teichman, M., & Foa, U. G. (1972). Depreciation and accusation tendencies: Empirical support. *Journal of Individual Psychology, 28,* 48–50.

Terner, J., & Pew, W. L. (1978). *The courage to be imperfect: The life and work of Rudolf Dreikurs.* New York: Hawthorn.

Thoreau, H. D. (1991). *Walden.* New York: Random House. (Original work published 1854)

Trentzsch, P. J. (1928). Detection of early symptoms of psychosis. *Internationale Zeitschrift für Individalpsychologie, 6,* 251–257.

Vaihinger, H. (1965). *The philosophy of "as if."* (C. K. Ogden, Trans.). London: Routledge & Kegan Paul. (Original work published 1911)

van Dusen, W. (1959). Adler and existence analysis. *Journal of Individual Psychology, 15,* 100–111.

Wachtel, P. L. (1977). *Psychoanalysis and behavior therapy.* New York: Basic Books.

Walton, F. X., & Powers, R. L. (1974). *Winning children over: A manual for teachers, counselors, principals and parents.* Chicago: Practical Psychology Associates.

Way, L. (1950). *Adler's place in psychology.* London: Allen & Unwin.

Weinhaus, E. (1977). *A practical guide for family meetings.* St. Louis: Author.

West, G. K. (1986). *Parenting without guilt: The predictable and situational misbehaviors of childhood.* Springfield, IL: Charles C. Thomas.

Wexberg, E. (1928). Zur Frage der Psychosen [The question of the psychoses]. *Internationale Zeitschrift für Individualpsychologie, 6,* 280–289.

Wexberg, E. (1929). *Individual Psychology* (W. B. Wolfe, Trans.). New York: Cosmopolitan.

Wexberg, E. (1947). *Introduction to medical psychology.* New York: Grune & Stratton.

Wilde, O. (1992). *The ballad of Reading Gaol.* New York: Dover. (Original work published 1898)

Williams, R. (1989). *The trusting heart.* New York: Times Books.

Wilson, F. R. (1975). TA and Adler. *Transactional Analysis Journal, 5,* 117–122.

Wolfe, W. B. (1932). *How to be happy though human.* New York: Penguin.

Wordsworth, W. (1979). The prelude. In M. H. Abrams (Eds.), *The Norton anthology of English literature* (4th ed., Vol. 2, pp. 230–313). New York: W. W. Norton. (Original work published 1850)

Wylie, P. (1994). *Generation of vipers.* Catchogue, NY: Buccaneer Books.

Yalom, I. D. (1980). *Existential psychotherapy.* New York: Basic Books.

Zborowski, R. M. (1997). *The phenomenon of transference: An Adlerian perspective.* Unpublished doctoral dissertation, Adler School of Professional Psychology, Chicago.

Zeigarnik, B. (1927). Das Behalten erledigter und unerledigter Handlungen [The remembrance of complete and incomplete acts]. *Psychologisches Forschung, 9,* 1–85.

Zuckerman, M. (1979). *Sensation seeking.* Hillsdale, NJ: Lawrence Erlbaum.

INDEX